Ryan Adams GOLD

Bug Music Limited

GUITAR TABLATURE EXPLAINED

Guitar music can be notated three different ways: on a musical stave, in tablature, and in rhythm slashes

RHYTHM SLASHES are written above the stave. Strum chords in the rhythm indicated. Round noteheads indicate single notes.

THE MUSICAL STAVE shows pitches and rhythms and is divided by lines into bars. Pitches are named after the first seven letters of the alphabet.

TABLATURE graphically represents the guitar fingerboard. Each horizontal line represents a string, and each number represents a fret.

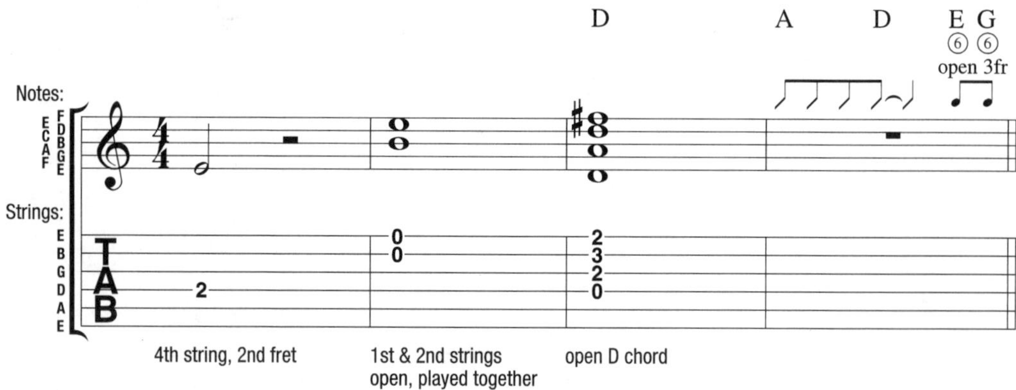

DEFINITIONS FOR SPECIAL GUITAR NOTATION

SEMI-TONE BEND: Strike the note and bend up a semi-tone (1/2 step).

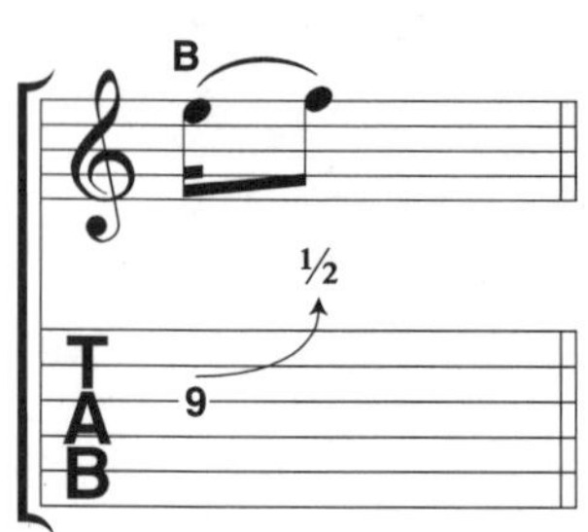

WHOLE-TONE BEND: Strike the note and bend up a whole-tone (whole step).

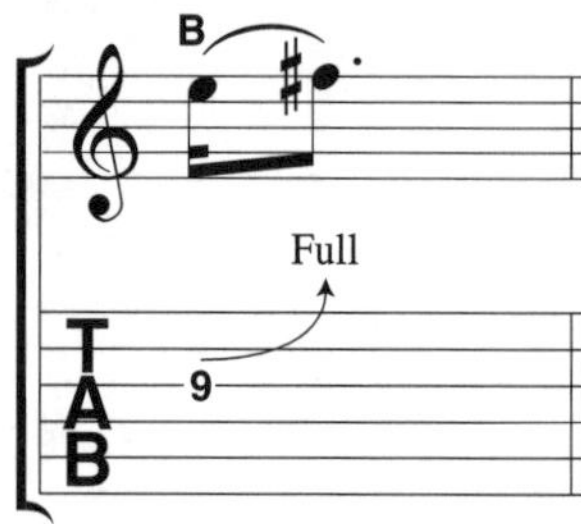

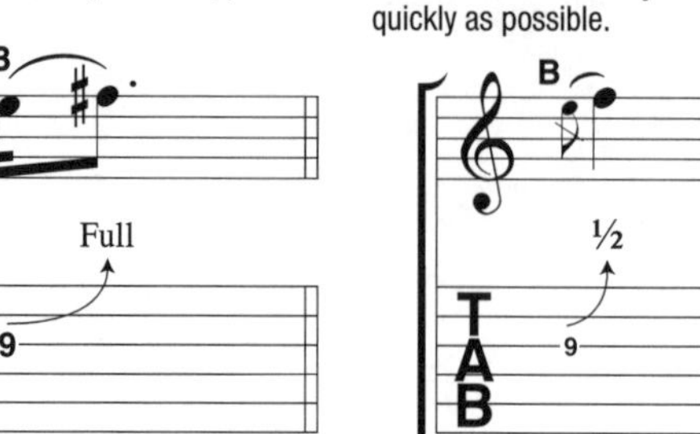

GRACE NOTE BEND: Strike the note and bend as indicated. Play the first note as quickly as possible.

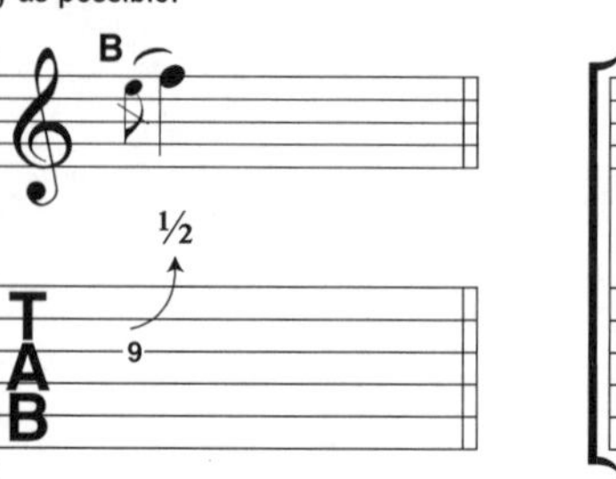

QUARTER-TONE BEND: Strike the note and bend up a 1/4 step.

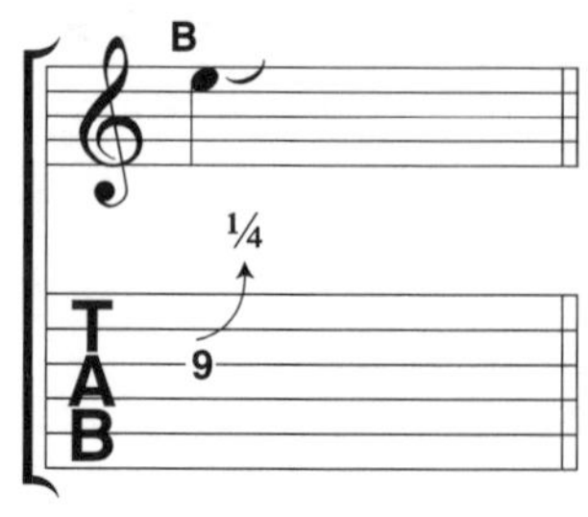

BEND & RELEASE: Strike the note and bend up as indicated, then release back to the original note.

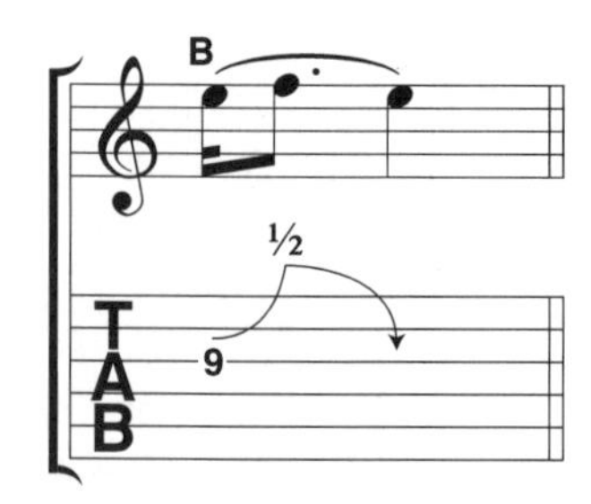

COMPOUND BEND & RELEASE: Strike the note and bend up and down in the rhythm indicated.

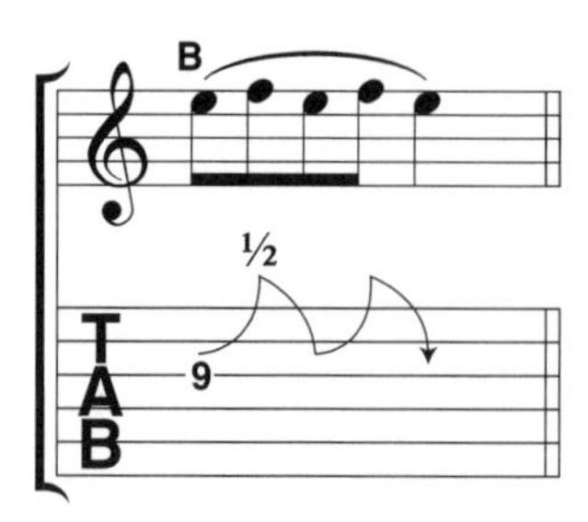

PRE-BEND: Bend the note as indicated, then strike it.

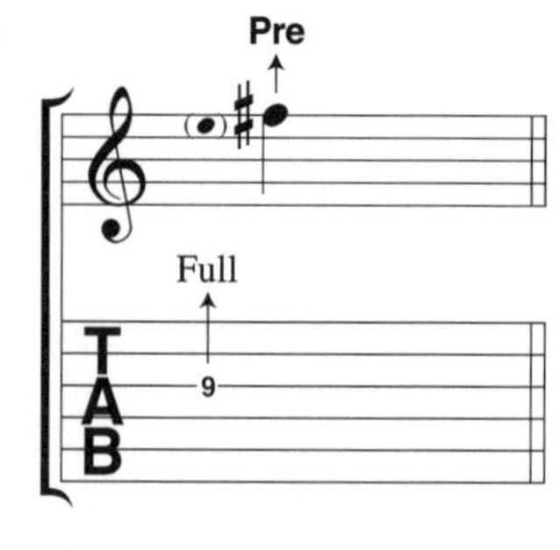

PRE-BEND & RELEASE: Bend the note as indicated. Strike it and release the note back to the original pitch.

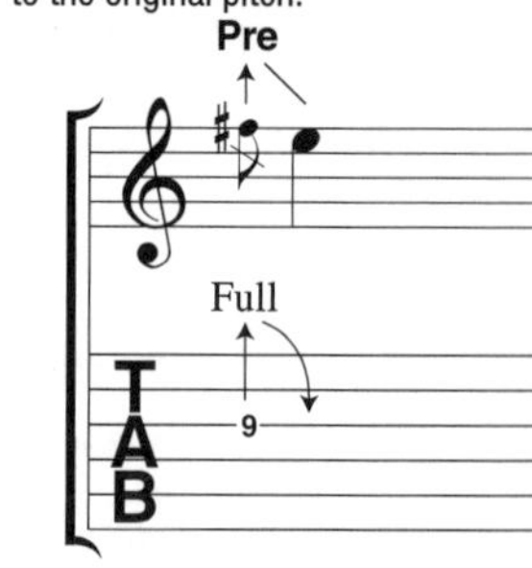

UNISON BEND: Strike the two notes simultaneously and bend the lower note up to the pitch of the higher.

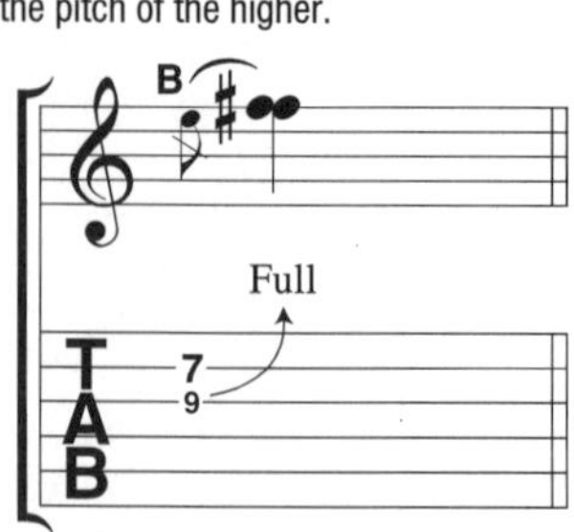

BEND & RESTRIKE: Strike the note and bend as indicated then restrike the string where the symbol occurs.

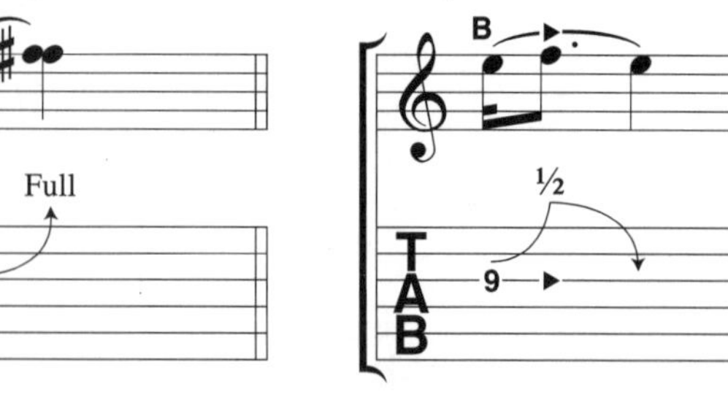

BEND, HOLD AND RELEASE: Same as bend and release but hold the bend for the duration of the tie.

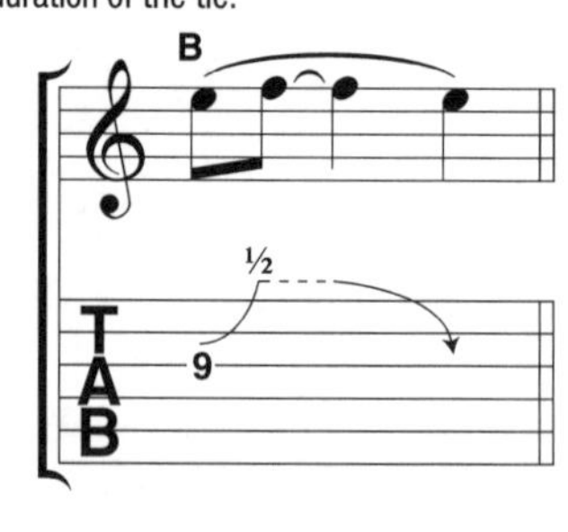

BEND AND TAP: Bend the note as indicated and tap the higher fret while still holding the bend.

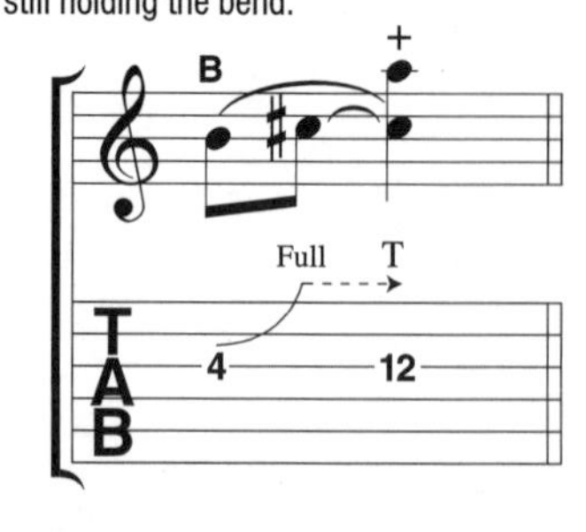

VIBRATO: The string is vibrated by rapidly bending and releasing the note with the fretting hand.

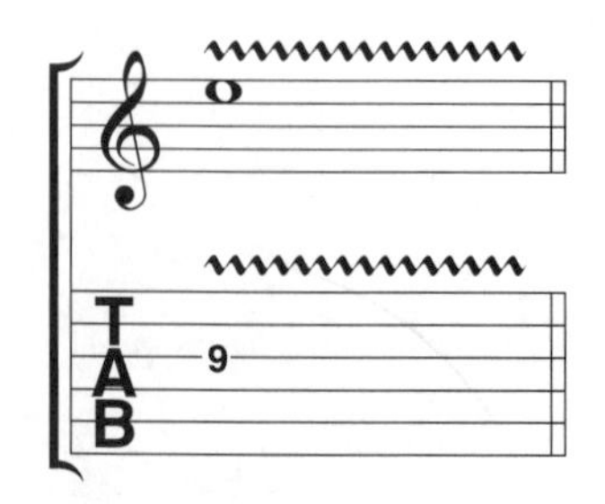

HAMMER-ON: Strike the first (lower) note with one finger, then sound the higher note (on the same string) with another finger by fretting it without picking.

9 11

PULL-OFF: Place both fingers on the notes to be sounded, Strike the first note and without picking, pull the finger off to sound the second (lower) note.

11 9

LEGATO SLIDE (GLISS): Strike the first note and then slide the same fret-hand finger up or down to the second note. The second note is not struck.

7 9

NOTE: The speed of any bend is indicated by the music notation and tempo.

SHIFT SLIDE (GLISS & RESTRIKE): Same as legato slide, except the second note is struck.

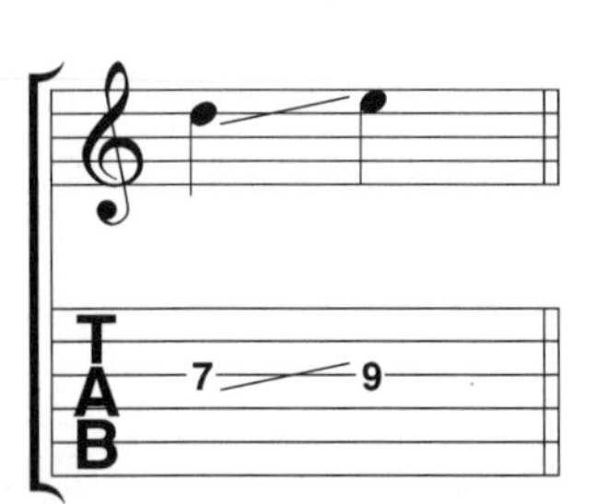

TRILL: Very rapidly alternate between the notes indicated by continuously hammering on and pulling off.

TAPPING: Hammer ("tap") the fret indicated with the pick-hand index or middle finger and pull off to the note fretted by the fret hand.

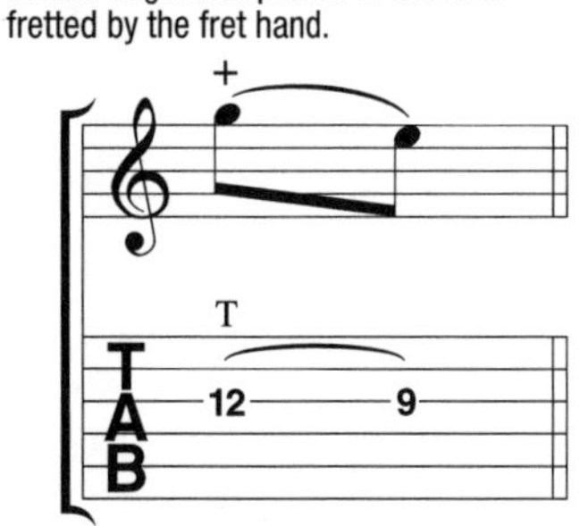

PICK SCRAPE: The edge of the pick is rubbed down (or up) the string, producing a scratchy sound.

MUFFLED STRINGS: A percussive sound is produced by laying the fret hand across the string(s) without depressing, and striking them with the pick hand.

NATURAL HARMONIC: Strike the note while the fret-hand lightly touches the string directly over the fret indicated.

Harm.

12

PINCH HARMONIC: The note is fretted normally and a harmonic is produced by adding the edge of the thumb or the tip of the index finger of the pick hand to the normal pick attack.

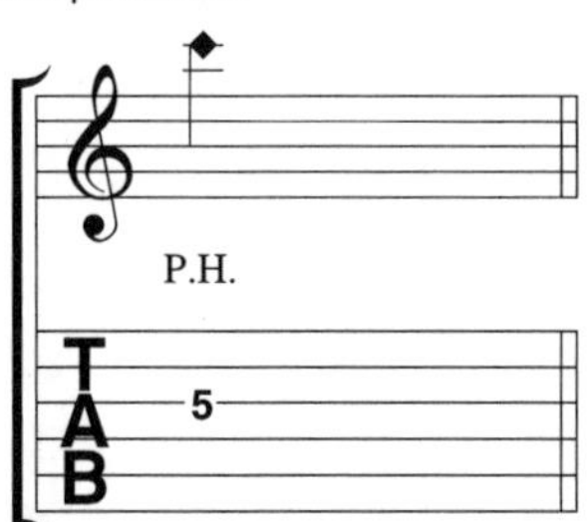

HARP HARMONIC: The note is fretted normally and a harmonic is produced by gently resting the pick hand's index finger directly above the indicated fret (in parentheses) while the pick hand's thumb or pick assists by plucking the appropriate string.

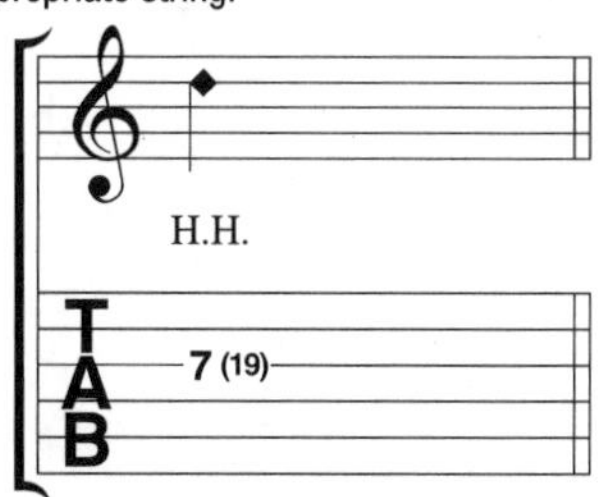

PALM MUTING: The note is partially muted by the pick hand lightly touching the string(s) just before the bridge.

P.M.

0 0 0 0

RAKE: Drag the pick across the strings indicated with a single motion.

rake

5

TREMOLO PICKING: The note is picked as rapidly and continuously as possible.

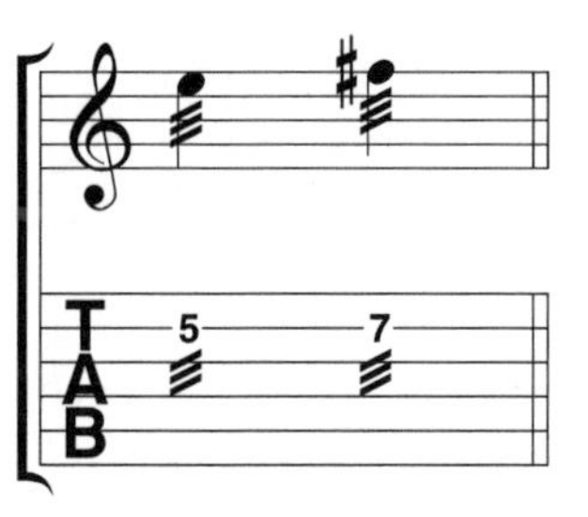

ARPEGGIATE: Play the notes of the chord indicated by quickly rolling them from bottom to top.

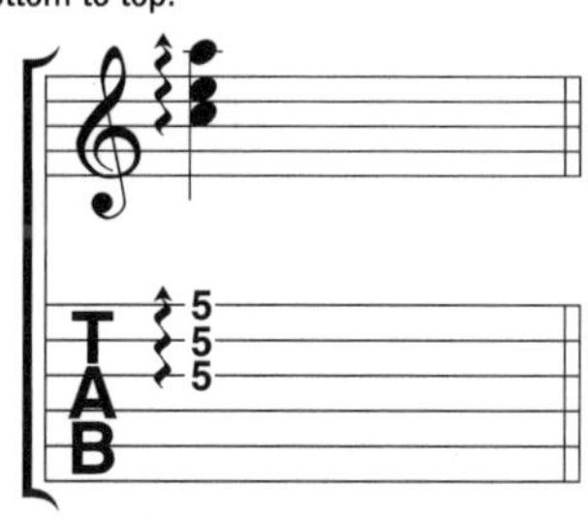

SWEEP PICKING: Rhythmic downstroke and/or upstroke motion across the strings.

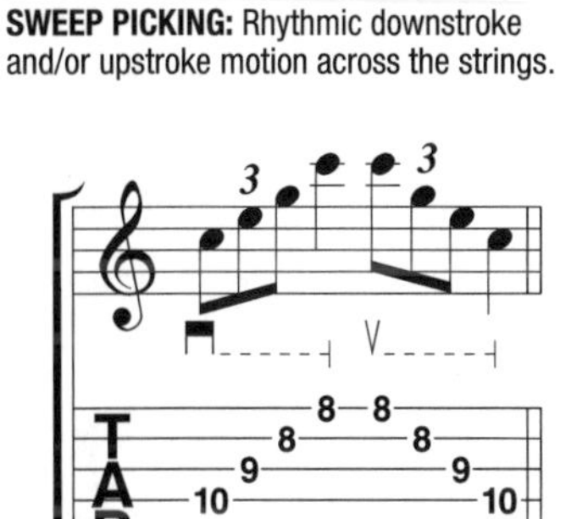

VIBRATO DIVE BAR AND RETURN: The pitch of the note or chord is dropped a specific number of steps (in rhythm) then returned to the original pitch.

w/bar

0 (0)

-1

VIBRATO BAR SCOOP: Depress the bar just before striking the note, then quickly release the bar.

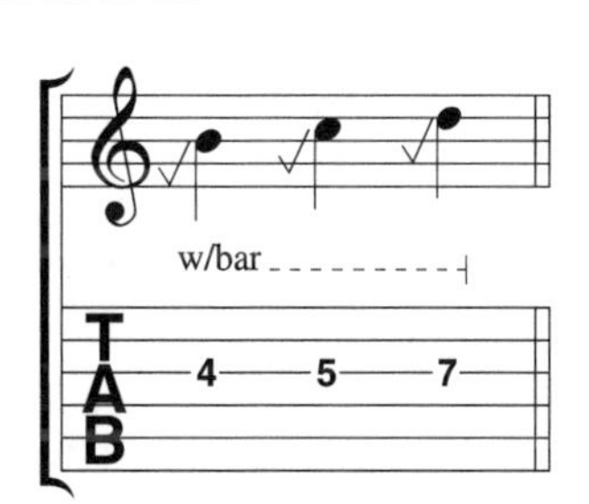

VIBRATO BAR DIP: Strike the note and then immediately drop a specific number of steps, then release back to the original pitch.

-½ -½ -½

w/bar

7 7 7

ADDITIONAL MUSICAL DEFINITIONS

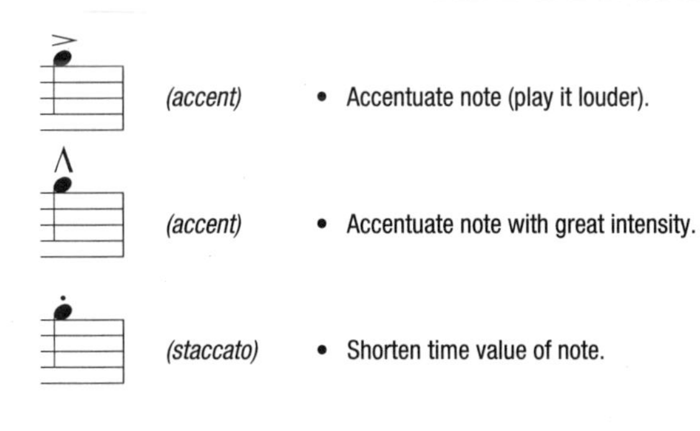

(accent) • Accentuate note (play it louder).

(accent) • Accentuate note with great intensity.

(staccato) • Shorten time value of note.

• Downstroke

• Upstroke

D.𝄋. al Coda • Go back to the sign (𝄋), then play until the bar marked ***To Coda*** ⊕ then skip to the section marked ⊕ ***Coda***.

D.C. al Fine • Go back to the beginning of the song and play until the bar marked ***Fine*** (end).

tacet • Instrument is silent (drops out).

• Repeat bars between signs.

1. 2.

• When a repeated section has different endings, play the first ending only the first time and the second ending only the second time.

NOTE: Tablature numbers in parentheses mean:
1. The note is sustained, but a new articulation (such as hammer on or slide) begins.
2. A note may be fretted but not necessarily played.

Exclusive distributors:
Music Sales Limited, 8/9 Frith Street, London W1B 3JB, England.
Music Sales Pty Limited, 120 Rothschild Avenue, Rosebery, NSW 2018, Australia.

Order No. AM974028 ISBN 0-7119-9403-X

Music arrangements by Matt Cowe. Music processed by Digital Music Art.
Printed in the United Kingdom by Printwise (Haverhill) Limited, Haverhill, Suffolk.

'GOLD' is available now on Lost Highway Records
www.losthighwayrecords.com

Ryan loves just about everybody including...Glyn Johns & Glynis, Alanis Morissette, Adam Duritz, Lynette Nutter, THE FRANKS, THE JOSH, THE LUKE & THE LYOR, JIMBO CAPARRO. Amy Lombardi, my bestest friend Billy Mercer, my other bestest friend, The Kidd, Alanis Morissette, Nan Warshaw, Rob Miller, Bloodshot Records, Brad Rice, Brian Walsby, Bucky Baxter and Hooterville, Carrie Hamilton, Chris Stills, Corey Parks, Darcy Hemley, Dawn Hill (Hi, Baby), Elton John you sweet sweet man, Alanis Morissette, ROSCOE, Ethan my brother... of course, the Mink, Gillian Welch and Dave Rawlings (f.y.i., I won the bet), Hannah, Jesse Klein, Mexico for being Mexico, Jesse Malin, Sally Timms - you rule, Juliet Malin, everybody at LAX, Keith Fuckin Morris, Kevn Kinney, Kyla Fairchild, Lisa Robinson (Loose Lips Sink Ships), Lucinda Williams, Margarette Simmons, Alanis Morissette, Matthew Smith and the best American band The Volebeats, Abbey Taylor and Detroit for making an Abbey Taylor, Melissa Auf Der Maur, Mike Fuckin Daly, Pamela Des Barres, Rami Jaffi, OASIS!!! Milo DeCruz, Rhett Miller and the 97s, Sal and the Viper Room, Vodka Tonics, Keith Richards, Sally Timms - you babe! Sheila "Where Am I?" Richman, Misty Lawrence, Brad "What would The Clash do?" Pemberton, Steve Earle, Richard Causon, Van Alston, SuperBidness, Kerri Leich, Sarah Ellis, the Lost Highway & Island Def Jam staffs. Trina Shoemaker, NATE, The Pink Hearts, Lauren Murphy, The Grateful Dead and Black Flag at the same time, Johnny B. and 12th & Porter, Sam McMillen, CORINA ROUND...I love you, girl. Alanis Morissette, James Minchin and the temple, Converse and cowboy boots, the Harlem Globetrotters, Anne Frank, the guy who gave me the tattoo of the "X" logo, MEG WHITE for saving Rock 'n' Roll, and Winona Ryder...damn girl.

Special love to Boardners Bar on Cherokee & Hollywood, The Hollywood Roosevelt Ghost Hunters Association, Los Burritos (#4 Huevos Rancheros), George Burns & Gracie Allen...goodnight Gracie...and, of course...MA! Oh, yeah, God Bless Stockholm and the entire country of Sweden!

Produced, Engineered and Mixed by Ethan Johns at the Sunset Sound Factory
Assistant Engineer and Additional Engineering by Steven Rhodes
Mastered by Doug Sax and Robert Hadley at the Mastering Lab, Hollywood, CA

Adam Duritz appears courtesy of Geffen Records
Chris Stills appears courtesy of Chris Stills

A&R and Artist Development: Frank Callari

Booking Information: Frank Riley, High Road Touring 415/332-9292

For More Information: Frank Callari 615/524 7800

Visit these websites:
www.losthighwayrecords.com and
www.ryan-adams.com

Art Direction: Ryan Adams & Karen Naff
Design: Karen Naff
Photography: James Minchin III

NEW YORK, NEW YORK

Words & Music by Ryan Adams

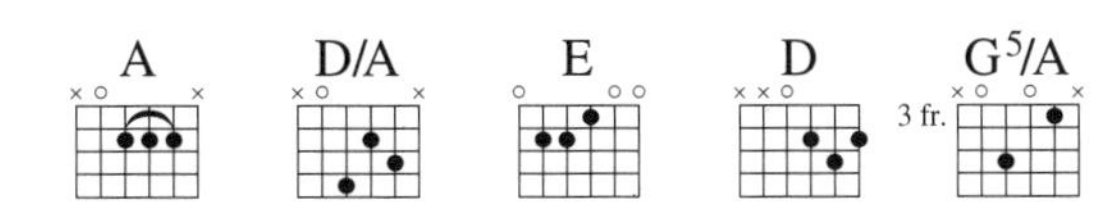

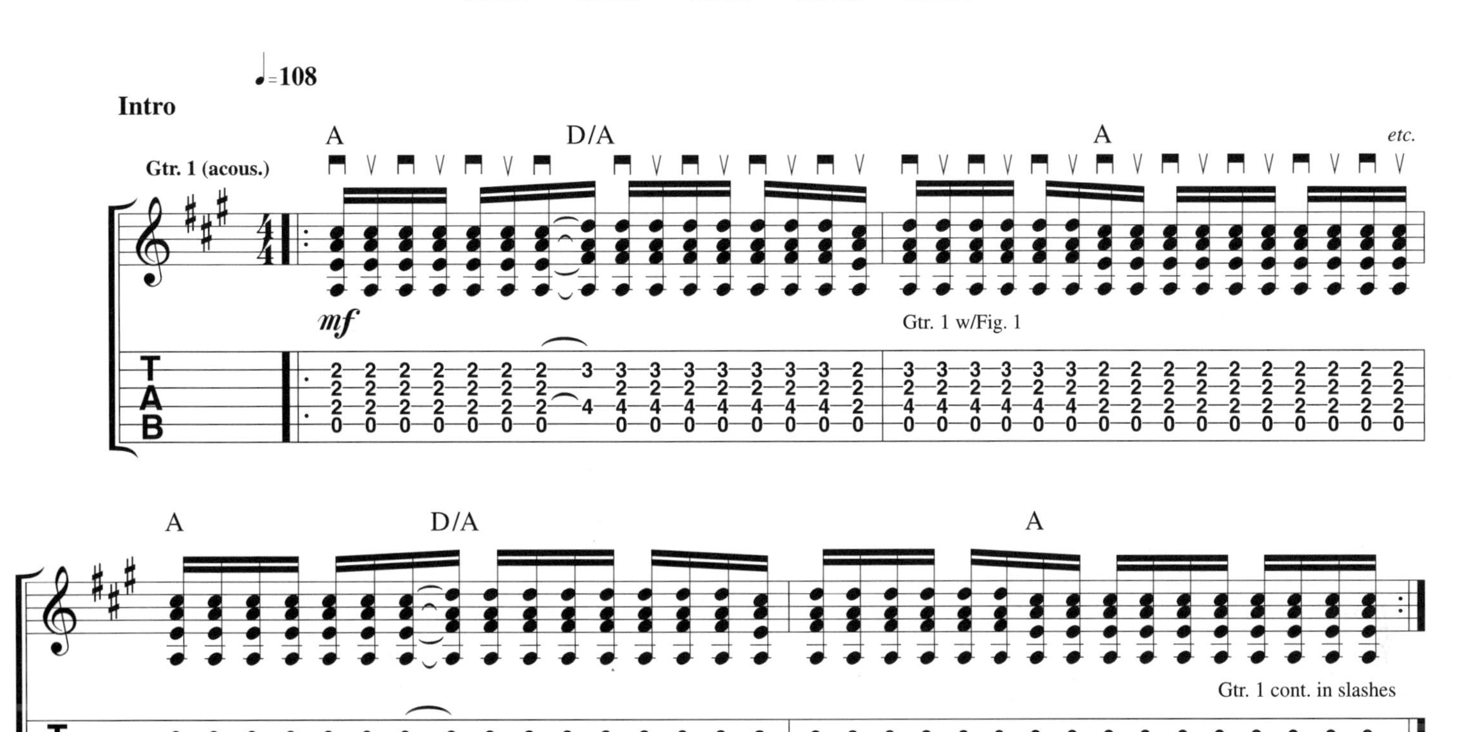

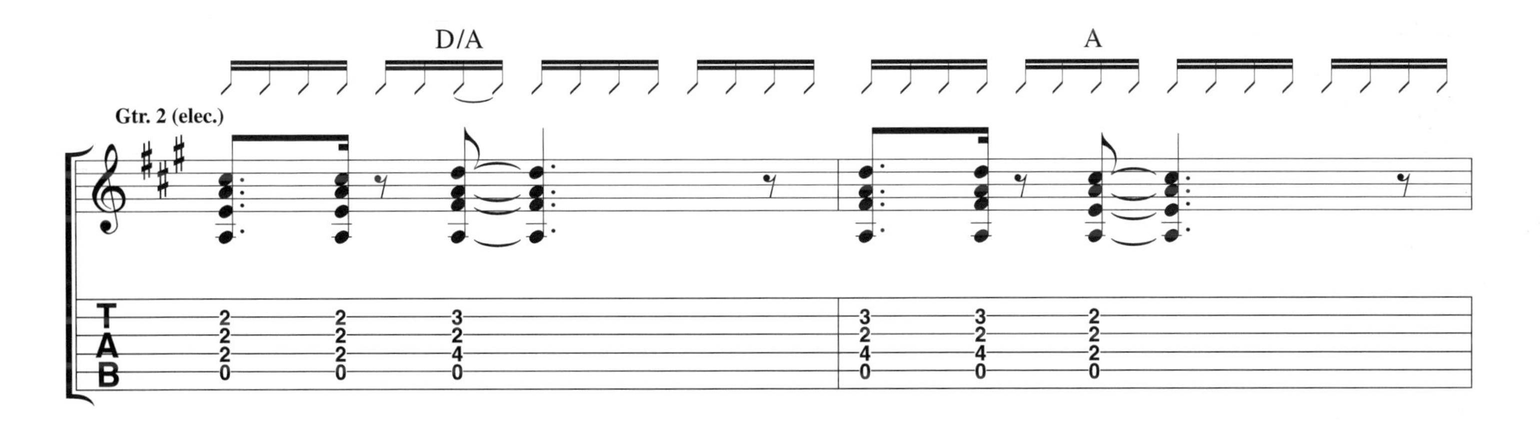

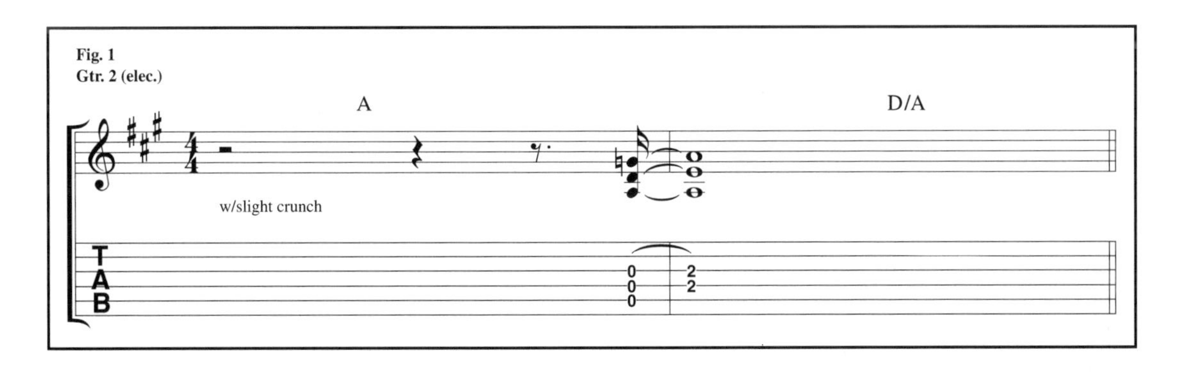

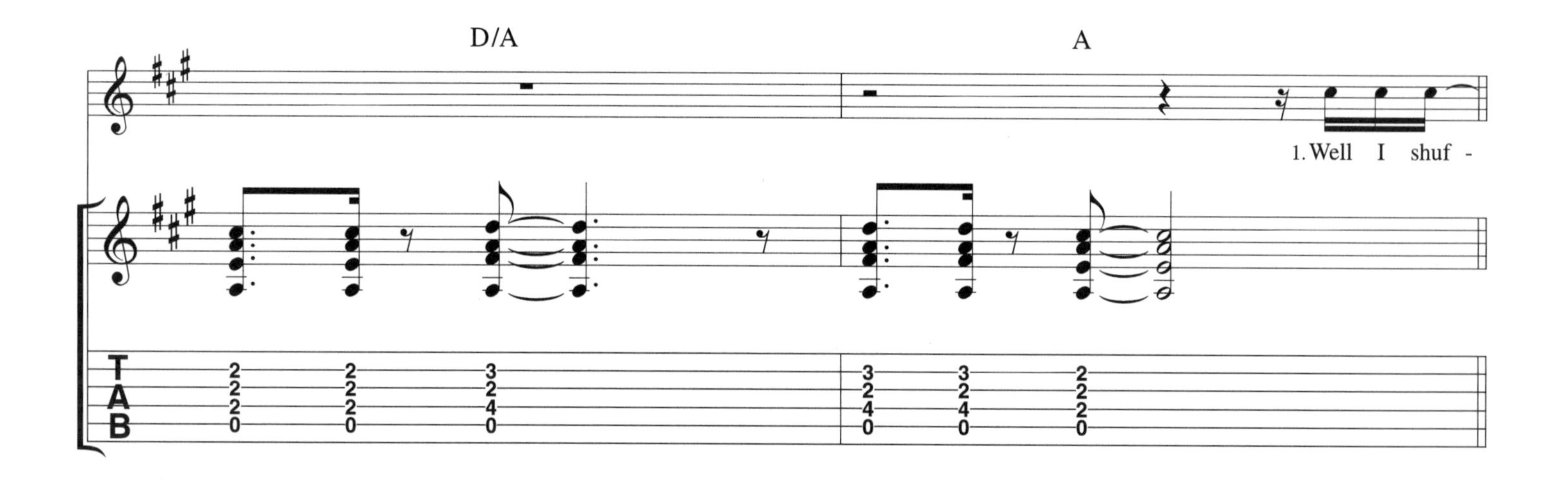
D/A
A
1. Well I shuf -
TAB

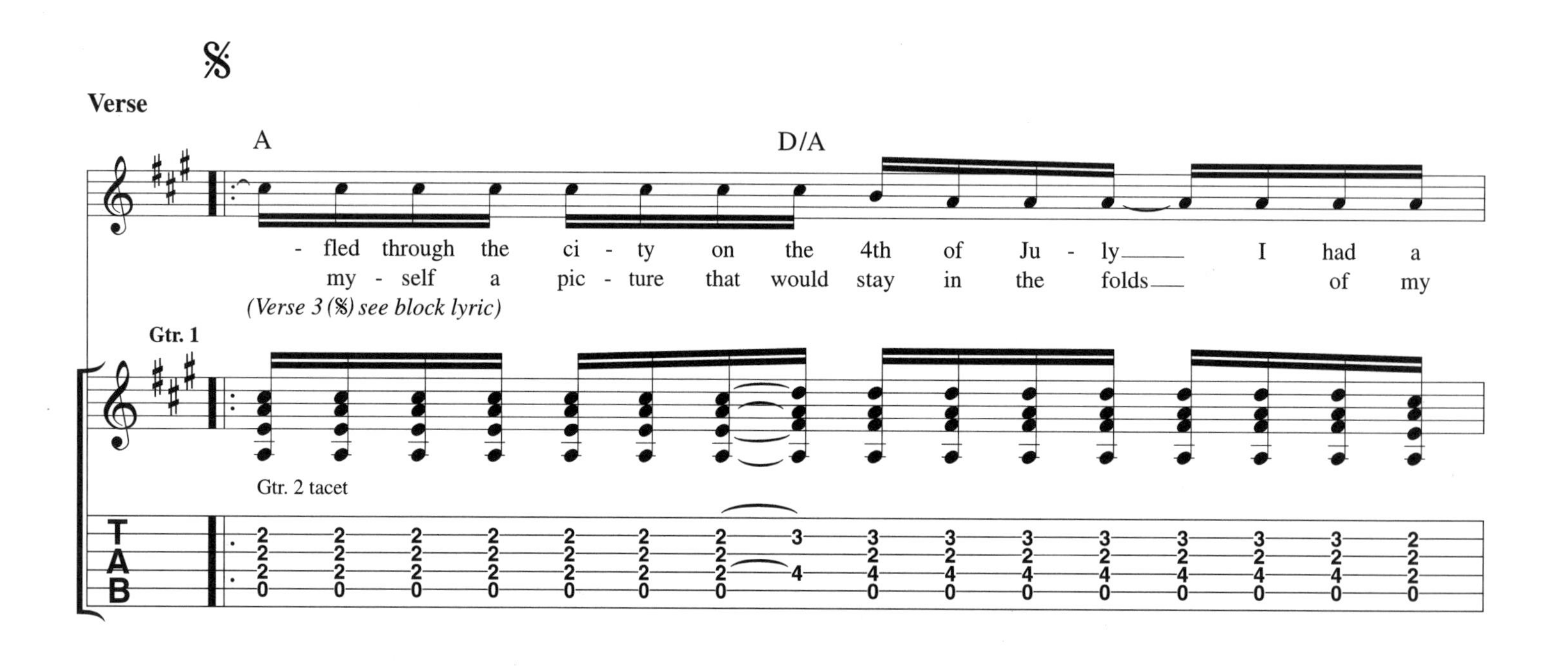
Verse
A
D/A
- fled through the ci - ty on the 4th of Ju - ly I had a
my - self a pic - ture that would stay in the folds of my
(Verse 3 (%) see block lyric)
Gtr. 1
Gtr. 2 tacet
TAB

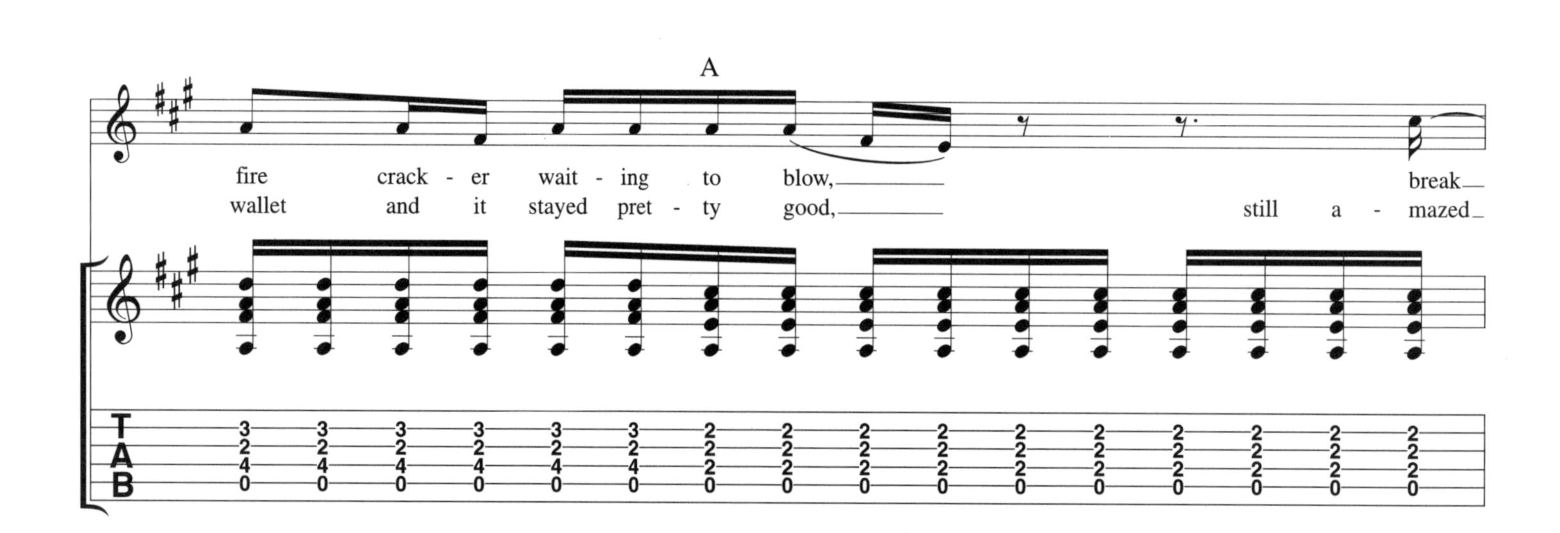
A
fire crack - er wait - ing to blow, break
wallet and it stayed pret - ty good, still a - mazed
TAB

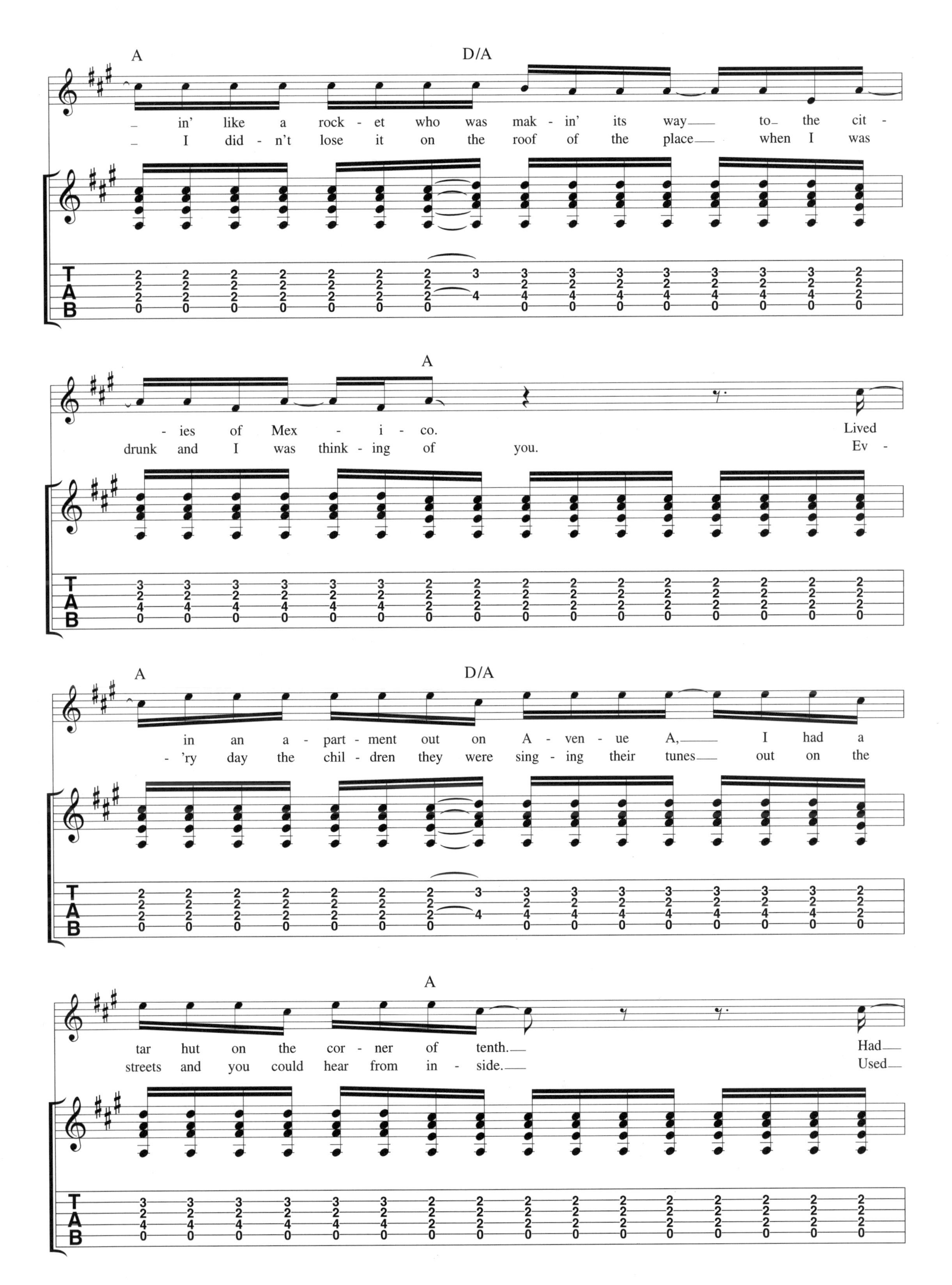
A
D/A
in' like a rock - et who was mak - in' its way to the cit -
I did - n't lose it on the roof of the place when I was
T
A
B
A
- ies of Mex - i - co.
Lived
drunk and I was think - ing of you.
Ev -
A
D/A
in an a - part - ment out on A - ven - ue A, I had a
- 'ry day the chil - dren they were sing - ing their tunes out on the
A
tar hut on the cor - ner of tenth.
Had
streets and you could hear from in - side.
Used

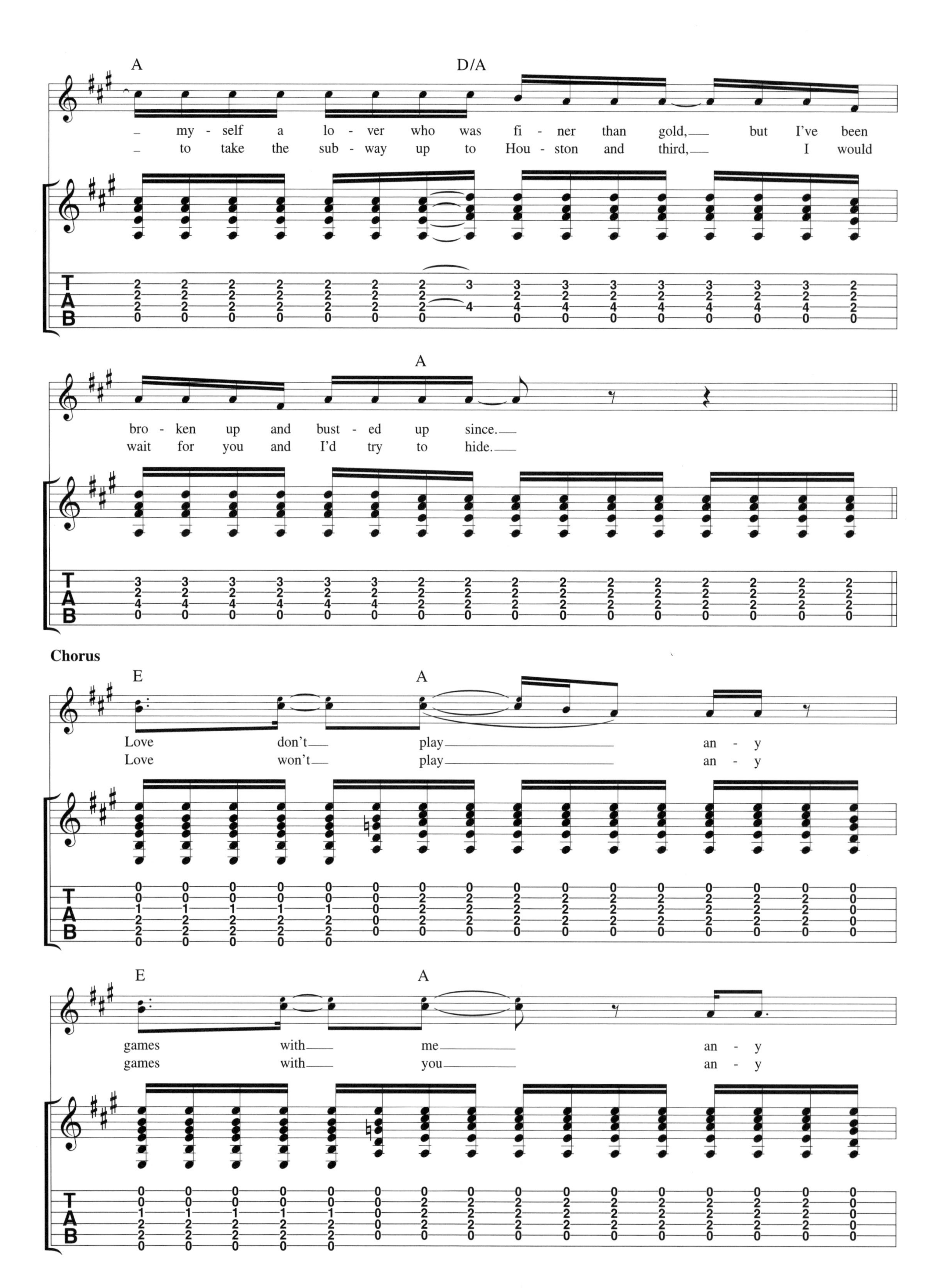
A
D/A
myself a lover who was finer than gold, but I've been
to take the subway up to Houston and third, I would
A
broken up and busted up since.
wait for you and I'd try to hide.
Chorus
E
A
Love don't play any
Love won't play any
E
A
games with me any
games with you any

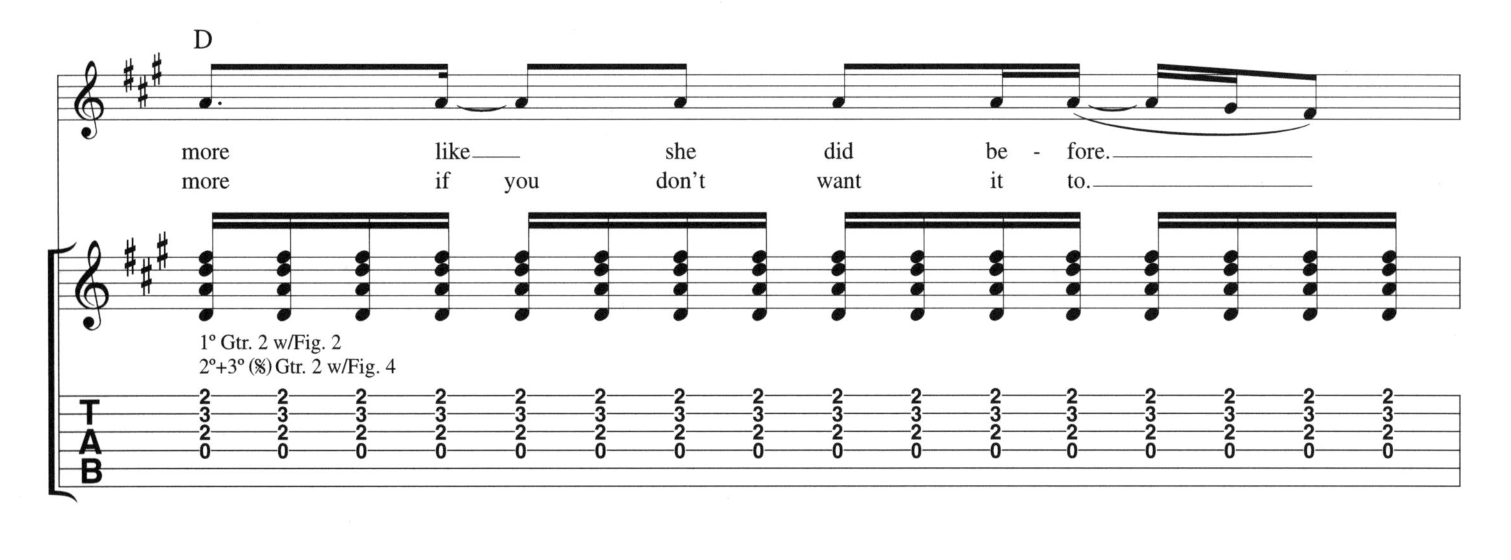
D
more like she did be - fore.
more if you don't want it to.
1º Gtr. 2 w/Fig. 2
2º+3º (𝄋) Gtr. 2 w/Fig. 4
T
A
B

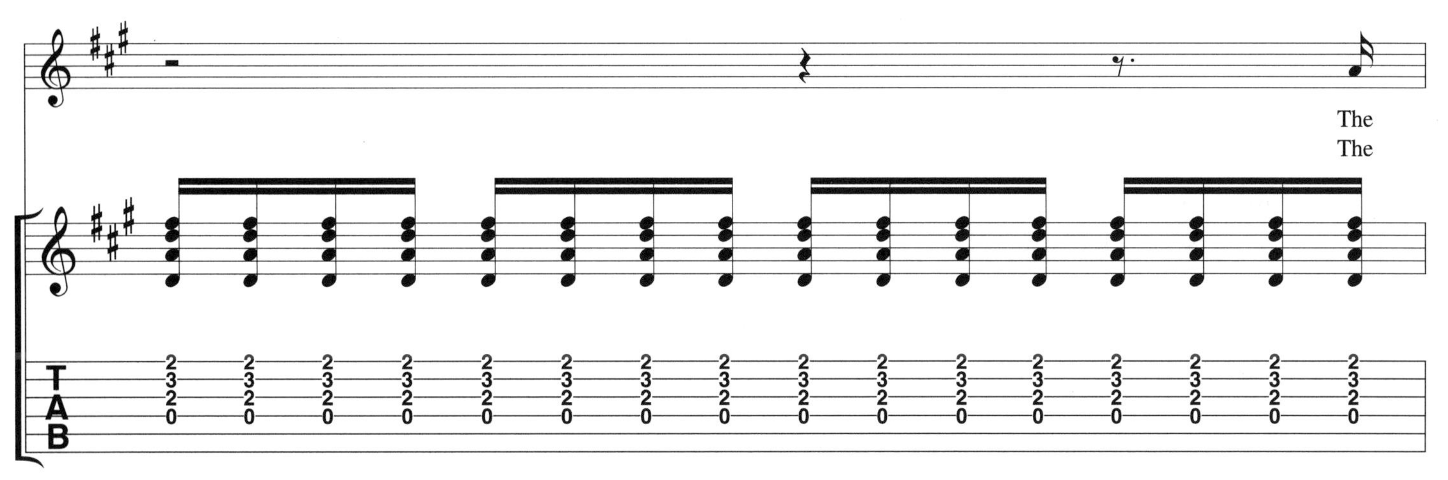
The
The
T
A
B

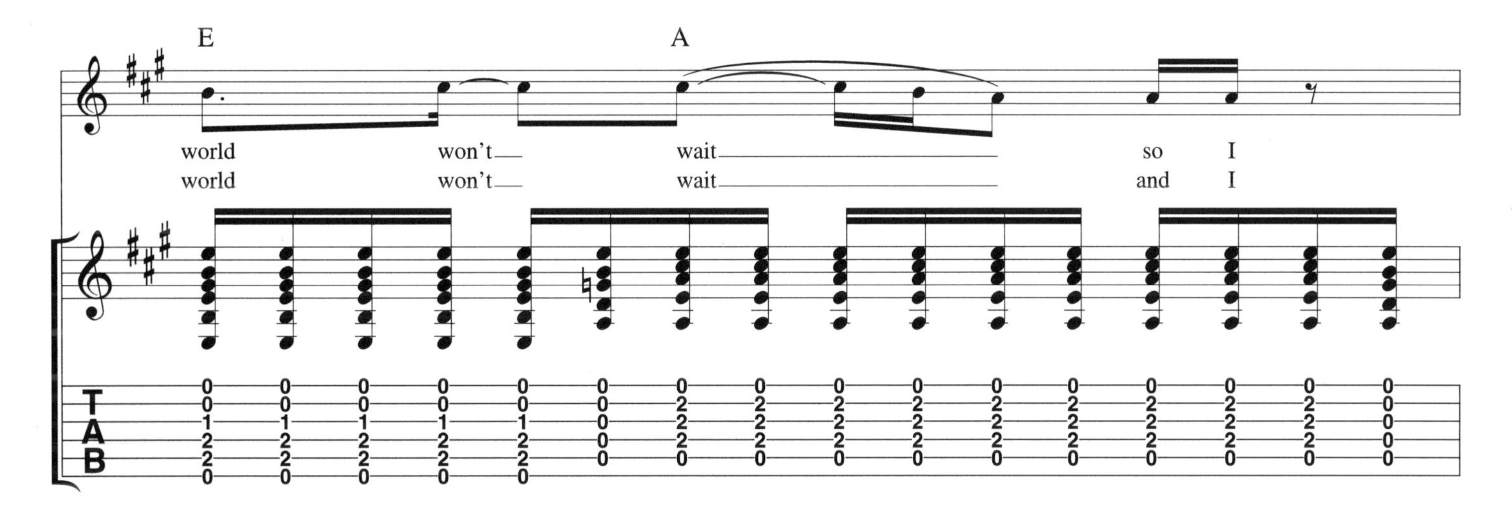
E
A
world won't wait so I
world won't wait and I
T
A
B

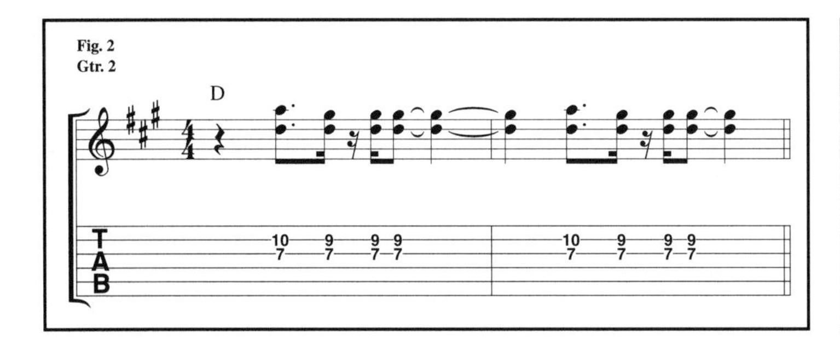
Fig. 2
Gtr. 2
D
T
A
B

Fig. 4
Gtr. 2
D
T
A
B

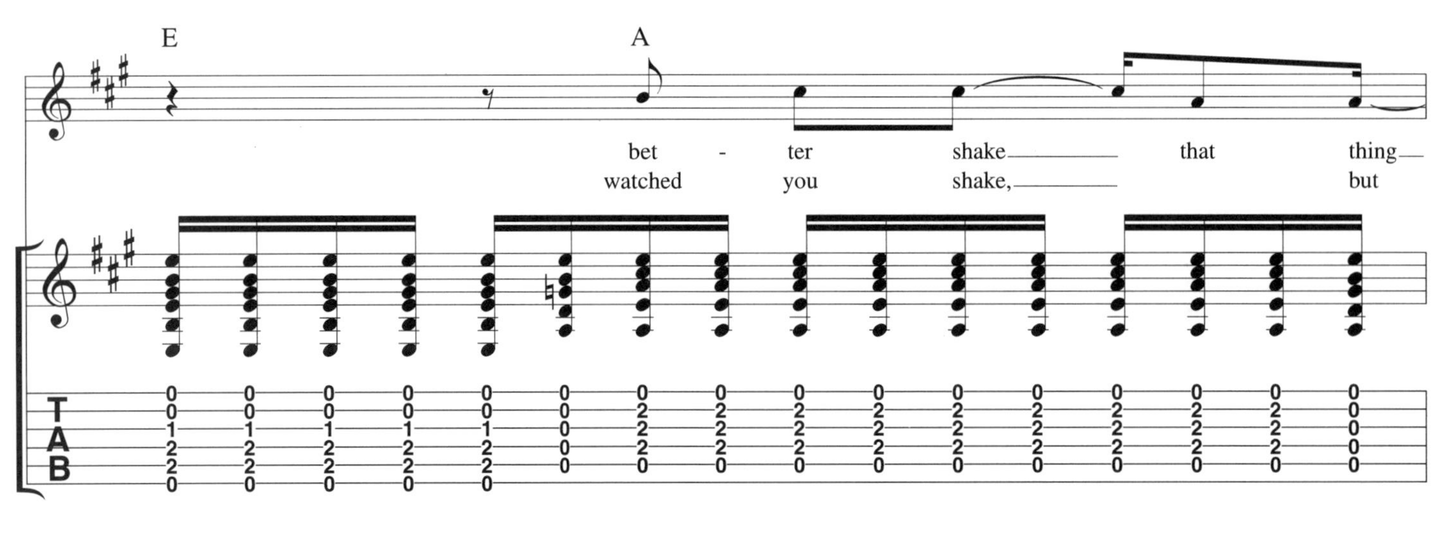
E
A
bet - ter shake that thing
watched you shake, but

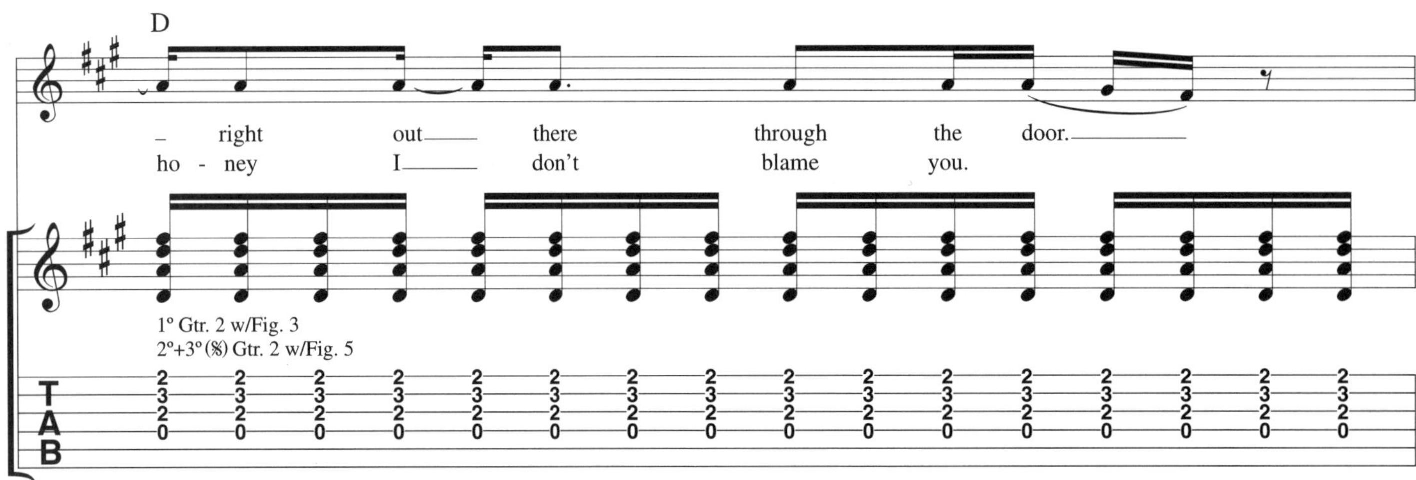
D
right out there through the door.
ho - ney I don't blame you.
1º Gtr. 2 w/Fig. 3
2º+3º (𝄋) Gtr. 2 w/Fig. 5

E
To Coda
Well I still love you New York.
Hell, I still love you New York.
Gtr. 1 cont. sim.

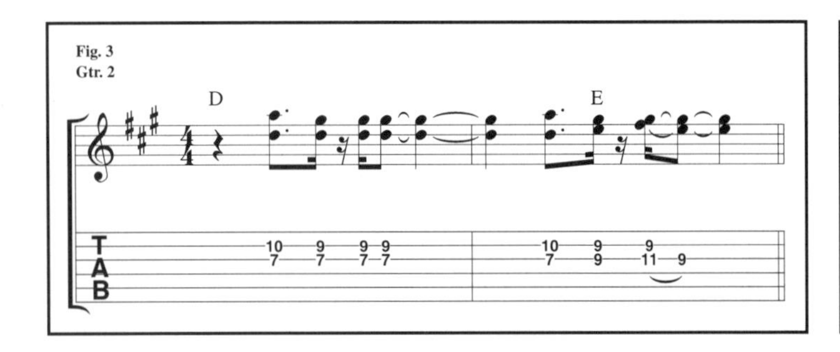
Fig. 3
Gtr. 2
D
E

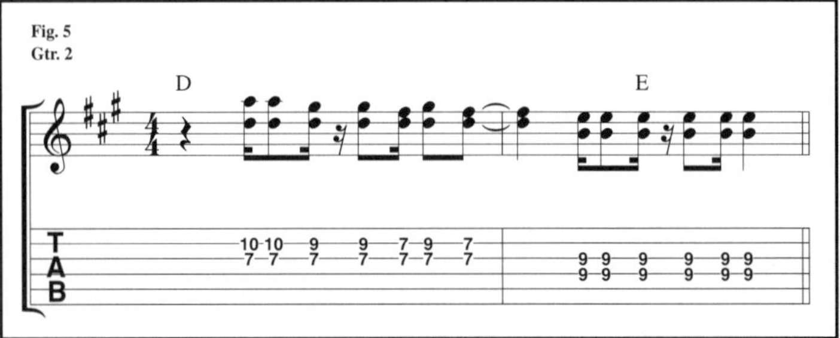
Fig. 5
Gtr. 2
D
E

Gtr. 1
Gtr. 2
A
D/A
1.
2.
2. Found
Hell, I still love you New York.
New York.
D.%. al Coda
3. I

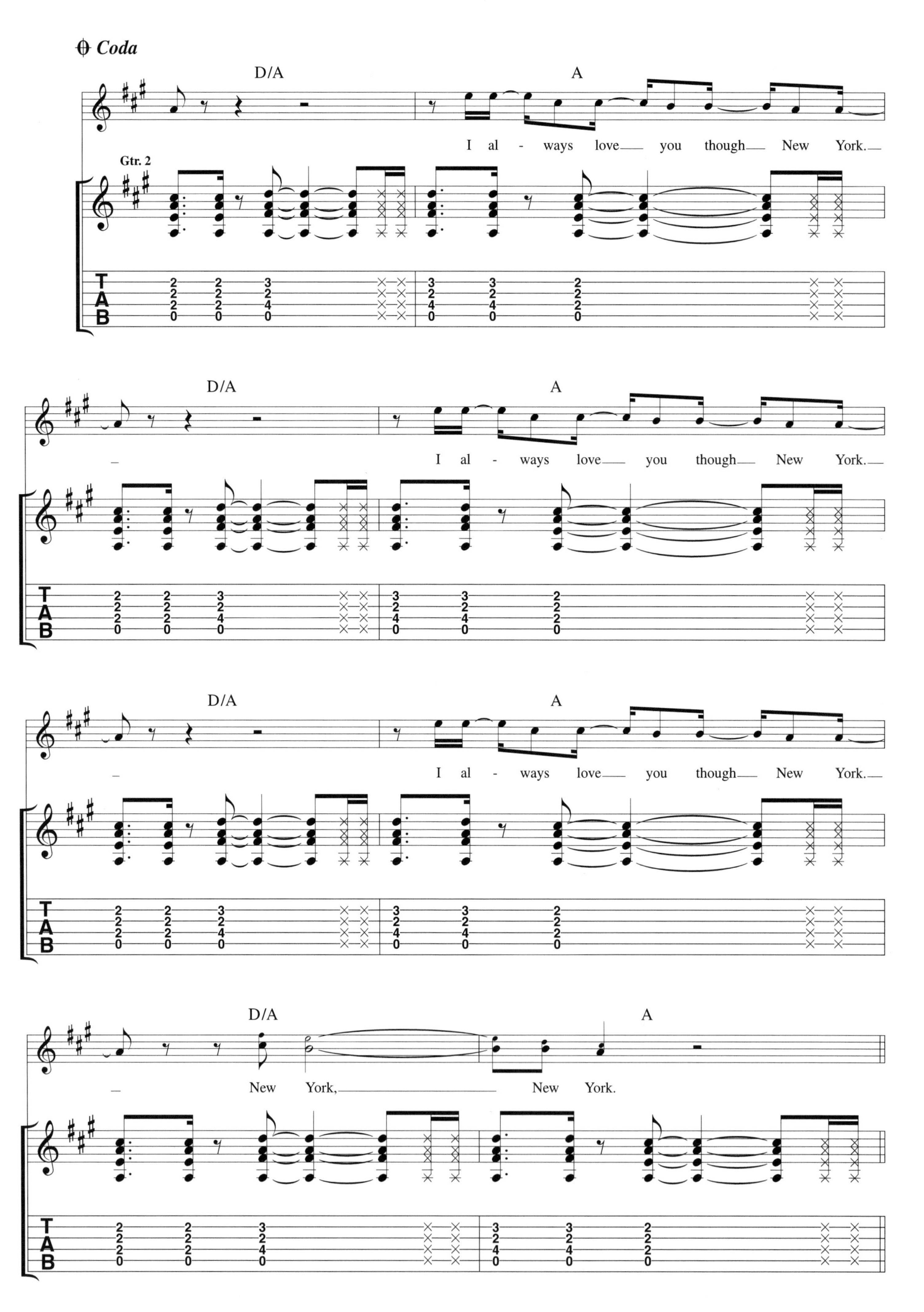
Coda
D/A
A
I al - ways love you though New York.
Gtr. 2
D/A
A
I al - ways love you though New York.
D/A
A
I al - ways love you though New York.
D/A
A
New York, New York.

Verse 3:

I remember Christmas in the blistering cold
In a church on the upper west side
Babe I stood there singin', I was holding your arm
You were holding my trust like a child
Found a lot of trouble out on Avenue B
But I tried to keep the overhead low
Farewell to the city and the love of my life
At least we left before we had to go.

And love won't play games with me anymore
If you don't want 'em to
So we better shake this old thing out the door
I'll always be thinking of you
I'll always love you though, New York
I'll always love you though, New York
New York, New York.

FIRECRACKER

Words & Music by Ryan Adams

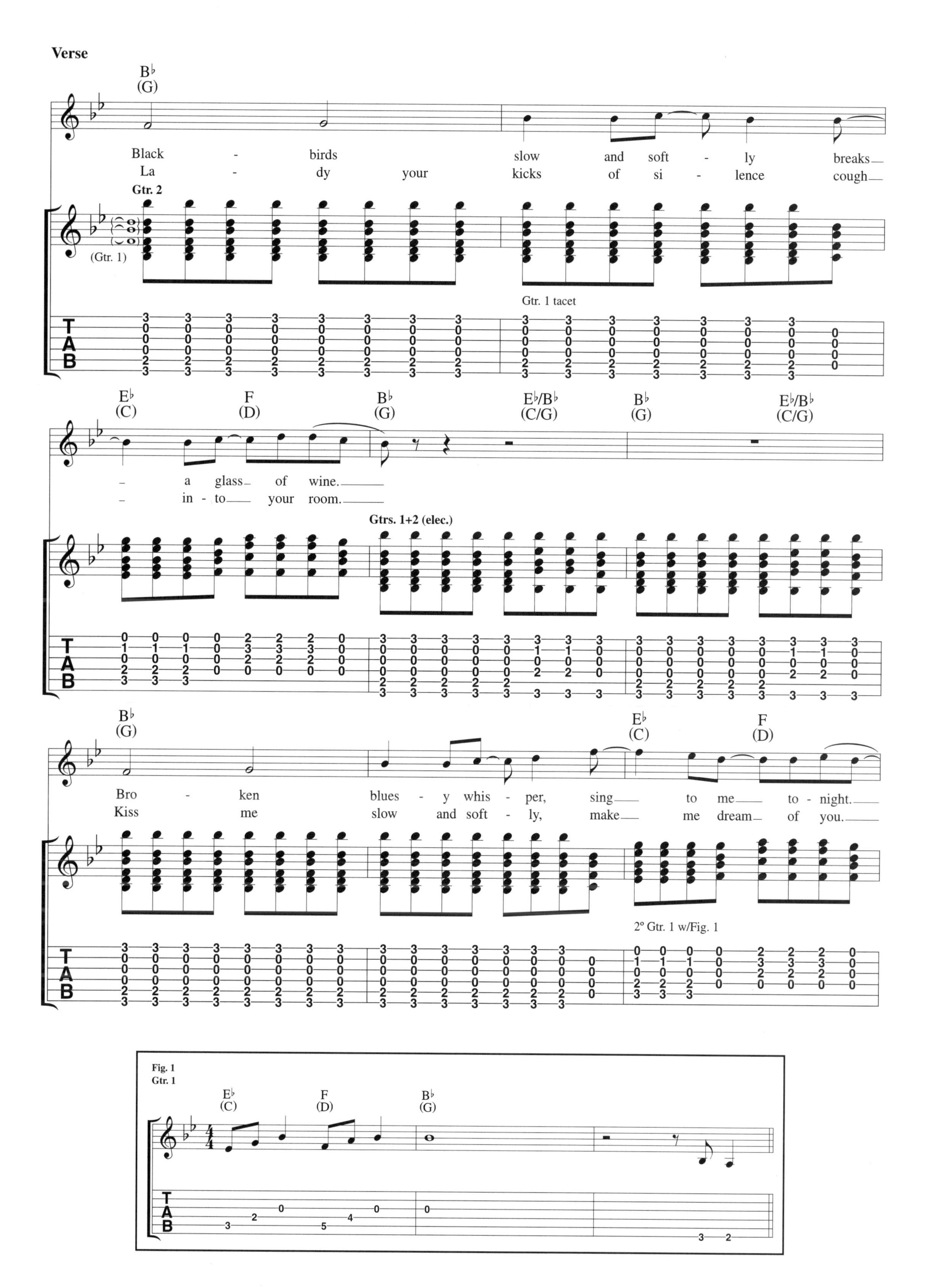
Verse
B♭
(G)
Black - birds slow and soft - ly breaks
La - dy your kicks of si - lence cough
Gtr. 2
(Gtr. 1)
Gtr. 1 tacet
E♭
(C)
F
(D)
B♭
(G)
E♭/B♭
(C/G)
B♭
(G)
E♭/B♭
(C/G)
a glass of wine.
in - to your room.
Gtrs. 1+2 (elec.)
B♭
(G)
E♭
(C)
F
(D)
Bro - ken blues - y whis - per, sing to me to - night.
Kiss me slow and soft - ly, make me dream of you.
2° Gtr. 1 w/Fig. 1
Fig. 1
Gtr. 1
E♭
(C)
F
(D)
B♭
(G)

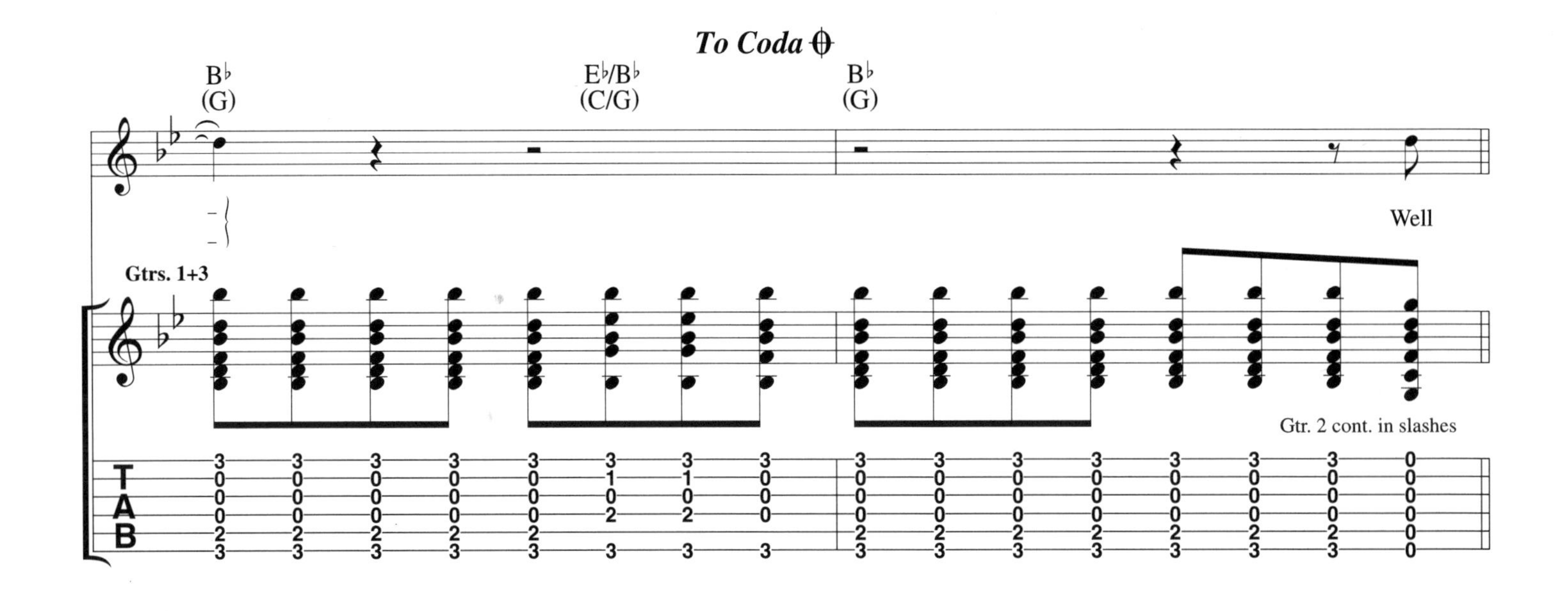
To Coda
B♭
(G)
E♭/B♭
(C/G)
B♭
(G)
Well
Gtrs. 1+3
Gtr. 2 cont. in slashes

Chorus

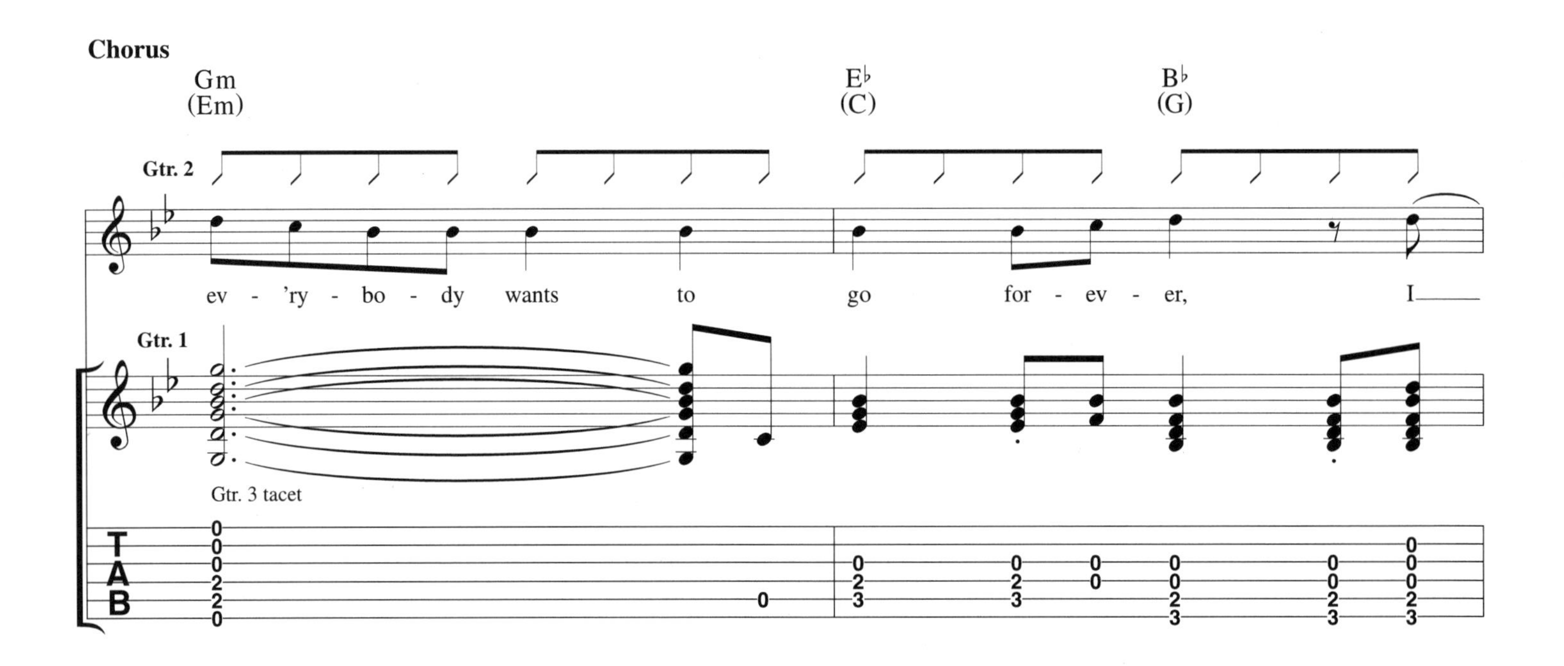
Gm
(Em)
E♭
(C)
B♭
(G)
Gtr. 2
ev - 'ry - bo - dy wants to go for - ev - er, I
Gtr. 1
Gtr. 3 tacet

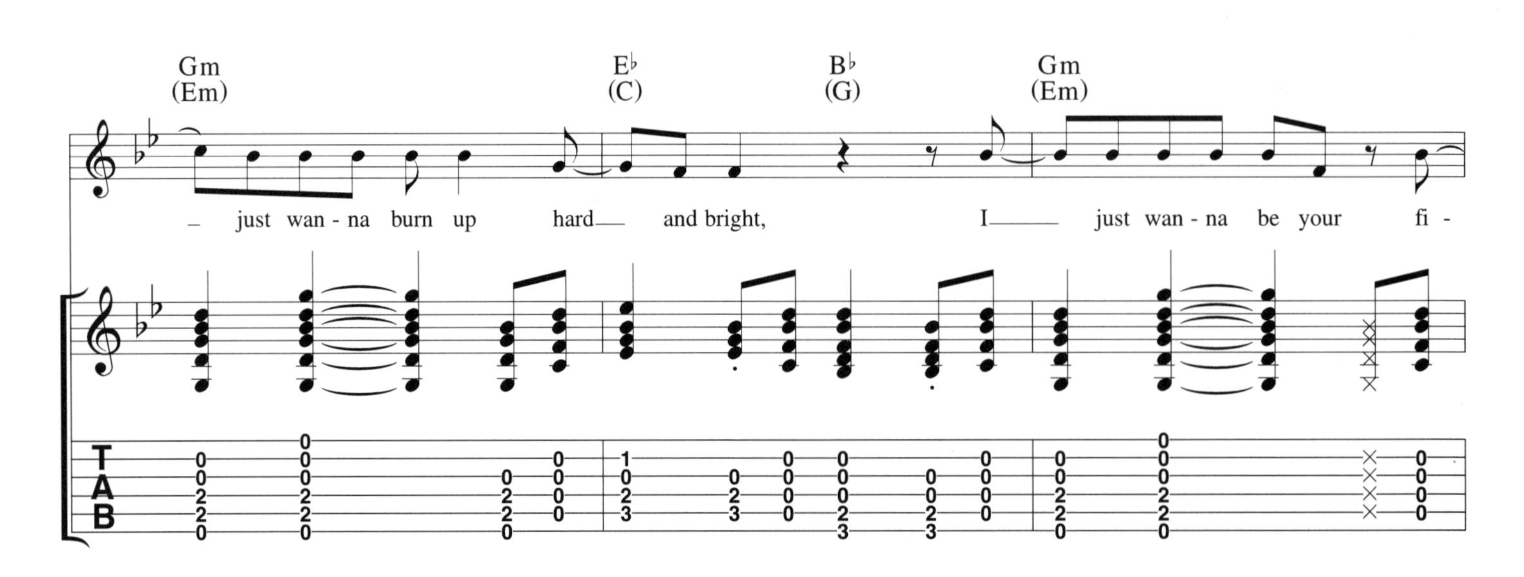
Gm
(Em)
E♭
(C)
B♭
(G)
Gm
(Em)
just wan - na burn up hard and bright, I just wan - na be your fi -

E♭ (C)
F (D)
Cm (Am)
E♭ (C)
-re - crack - er, may - be be your ba - by to - night.
May -
Cm (Am)
E♭ (C)
F (D)
- be be your ba - by to - night,
ah.
B♭ (G)
Harmonica
E♭ (C)
F (D)
B♭ (G)

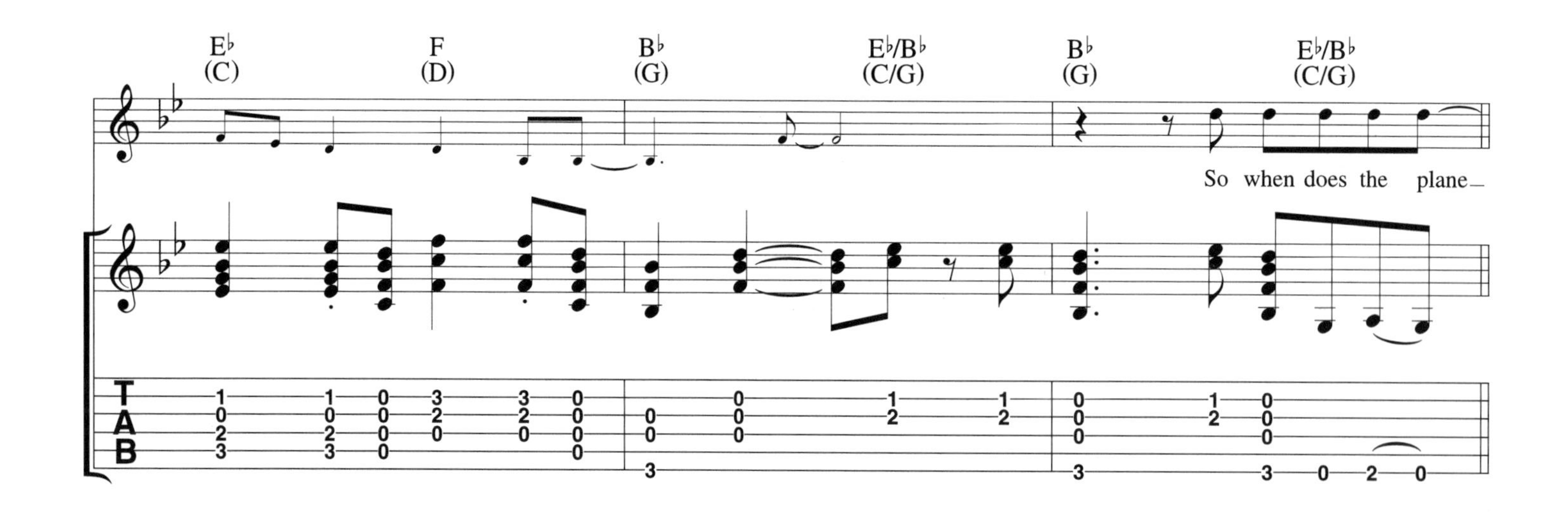
E♭ (C)
F (D)
B♭ (G)
E♭/B♭ (C/G)
B♭ (G)
E♭/B♭ (C/G)
So when does the plane

Bridge

Gm (Em)
B♭ (G)
go down?
'Cos I'm gon - na ride it till it hits the

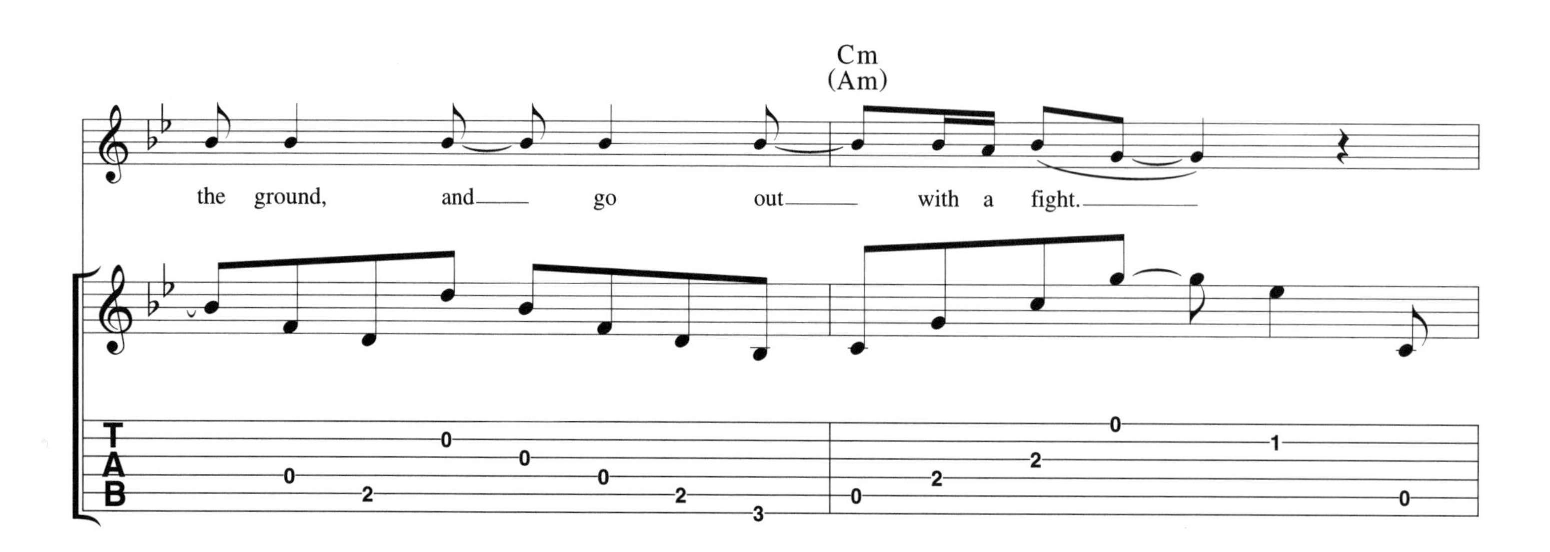
Cm (Am)
the ground, and go out with a fight.

B♭/D
(G/B)
E♭
(C)
F
(D)
'Cos I just wan - na be your ba - by__ to -
T
A
B

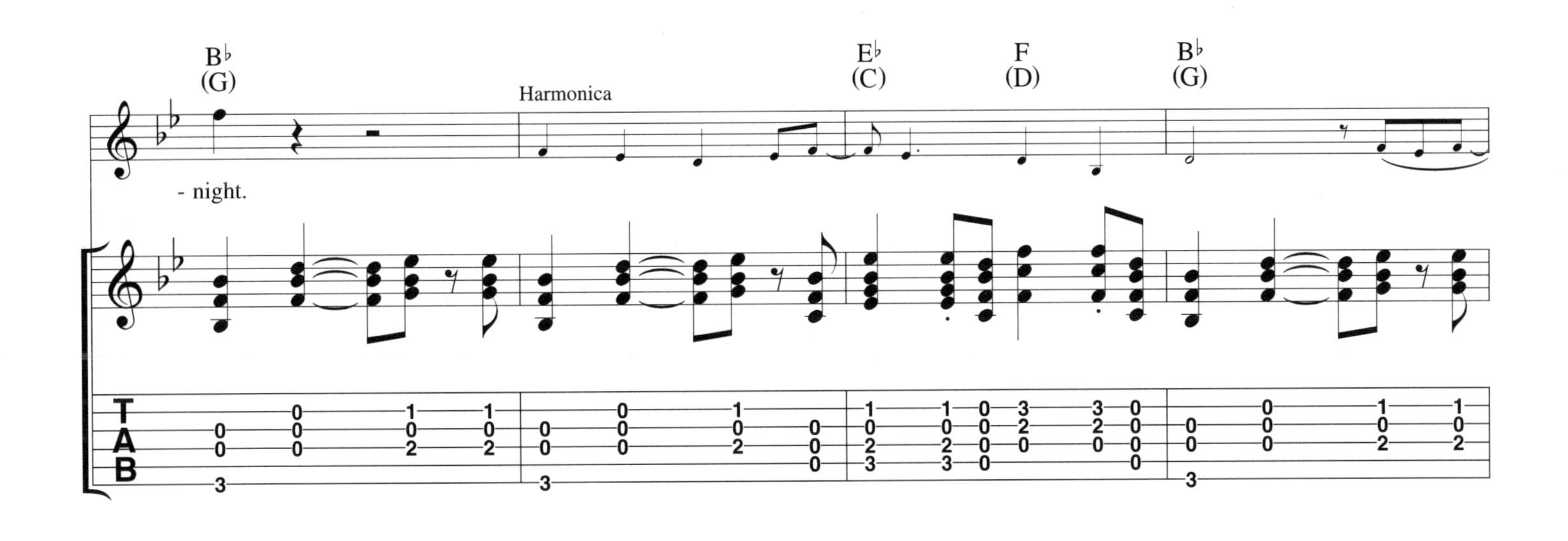
B♭
(G)
Harmonica
E♭
(C)
F
(D)
B♭
(G)
- night.
T
A
B

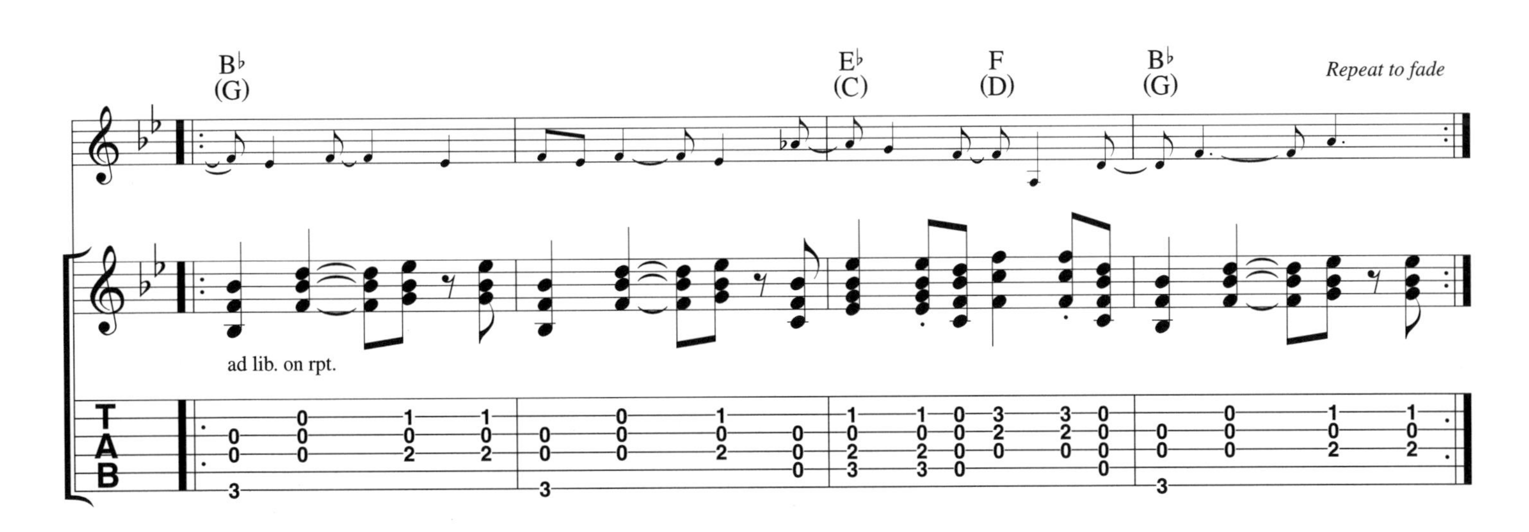
B♭
(G)
E♭
(C)
F
(D)
B♭
(G)
Repeat to fade
ad lib. on rpt.
T
A
B

ANSWERING BELL

Words & Music by Ryan Adams

G
Bm
C
Am
All's I know is I wake up here in my clothes to-mor - row.
The names are changed but the con-stel-la-tions are still fall-in'.

Chorus

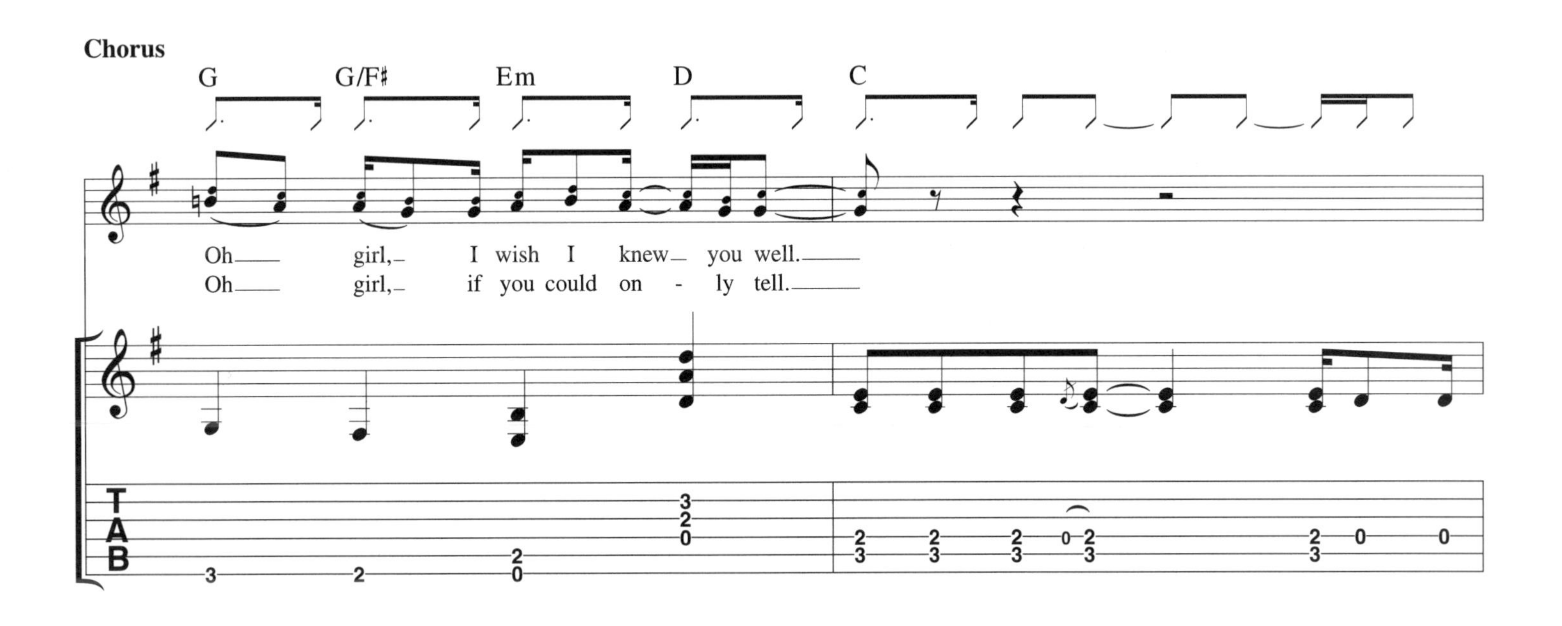
G
G/F♯
Em
D
C
Oh girl, I wish I knew you well.
Oh girl, if you could on - ly tell.

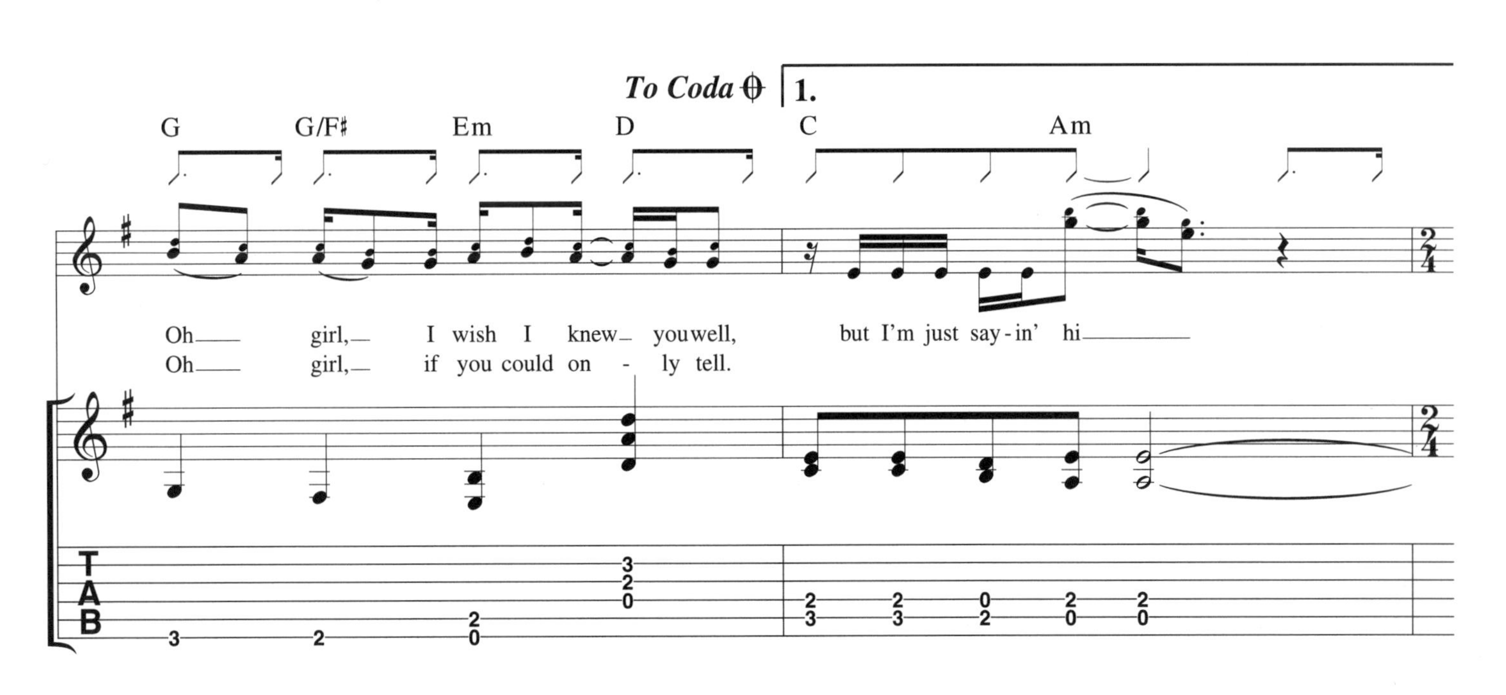
To Coda
1.
G
G/F♯
Em
D
C
Am
Oh girl, I wish I knew you well, but I'm just say-in' hi
Oh girl, if you could on - ly tell.

2.
C
Am
to your ans - wer - ing bell.
but I'm just say - in' hi.
Bridge
Bm
C
G
C/G
G
Let your tears fall and touch my skin,
then your thun - der clouds could rage and wail,
D
I will col - lect them all for you in but - ter - fly jars.
T
A
B

Chorus

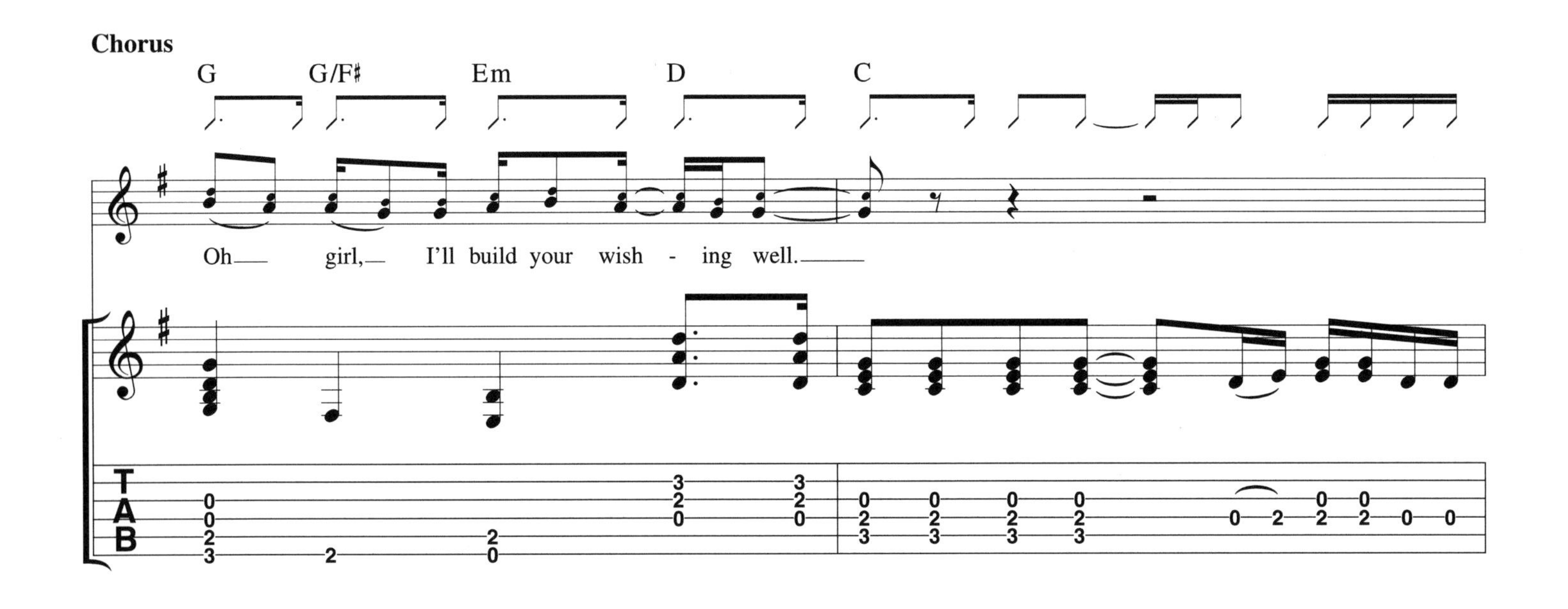
G G/F♯ Em D C
Oh girl, I'll build your wish - ing well.
T
A
B

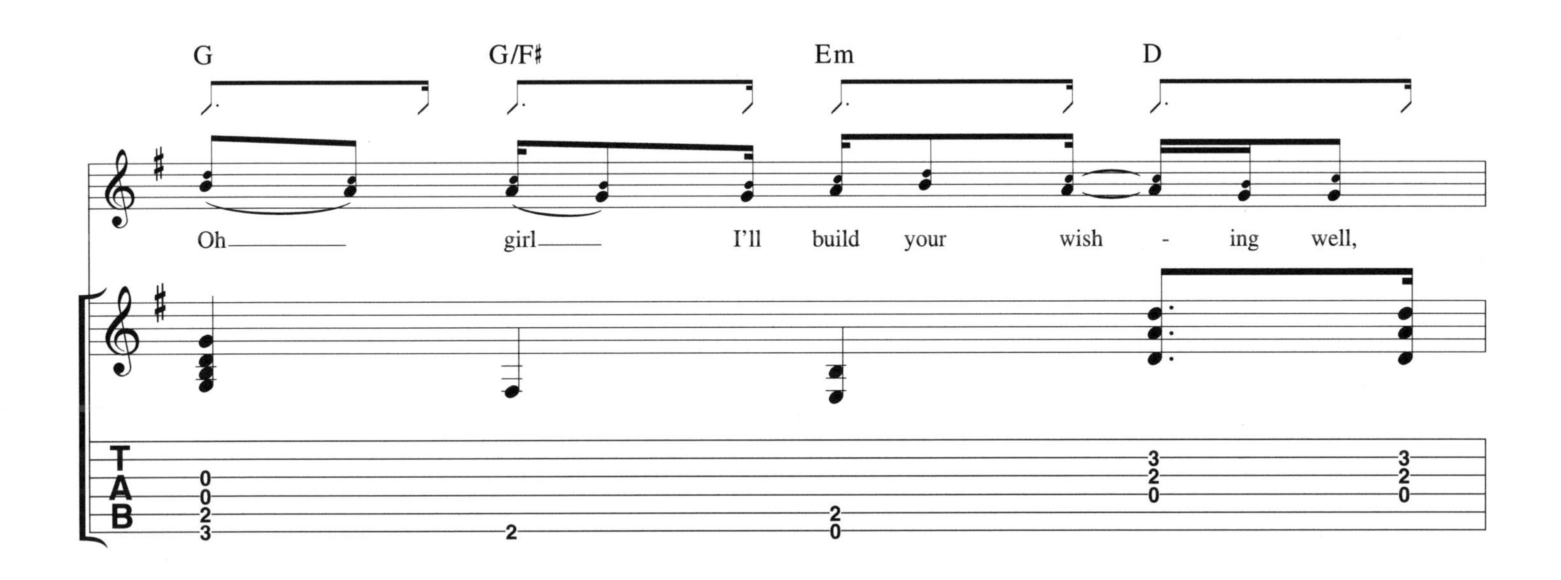
G G/F♯ Em D
Oh girl I'll build your wish - ing well,
T
A
B

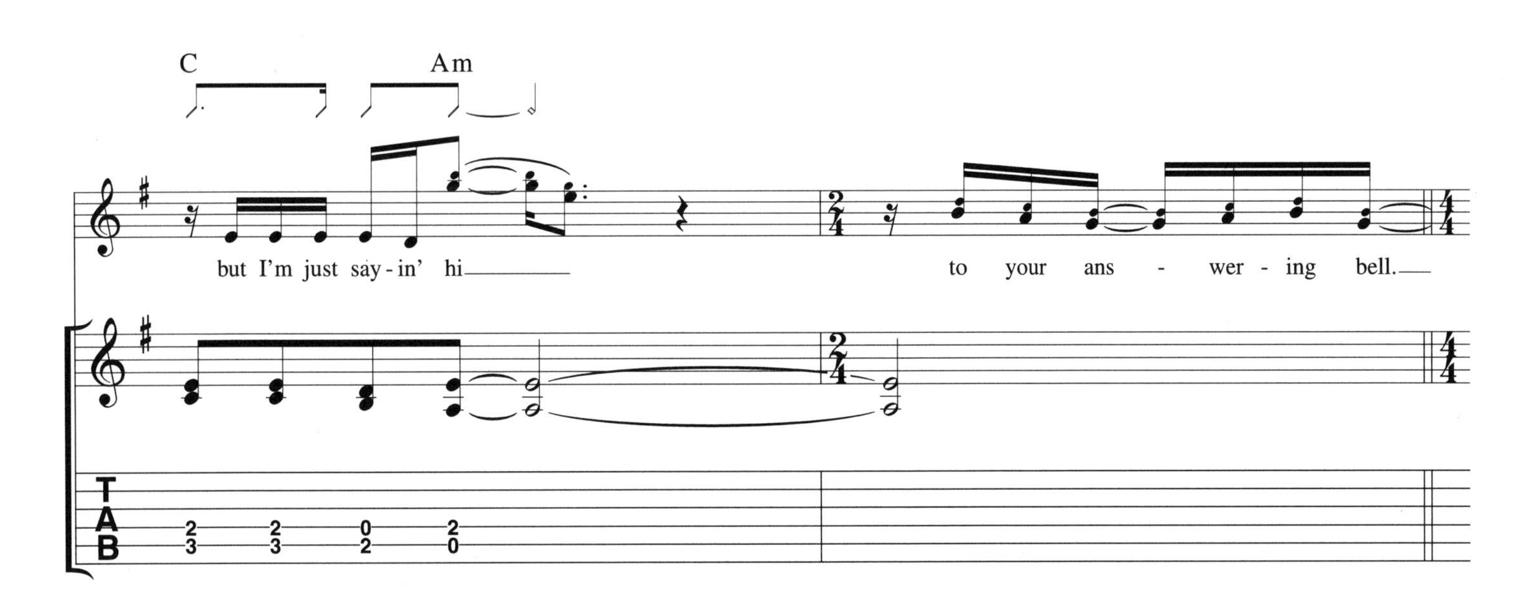
C Am
but I'm just say-in' hi
to your ans - wer - ing bell.
T
A
B

Instrumental

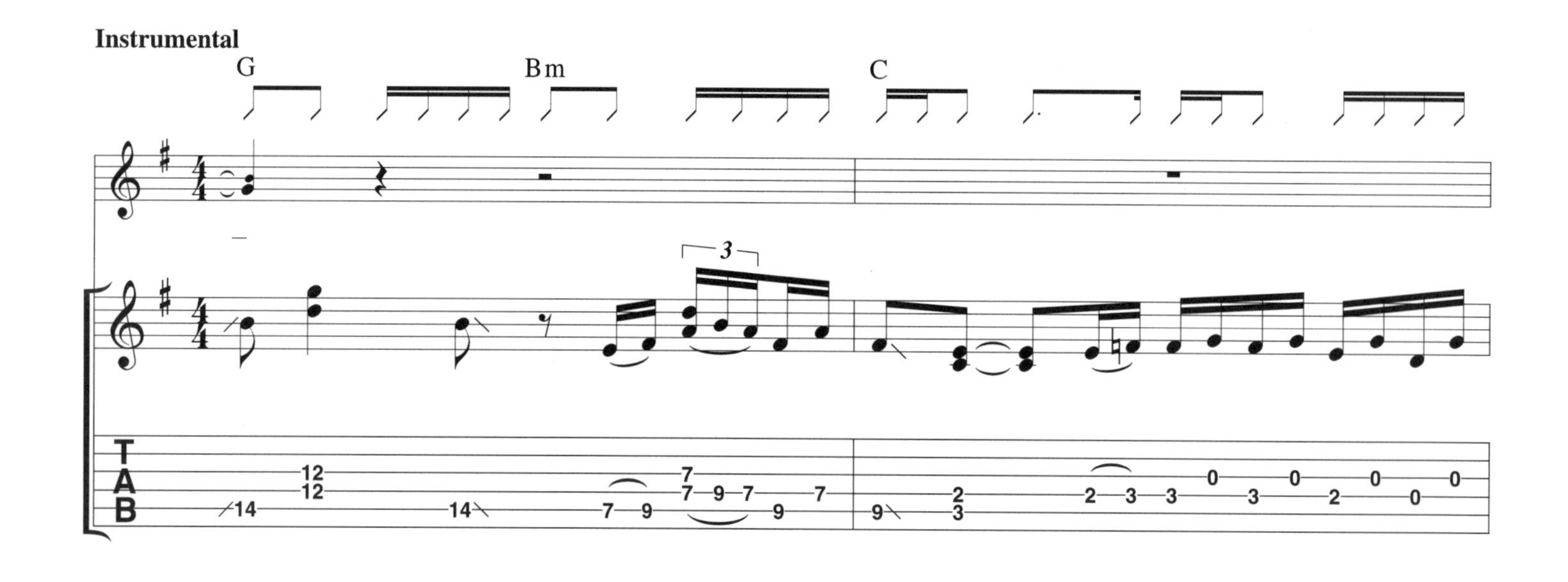

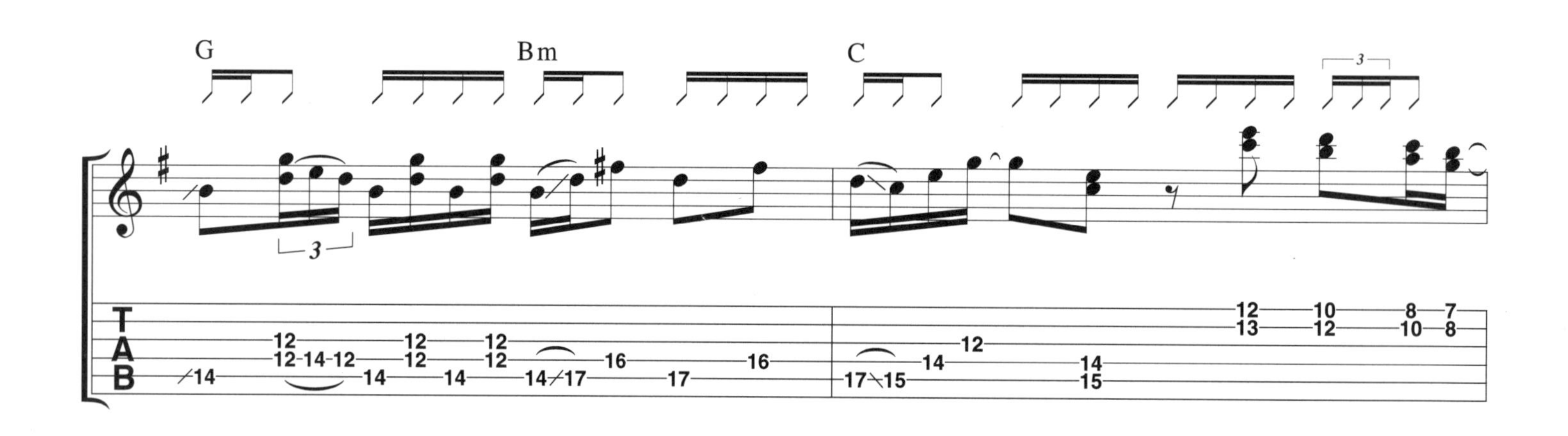

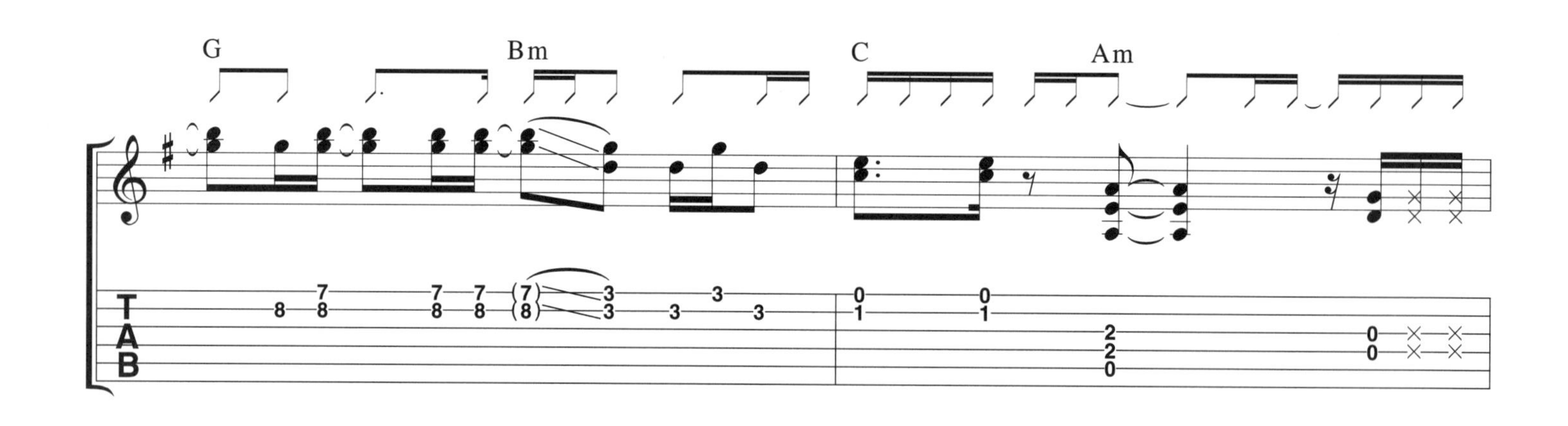

D.%. al Coda

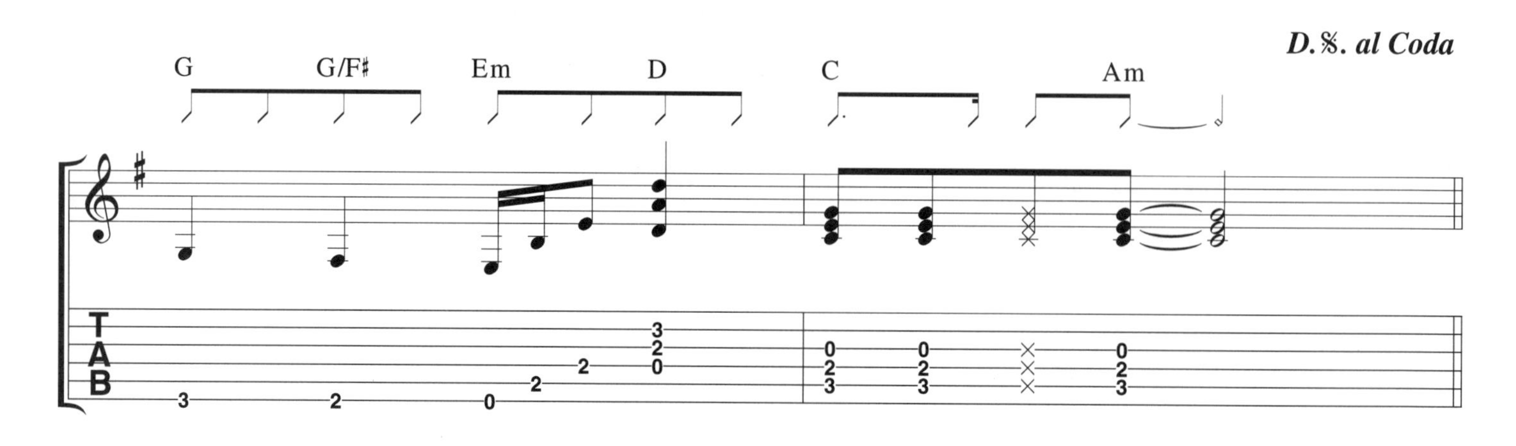

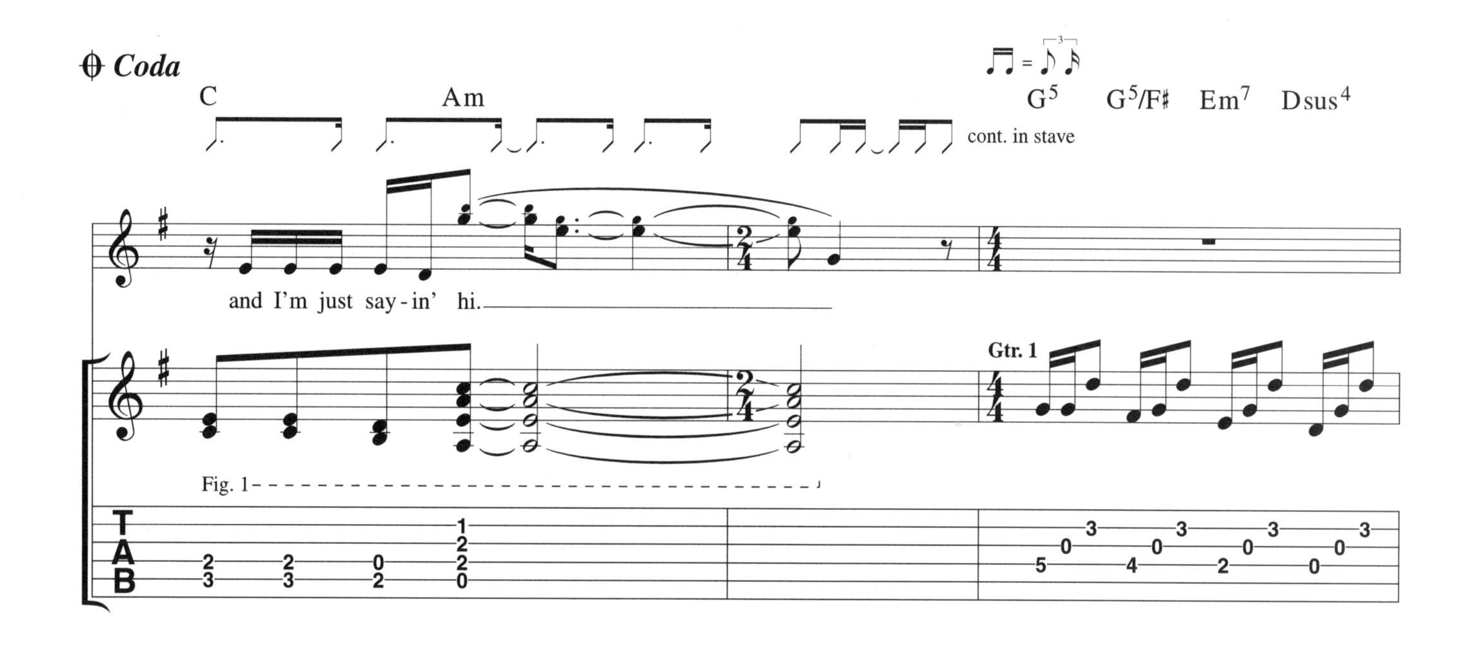

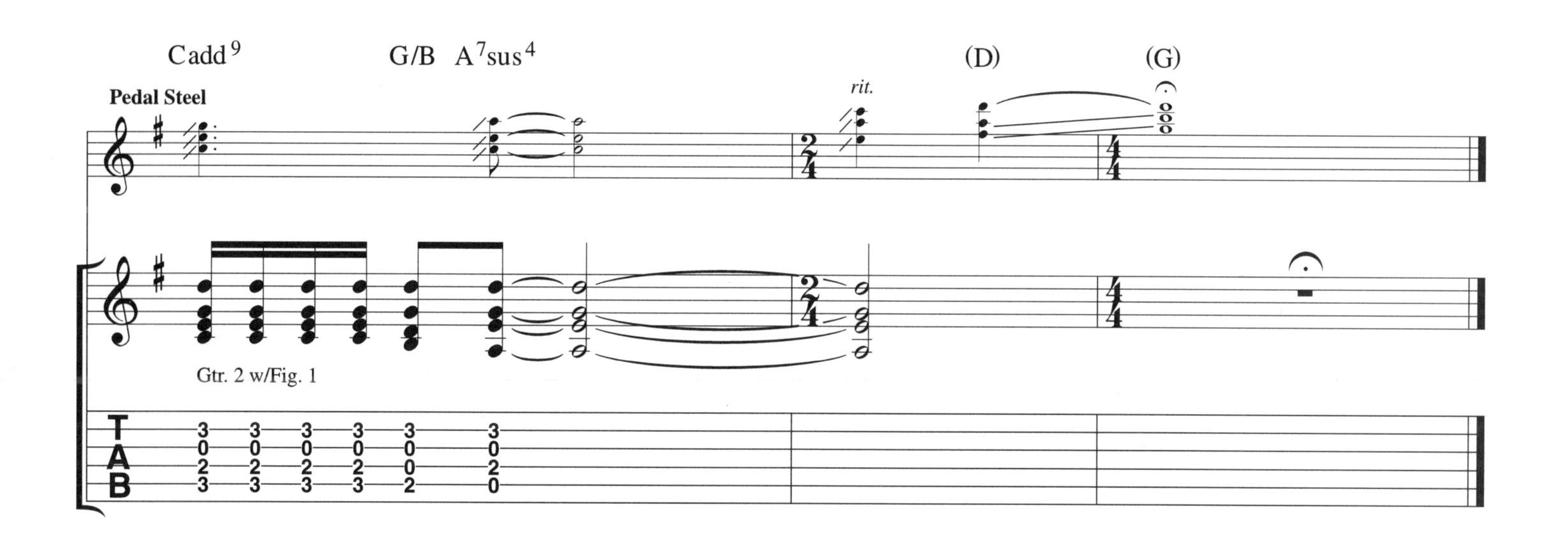

Verse 3:

Did I sleep?
'Cause I musta been dreamin'
Did I weep?
'Cause I cried like hell
All I want is your fortress of tears to crumble

And oh girl
I'd tear 'em down myself
And oh girl
The story's they could tell
But I'm just sayin' hi.

LA CIENEGA JUST SMILED

Words & Music by Ryan Adams

Capo 8th fret

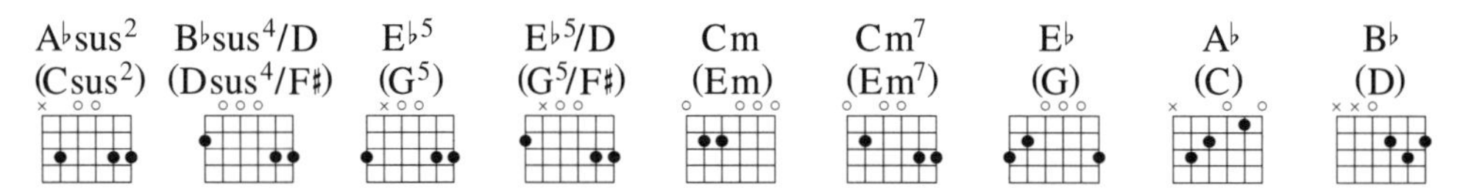

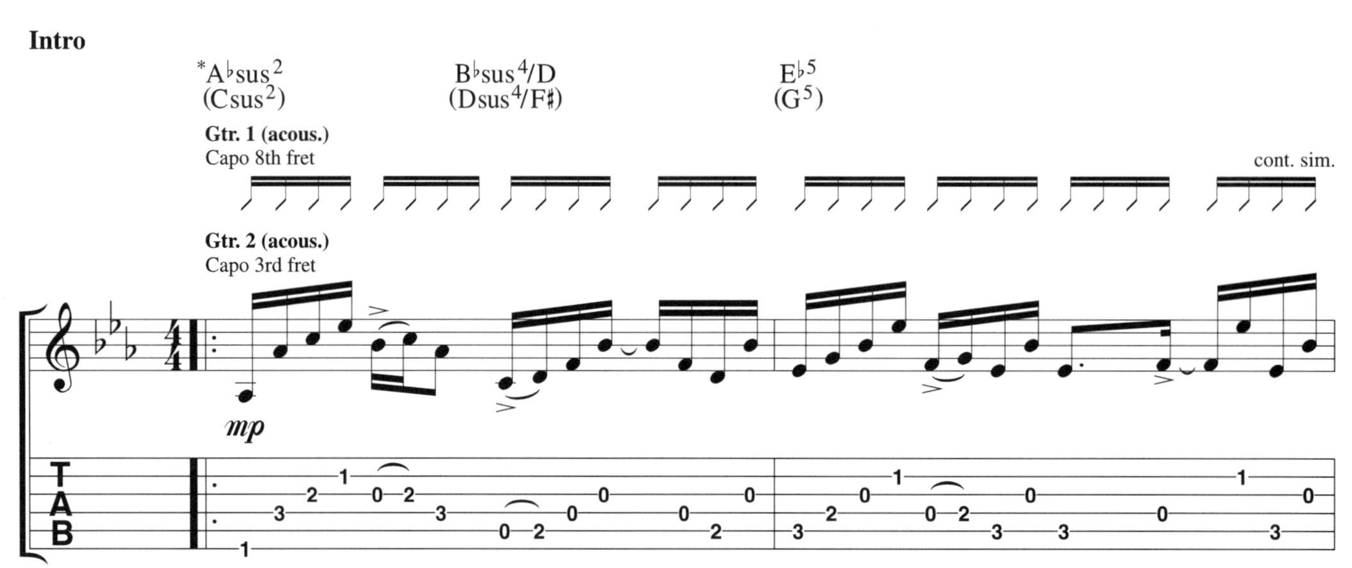

*Symbols in parentheses represent chord names with respect to capoed gtr.
Symbols above represent actual sounding chords

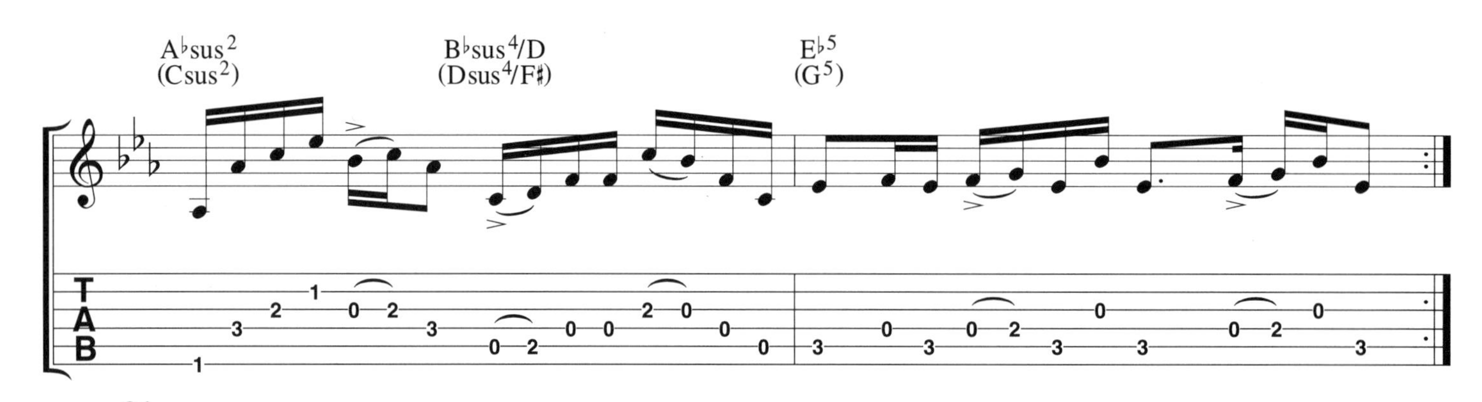

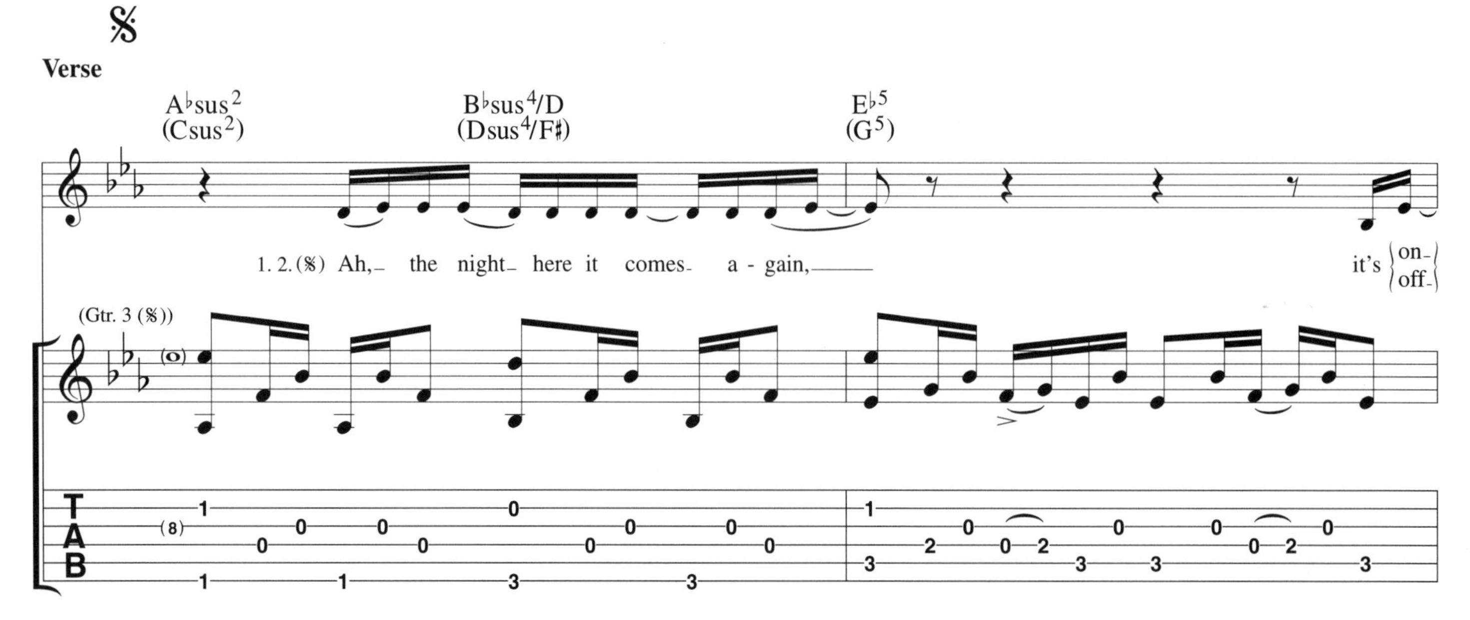

A♭sus2
(Csus2)
B♭sus4/D
(Dsus4/F♯)
E♭5
(G5)
with the jeans, the ja-cket and the shirt.
E♭5/D
(G5/F♯)
How'd I end up feel-ing so bad for such a lit-tle girl.
Cm
(Em)
And I
Chorus
(𝄋) hold you close in the back- of my- mind,
feels
hold you close in the back- of my- mind,
and raise

A♭sus2
(Csus2)
B♭sus4/D
(Dsus4/F♯)
E♭5
(G5)
so good, but damn, it makes me hurt. And I'm
my glass 'cos either way I'm dead.

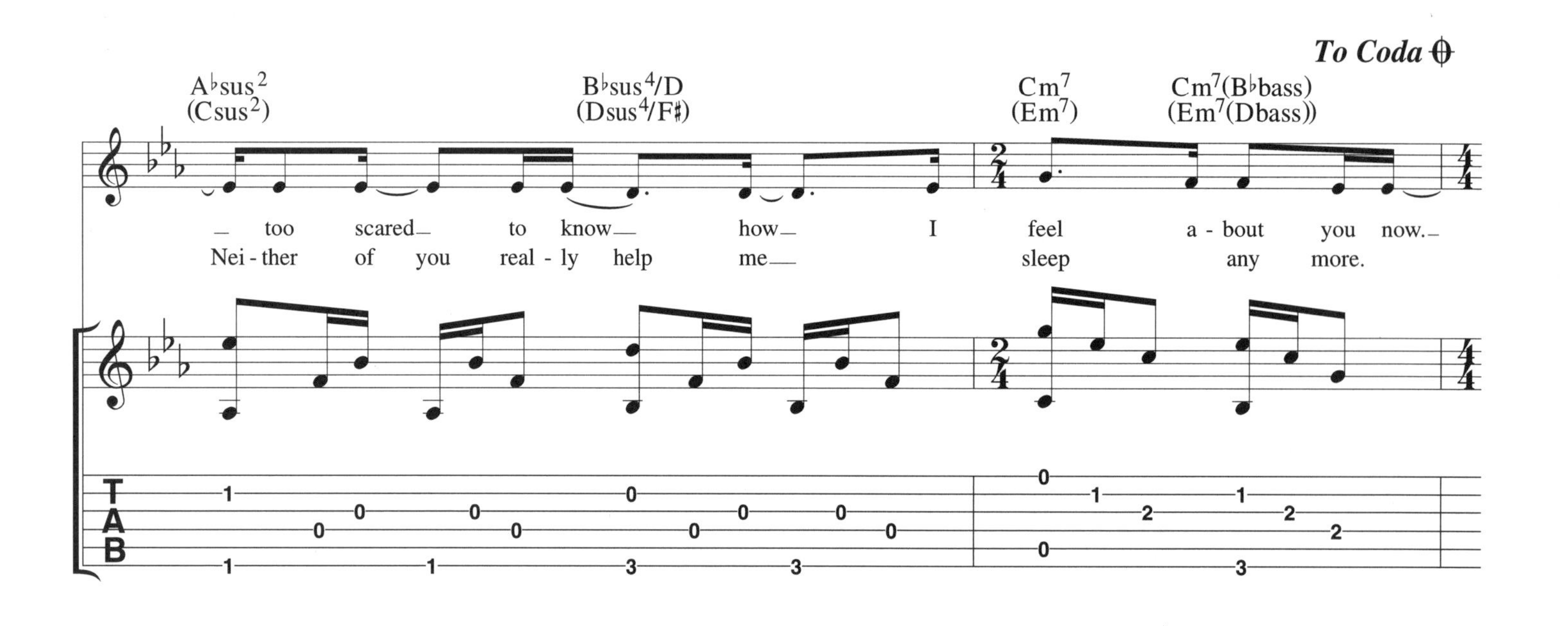
To Coda
A♭sus2
(Csus2)
B♭sus4/D
(Dsus4/F♯)
Cm7
(Em7)
Cm7(B♭bass)
(Em7(Dbass))
too scared to know how I feel a - bout you now.
Nei - ther of you real - ly help me sleep any more.

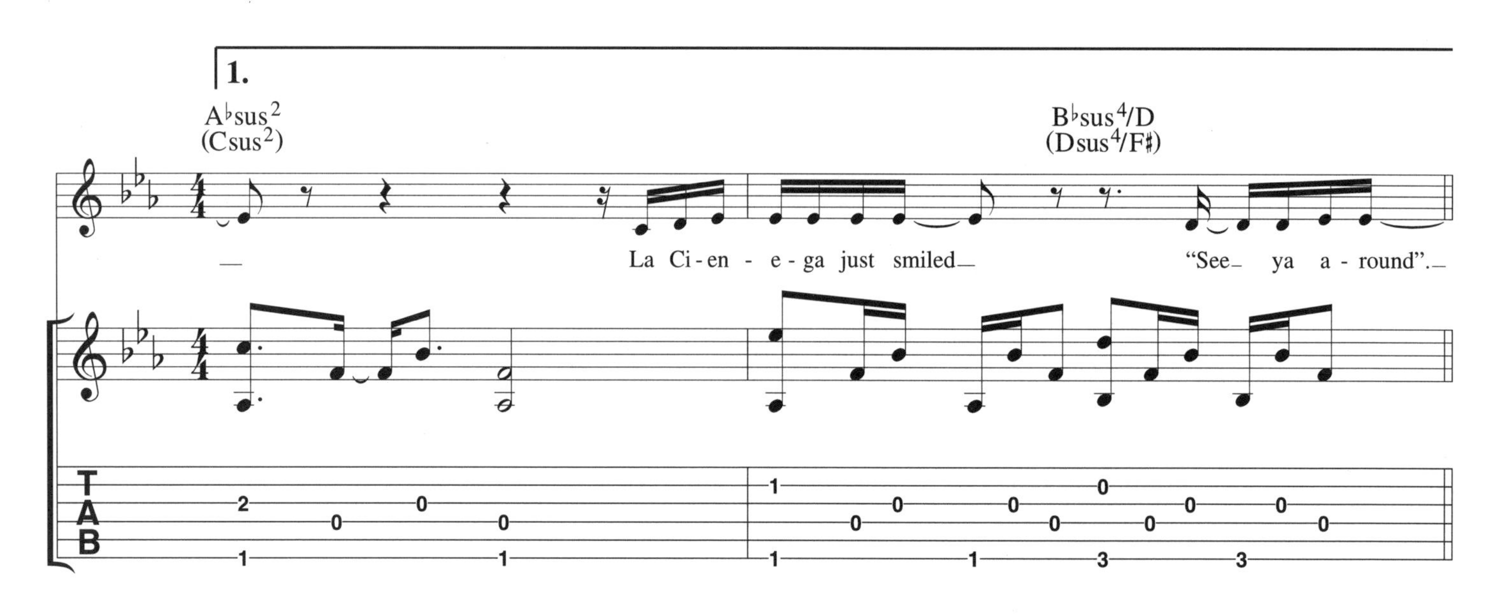
1.
A♭sus2
(Csus2)
B♭sus4/D
(Dsus4/F♯)
La Ci - en - e - ga just smiled "See ya a - round".

E♭
(G)
A♭
(C)
mf
And I
2.
A♭sus2
(Csus2)
Cm
(Em)
B♭
(D)
mp
One breaks my bo-dy and the oth-
-er breaks my soul.
La Ci-en-e-ga just smiled as it waves good-bye.
B♭sus4/D
(Dsus4/F♯)

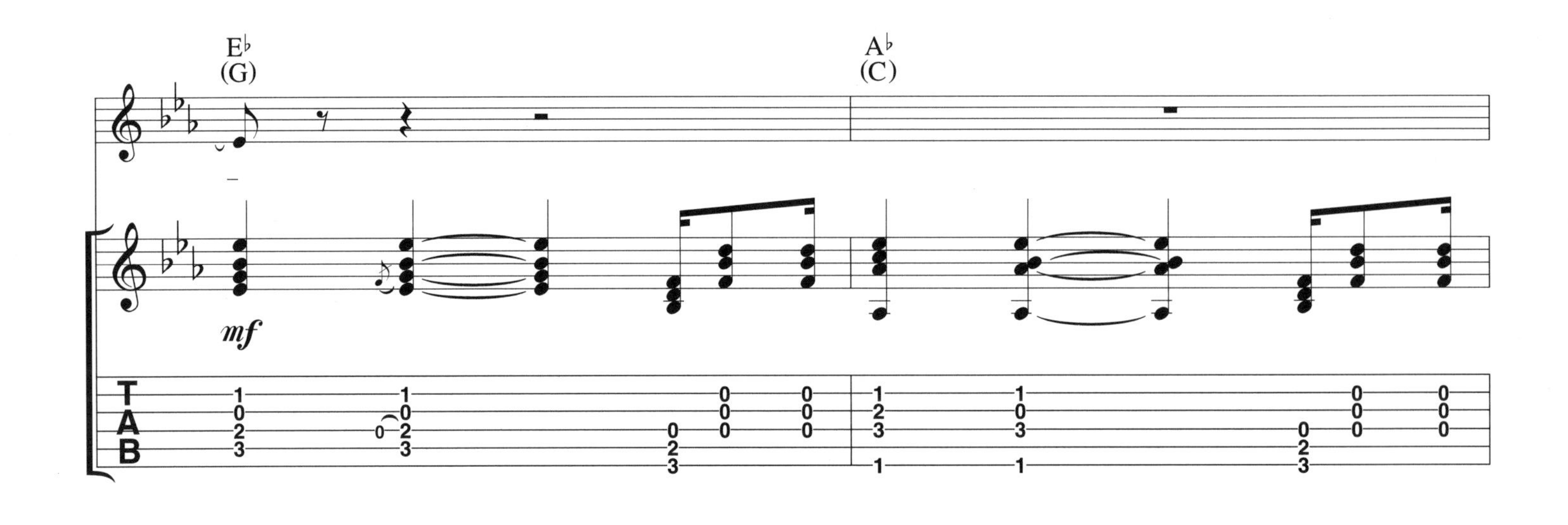
E♭
(G)
A♭
(C)
mf
TAB

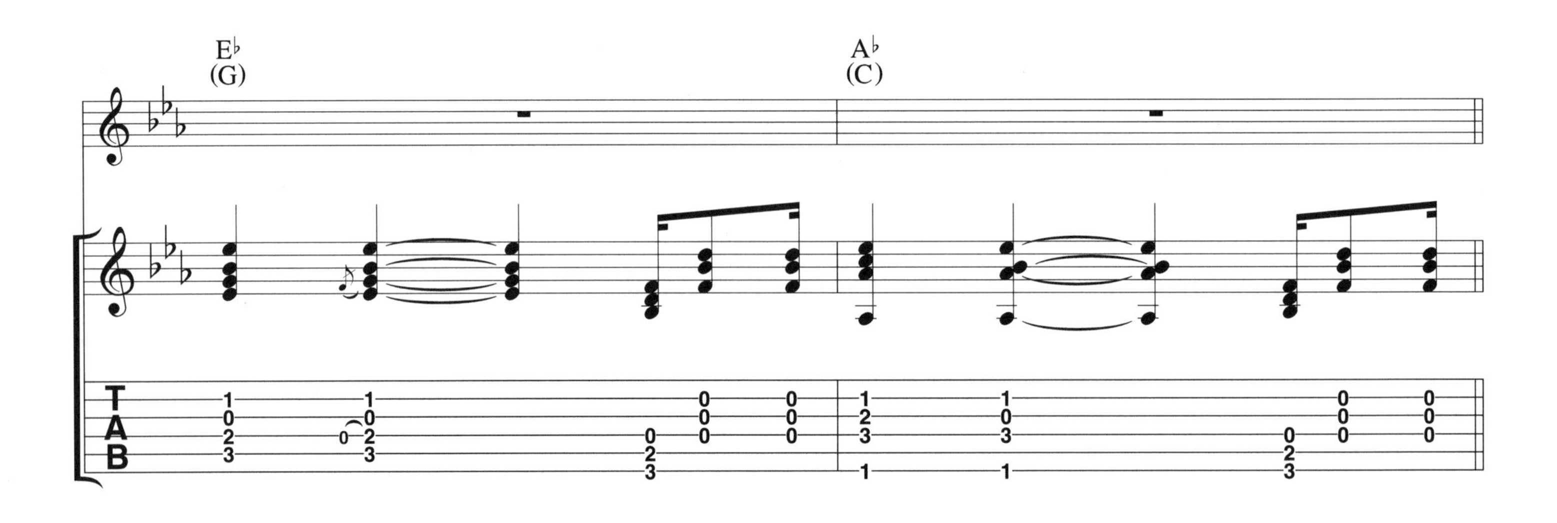
E♭
(G)
A♭
(C)
TAB

Solo

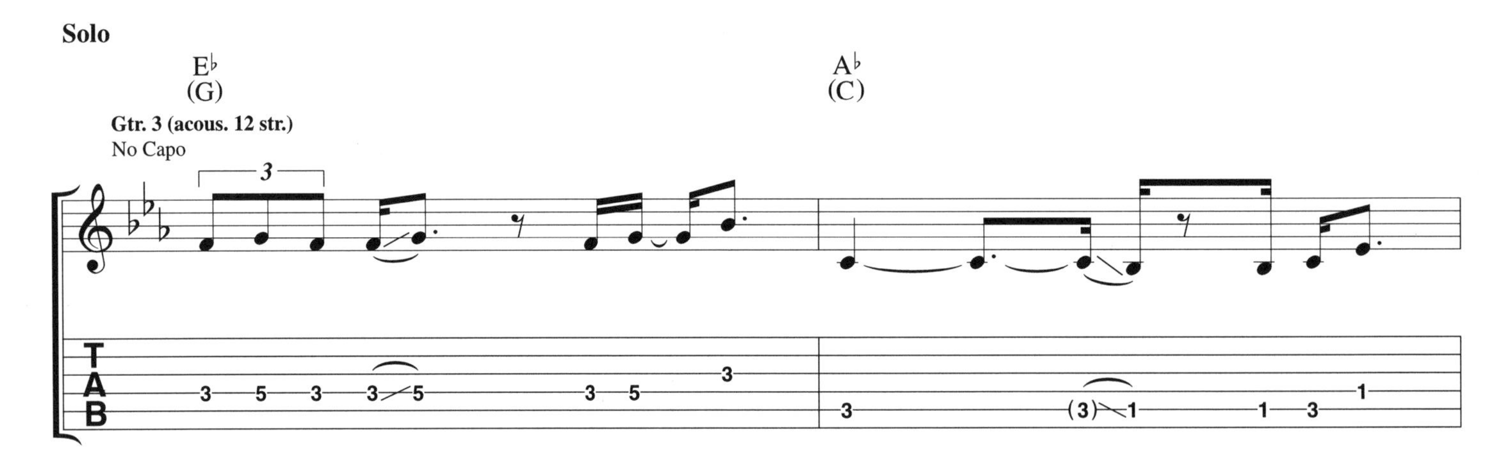
E♭
(G)
A♭
(C)
Gtr. 3 (acous. 12 str.)
No Capo
TAB

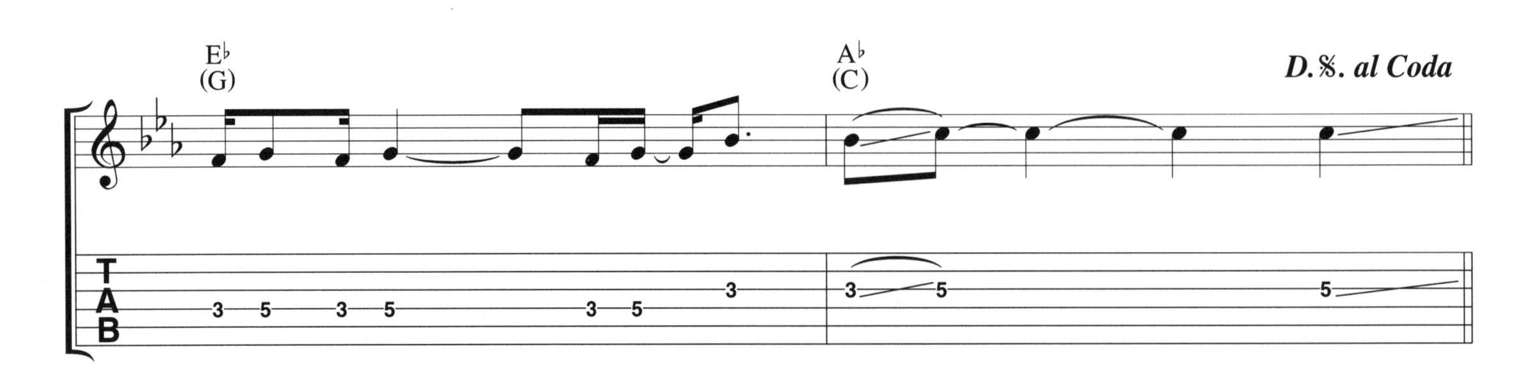
E♭
(G)
A♭
(C)
D.%. al Coda
TAB

Coda
A♭sus2 (Csus2)
Cm7 (Em7)
Cm7(B♭bass) (Em7(Dbass))
how I feel a - bout you now.
B♭sus4/D (Dsus4/F♯)
La Ci-en - e - ga just smiles and says "I'll see you a - round".
E♭ (G)
A♭ (C)
mf Fig. 1...
...Fig. 1 ends

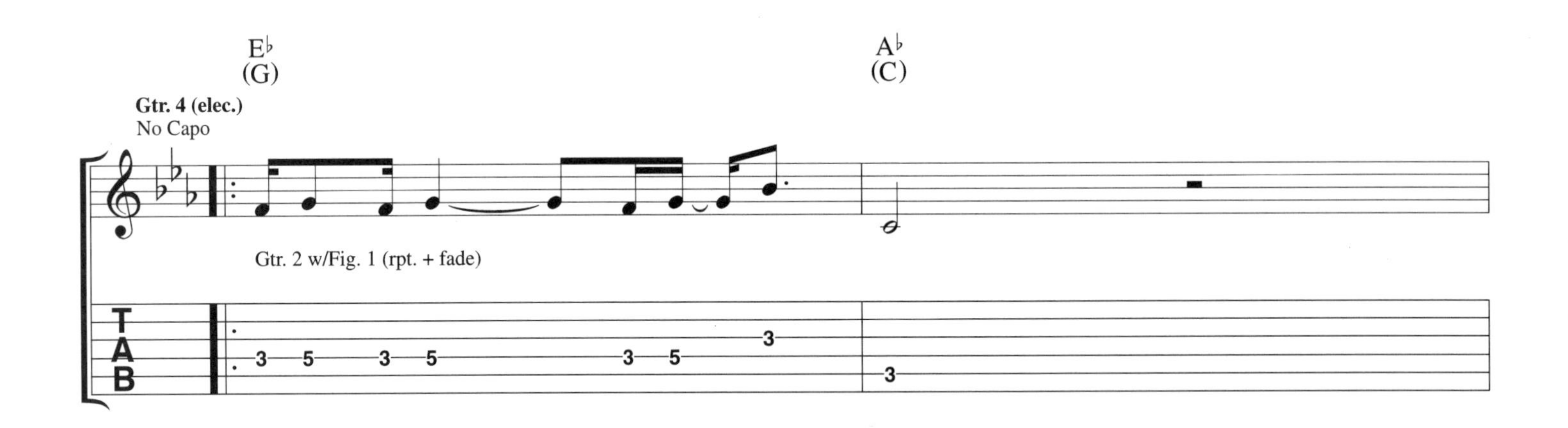
E♭
(G)
A♭
(C)
Gtr. 4 (elec.)
No Capo
Gtr. 2 w/Fig. 1 (rpt. + fade)
T
A
B

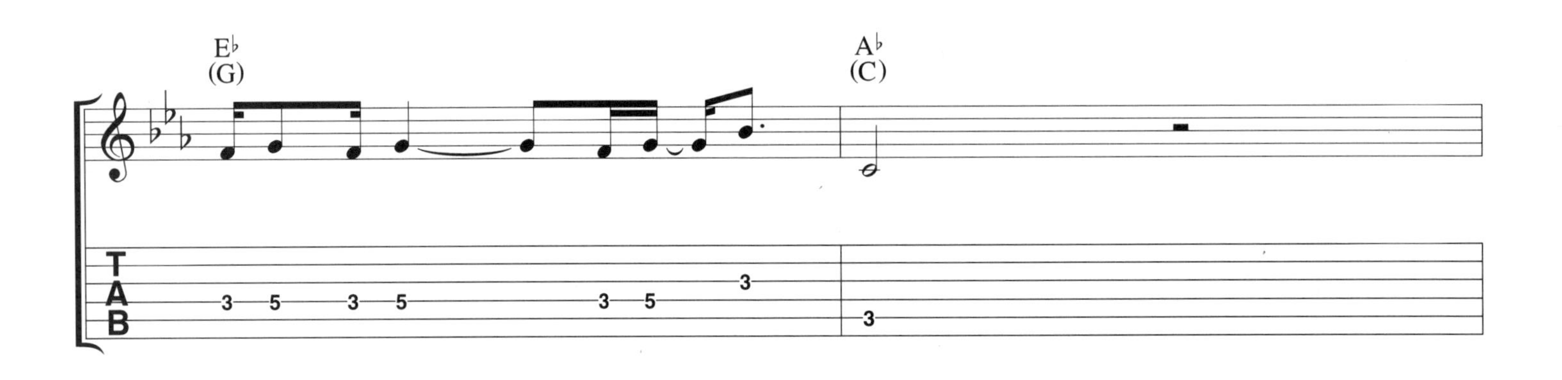
E♭
(G)
A♭
(C)
T
A
B

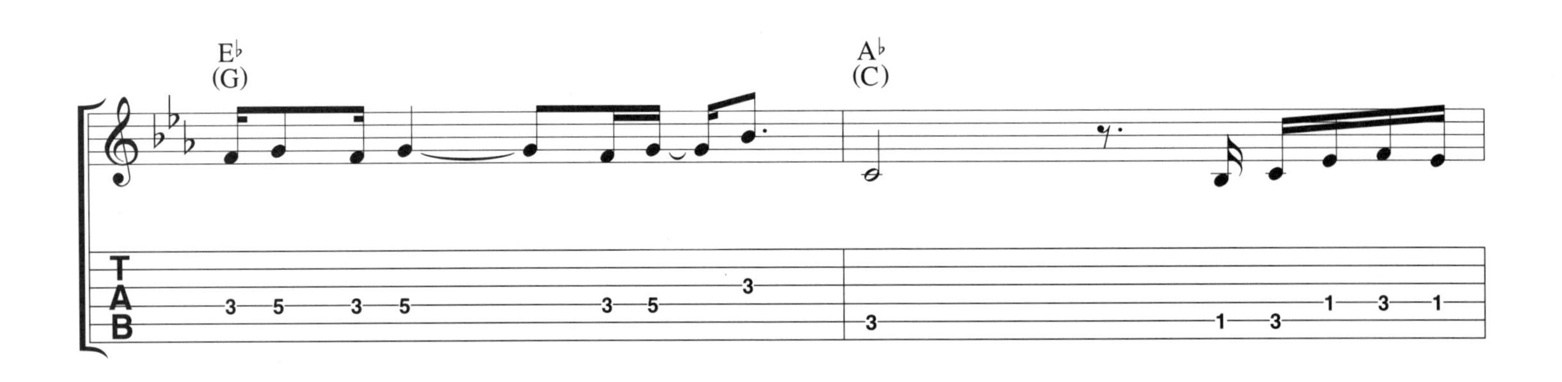
E♭
(G)
A♭
(C)
T
A
B

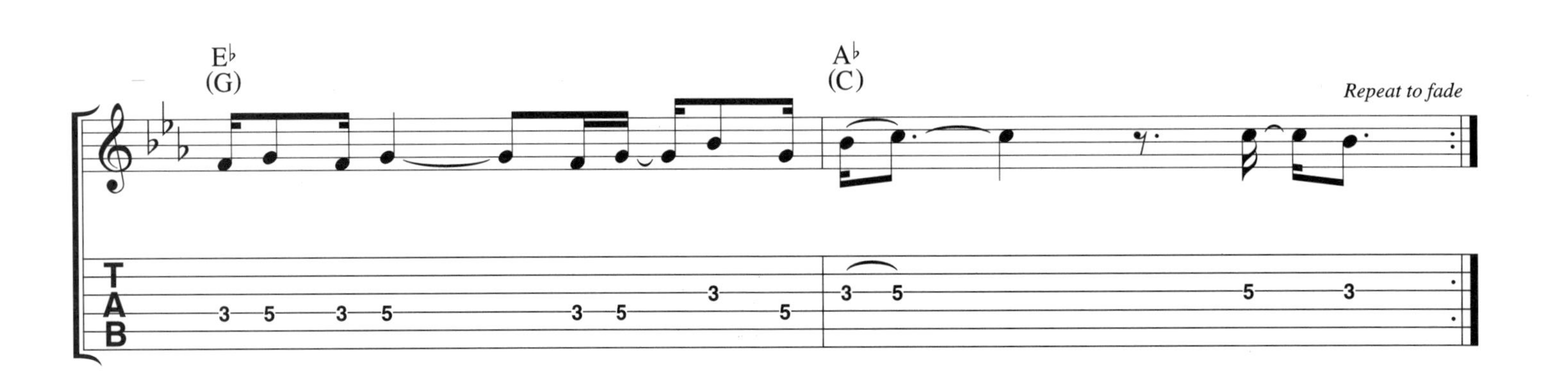
E♭
(G)
A♭
(C)
Repeat to fade
T
A
B

THE RESCUE BLUES

Words & Music by Ryan Adams

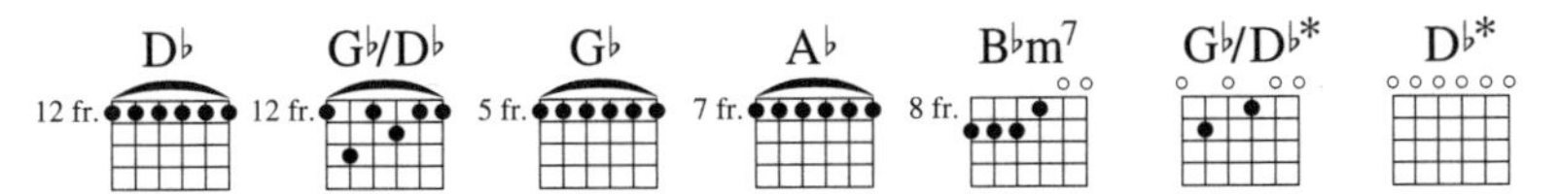

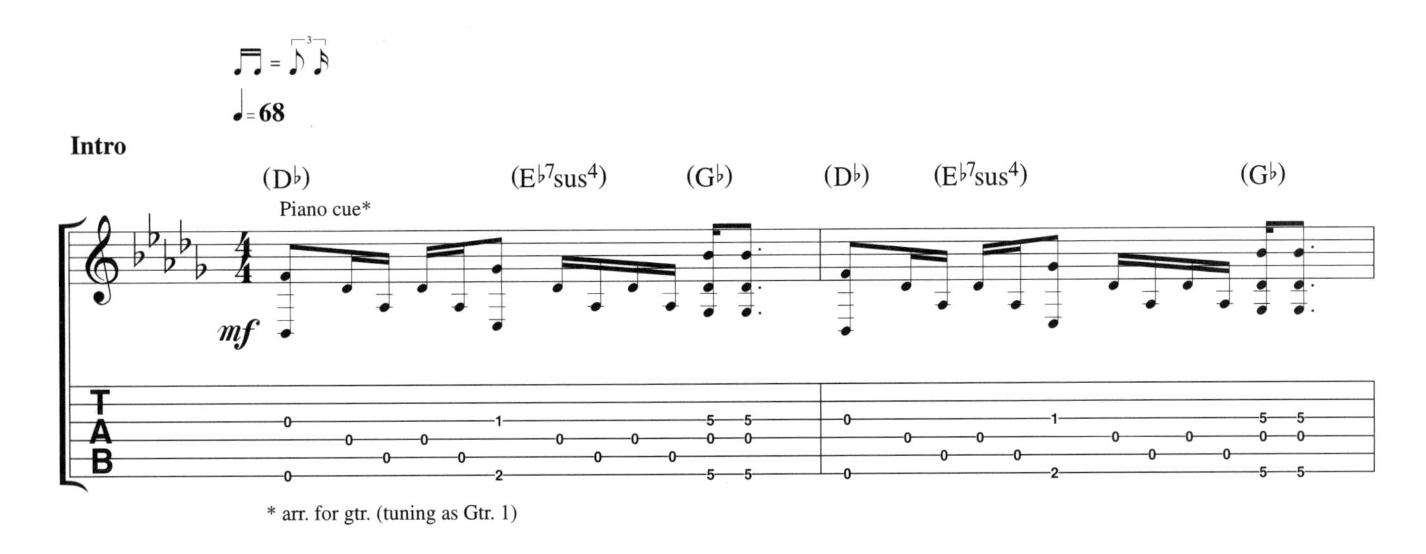

* arr. for gtr. (tuning as Gtr. 1)

† Gtrs. 1+2 tuned:
①=D♭ ④=D♭
②=A♭ ⑤=A♭
③=F ⑥=D♭

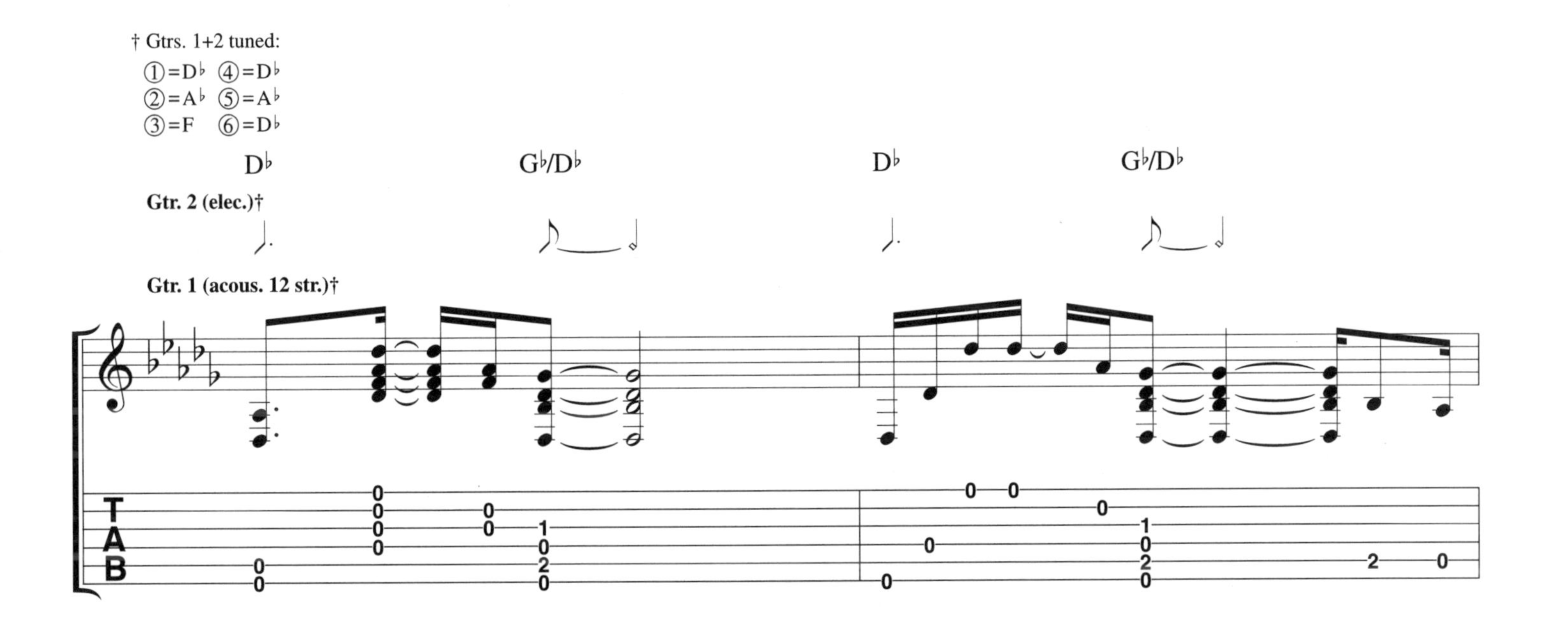

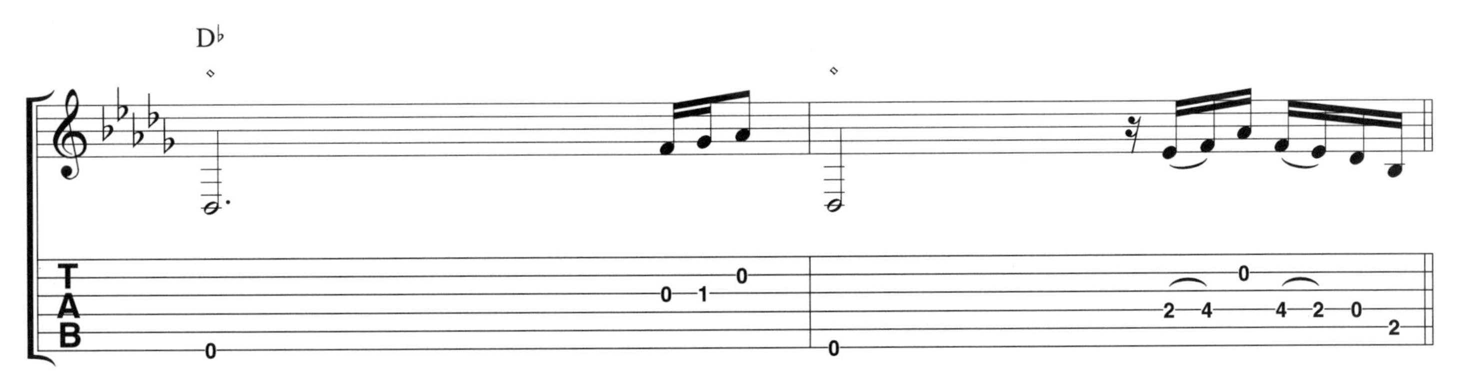

Verse

D♭
G♭/D♭
1. And ev - 'ry - bo - dy wants you to be spe - cial,
2. And ev - 'ry - bo - dy wants to see you suf - fer,
Gtr. 3 w/Fig. 1

D♭
G♭/D♭
and ev - 'ry - bo - dy wants you to be high.
they know that you need the pain so much.
2º Gtr. 3 w/Fig. 3

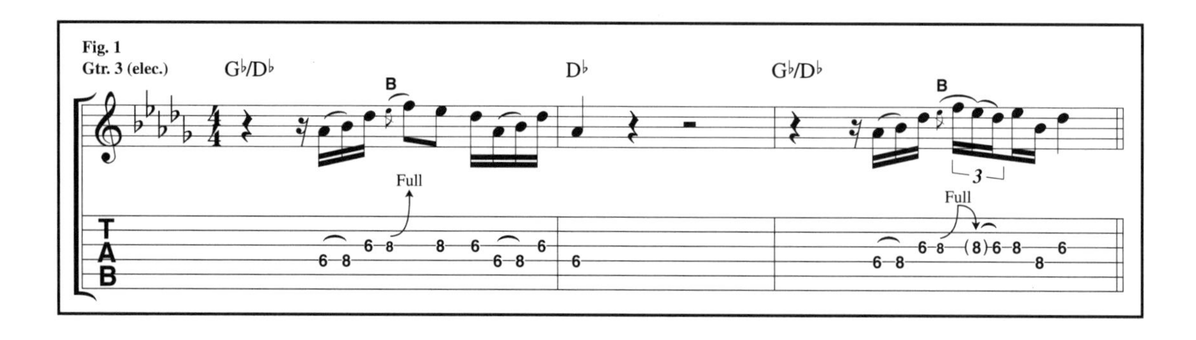
Fig. 1
Gtr. 3 (elec.)
G♭/D♭
D♭
G♭/D♭
Full
Full

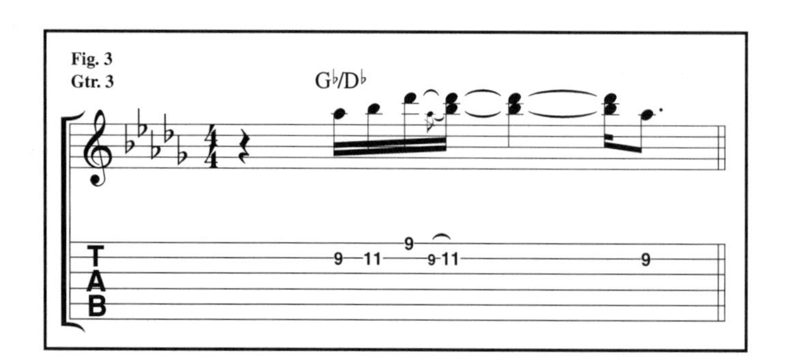
Fig. 3
Gtr. 3
G♭/D♭

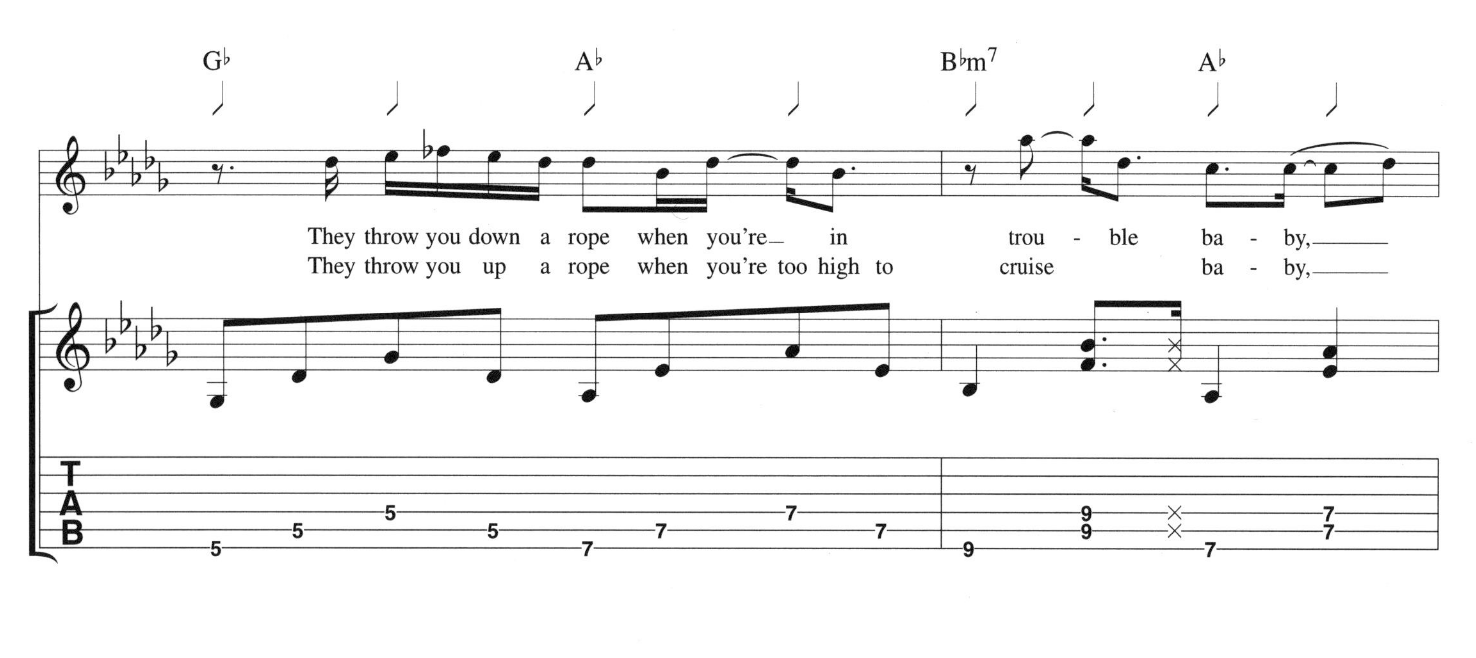
G♭
A♭
B♭m7
A♭
They throw you down a rope when you're in trou - ble ba - by,
They throw you up a rope when you're too high to cruise ba - by,
T
A
B

B♭m7
A♭
G♭
D♭
scream - in' "Save me",
Lord you lose la - dy,
then they charge you with the res-cue blues.
1º Gtr. 3 w/Fig. 2
2º Gtr. 3 w/Fig. 2 ad lib.
T
A
B

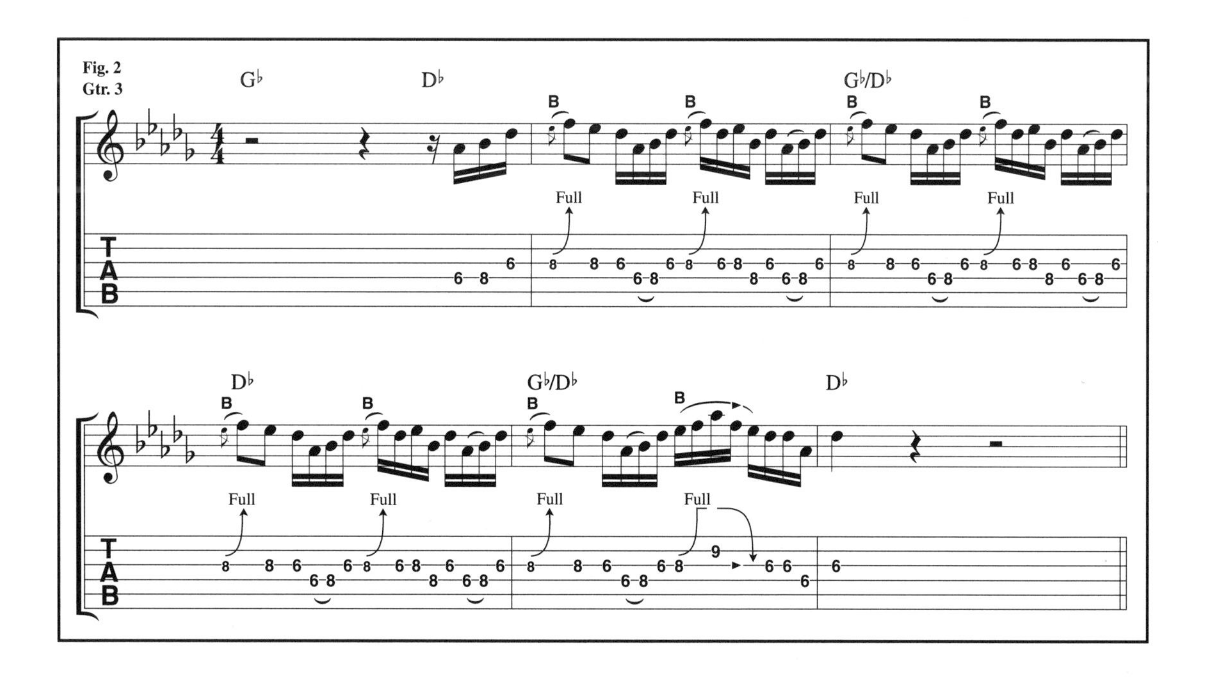
Fig. 2
Gtr. 3
G♭
D♭
G♭/D♭
D♭
G♭/D♭
D♭
B
Full
T
A
B

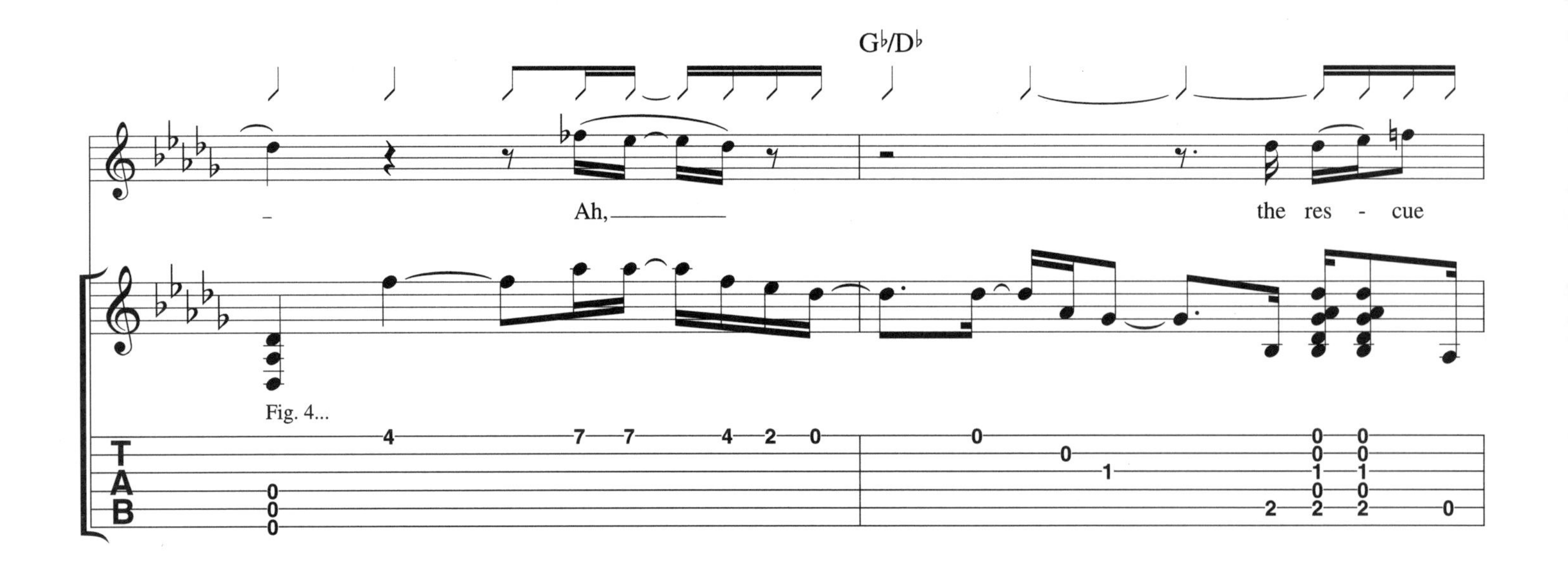
G♭/D♭
Ah,
the res - cue
Fig. 4...
T
A
B

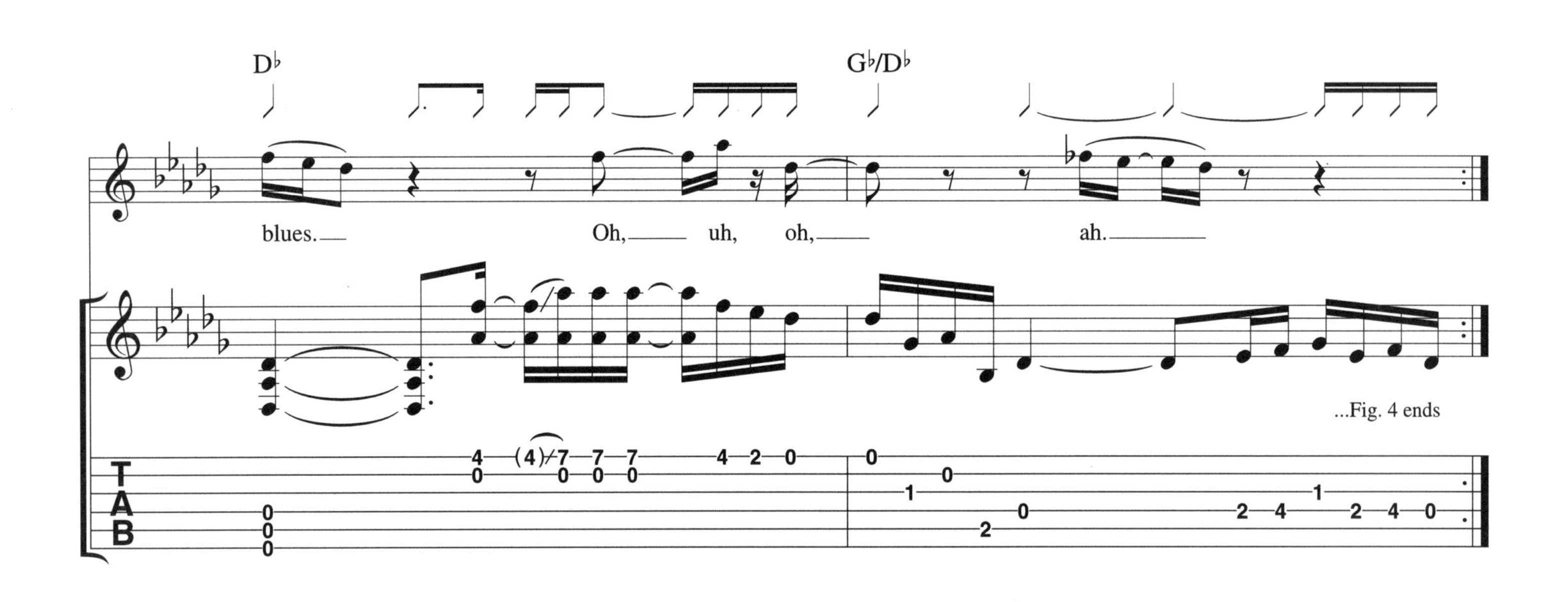
D♭
G♭/D♭
blues.
Oh, uh, oh,
ah.
...Fig. 4 ends
T
A
B

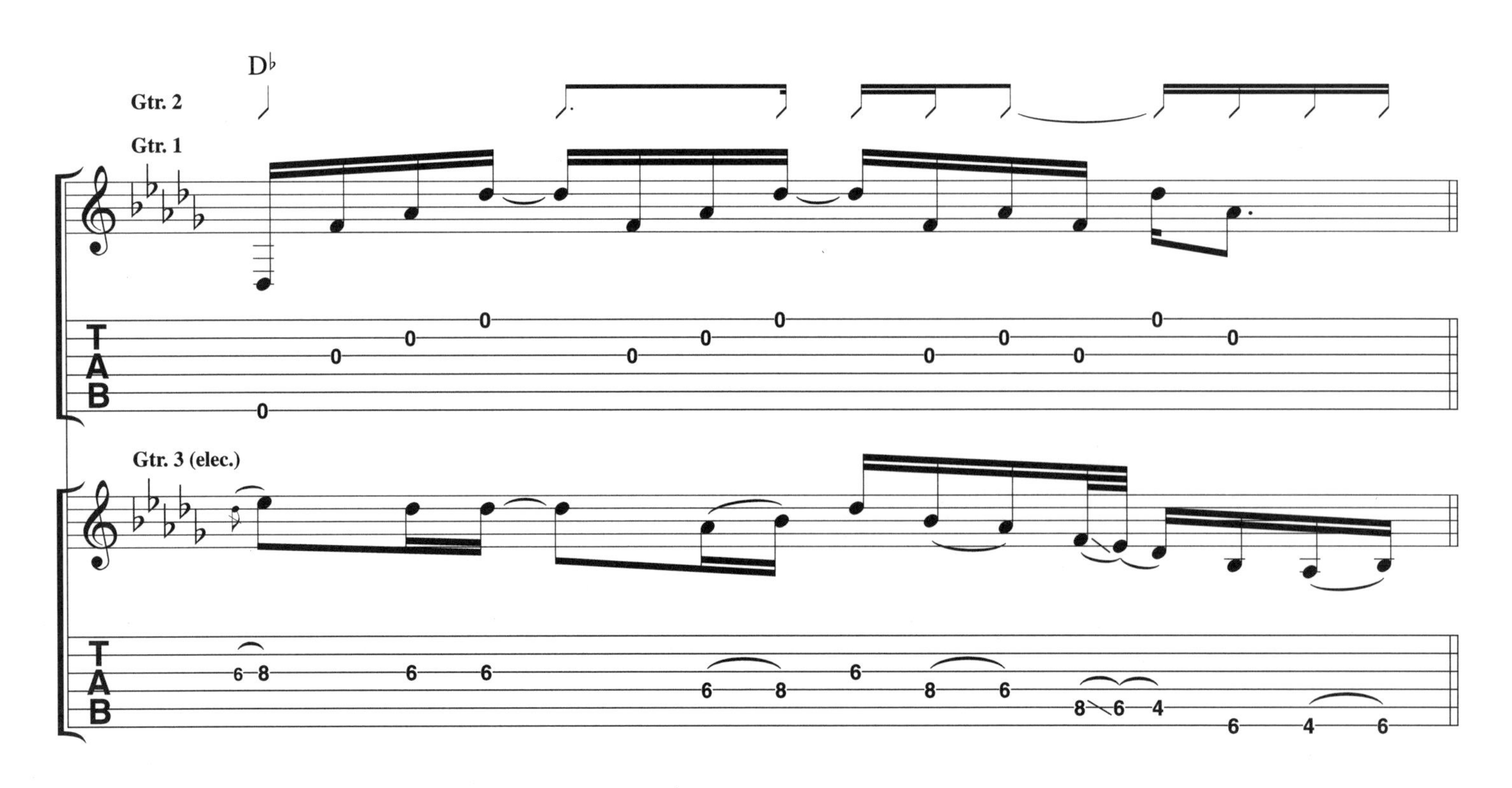
D♭
Gtr. 2
Gtr. 1
Gtr. 3 (elec.)
T
A
B

Bridge

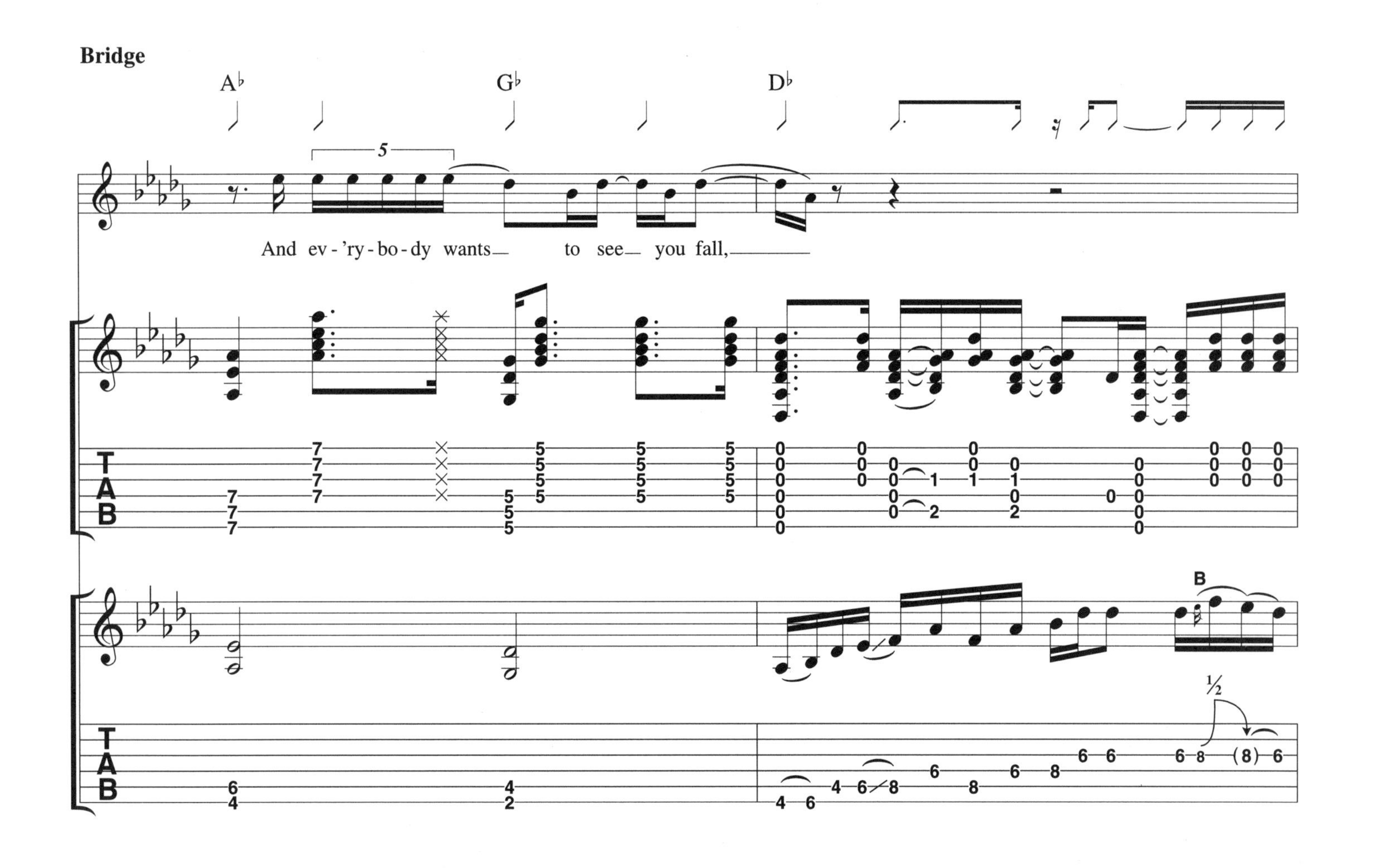
A♭
G♭
D♭
And ev - 'ry - bo - dy wants to see you fall,
B
½

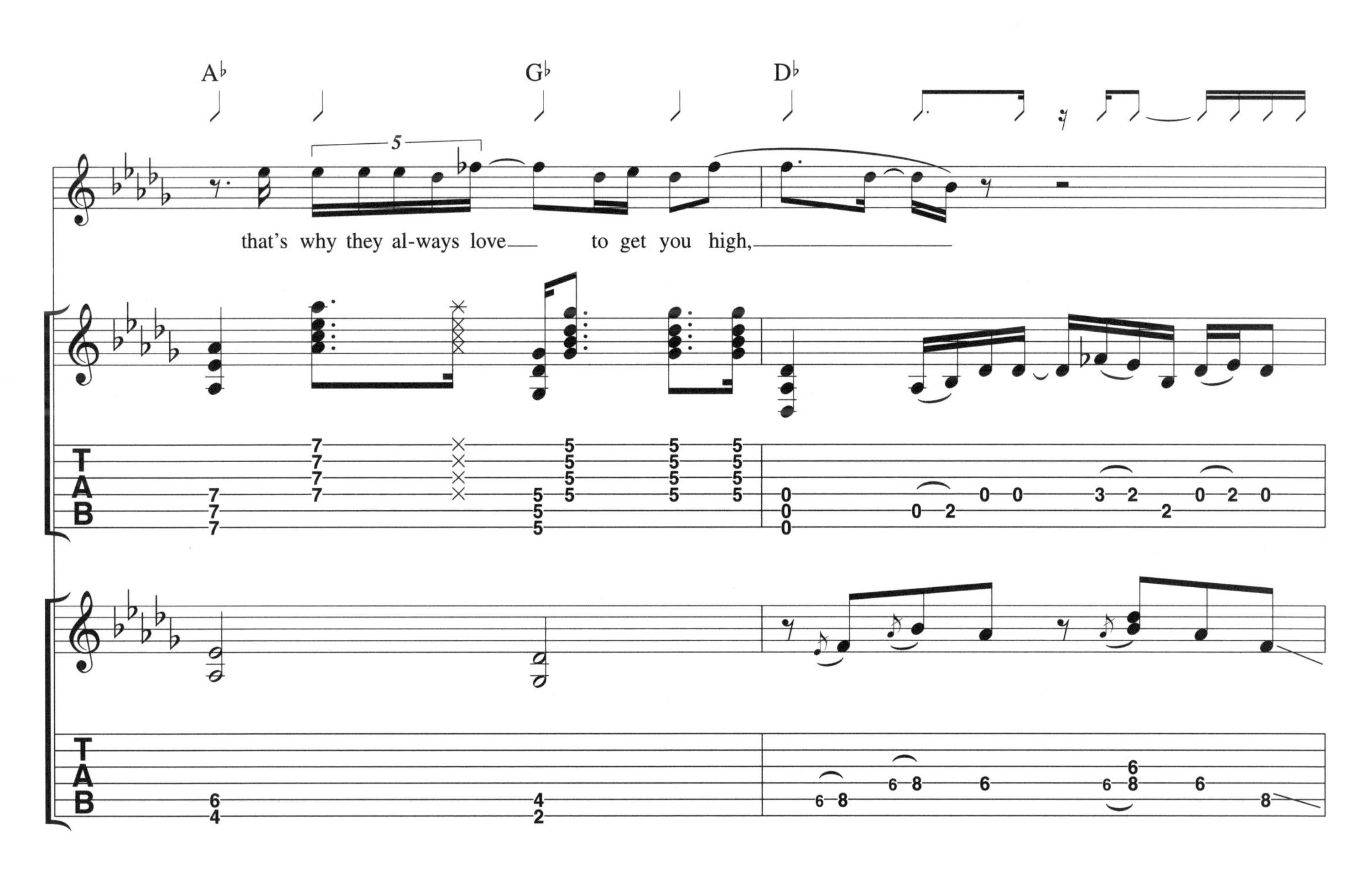
A♭
G♭
D♭
that's why they al - ways love to get you high,

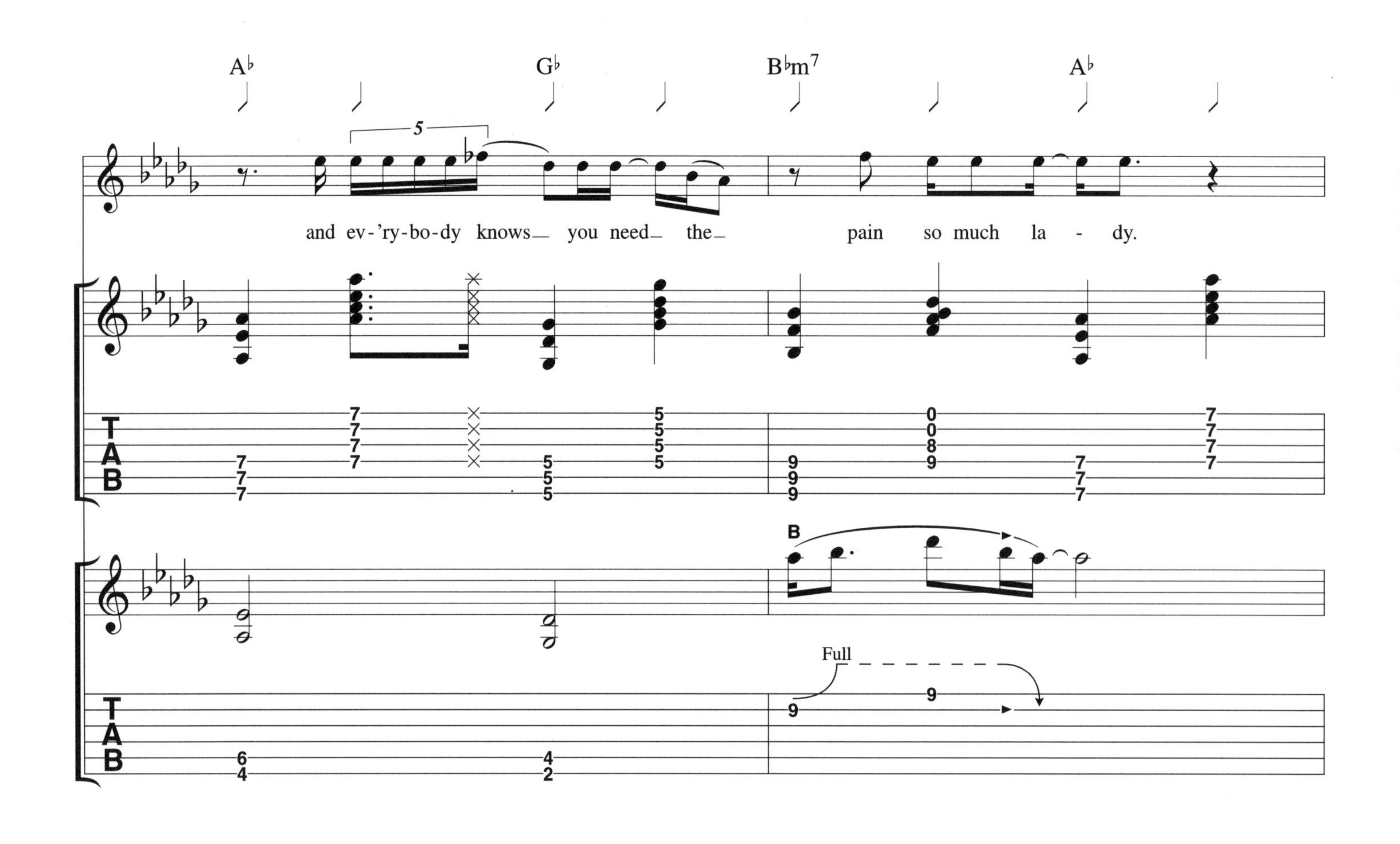
A♭
G♭
B♭m7
A♭
and ev-'ry-bo-dy knows you need the pain so much la - dy.
B
Full

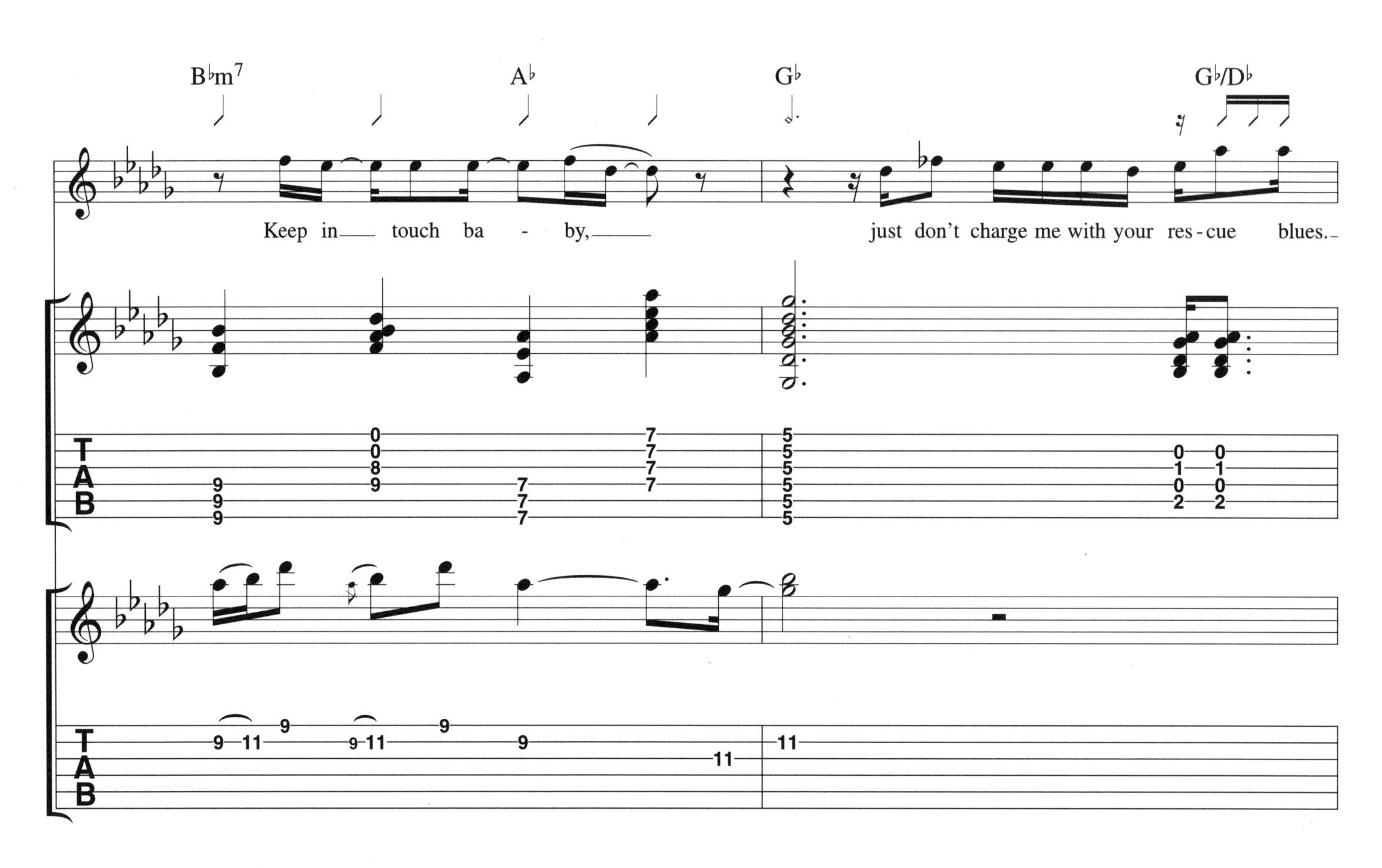
B♭m7
A♭
G♭
G♭/D♭
Keep in touch ba - by, just don't charge me with your res-cue blues.

D♭
G♭/D♭
cont. sim.
Ah,
ah,
res - cue blues.
Gtr. 3
Gtr. 1 w/Fig. 4 (x4)
Full
D♭
G♭/D♭
Ah.
Ah,
ah,
ah.
D♭
Gospel Choir
G♭/D♭
Ah,
ah,
ah,
ah.
D♭
G♭/D♭
Ah,
ah,
ah,
ah.

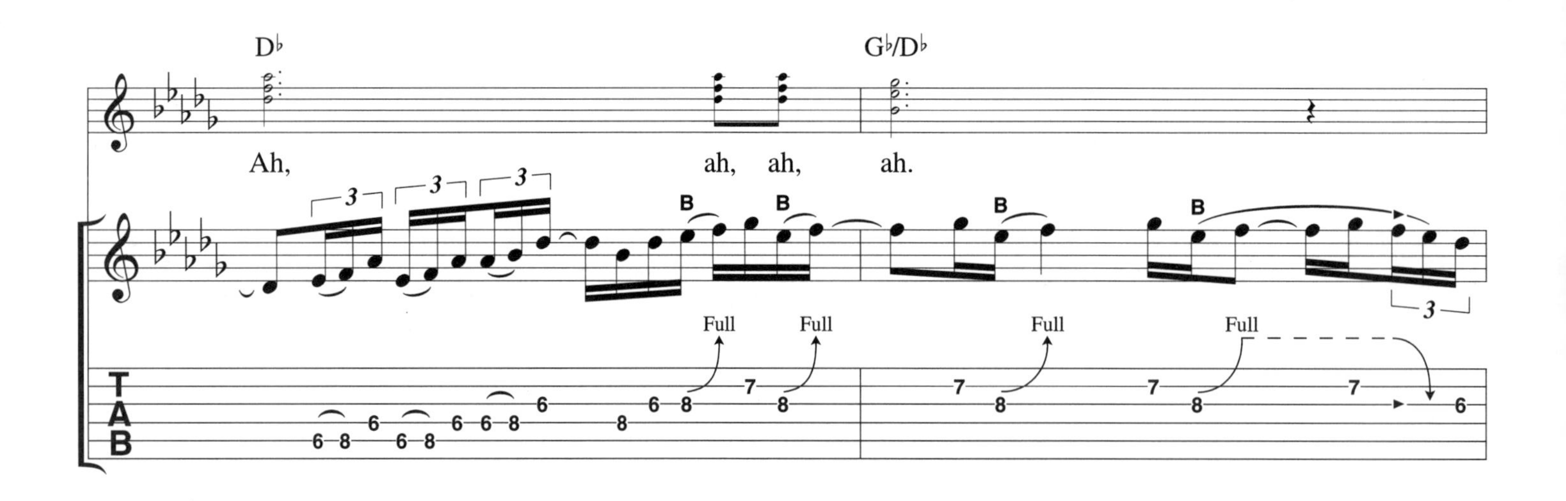
D♭
G♭/D♭
Ah,
ah, ah,
ah.
Full
Full
Full
Full

D♭
G♭/D♭
Ah,
ah, ah,
ah.
Full
Full
Full
Full
Full

D♭
G♭/D♭
Ah,
ah, ah,
ah.
Full
Full
Full
Full
Full
Full
Full

D♭
G♭/D♭
Ah,
ah, ah, ah.
Full
Full
Full
Full
rit.

D♭
G♭/D♭*
cont. sim. ad lib.
Ah.
Gtr. 1
(Gtr. 3)
mf
mp
Gtr. 2 tacet

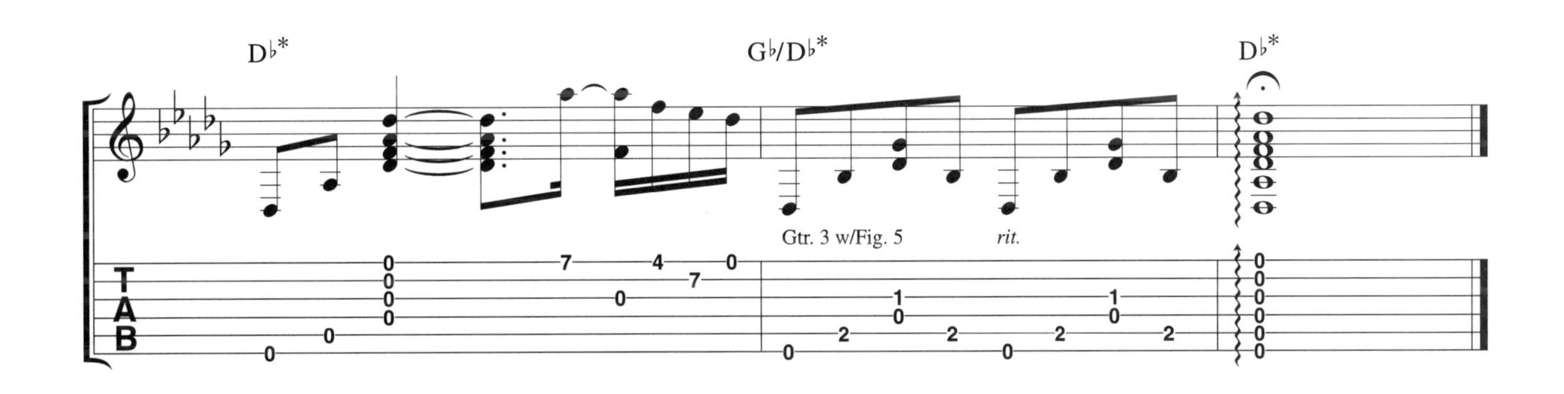
D♭*
G♭/D♭*
D♭*
Gtr. 3 w/Fig. 5
rit.

Fig. 5
Gtr. 3
G♭/D♭*
D♭*
Full
rit.

WHEN THE STARS GO BLUE

Words & Music by Ryan Adams

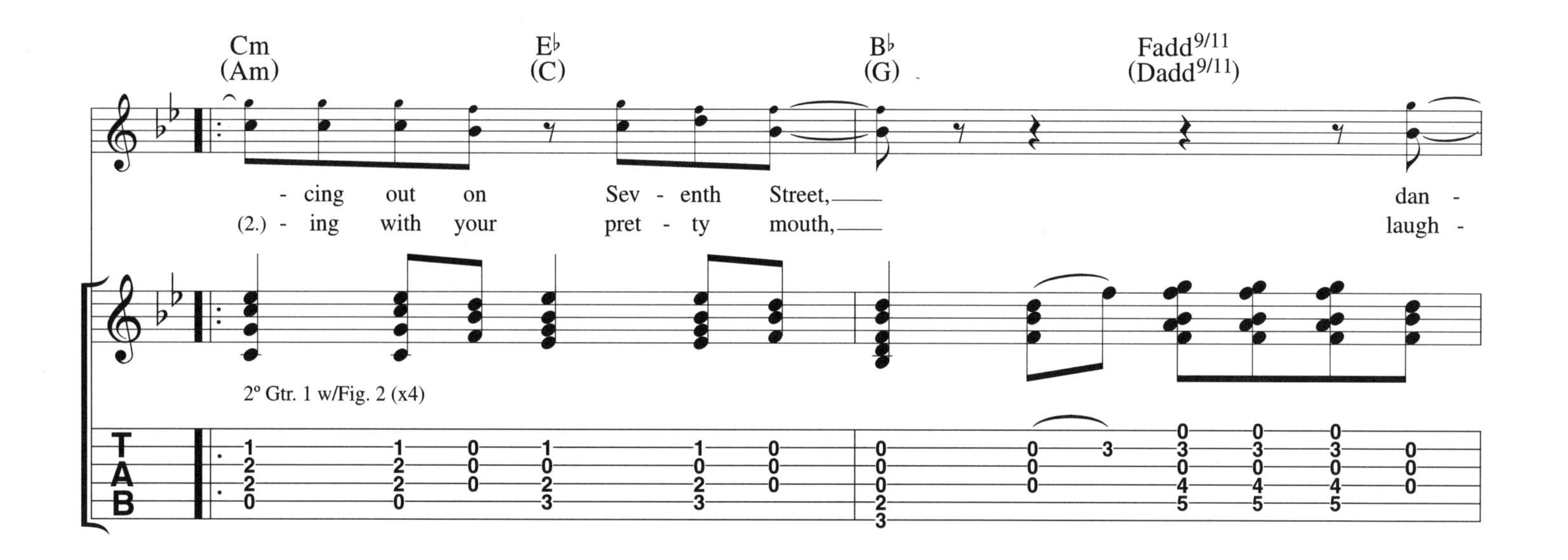

Cm
(Am)
E♭
(C)
B♭
(G)
Fadd9/11
(Dadd9/11)
- cing out on Sev - enth Street, dan -
(2.) - ing with your pret - ty mouth, laugh -
2º Gtr. 1 w/Fig. 2 (x4)
TAB

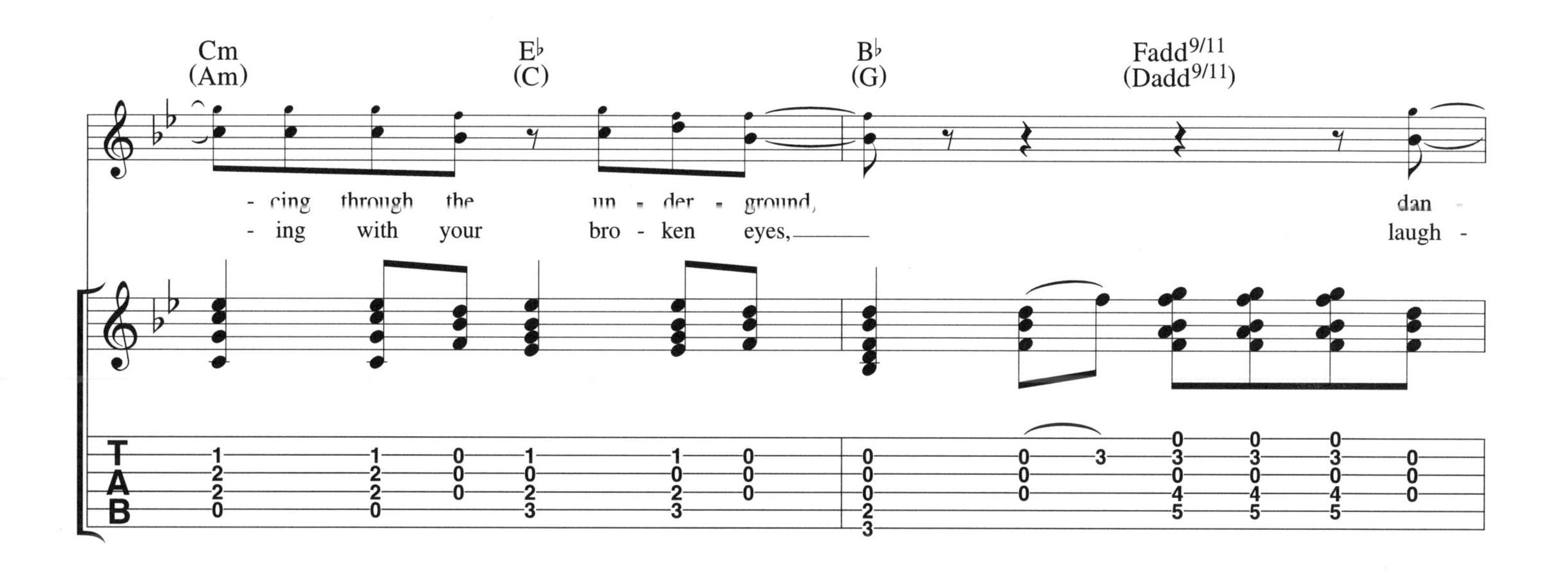

Cm
(Am)
E♭
(C)
B♭
(G)
Fadd9/11
(Dadd9/11)
- cing through the un - der - ground, dan -
- ing with your bro - ken eyes, laugh -
TAB

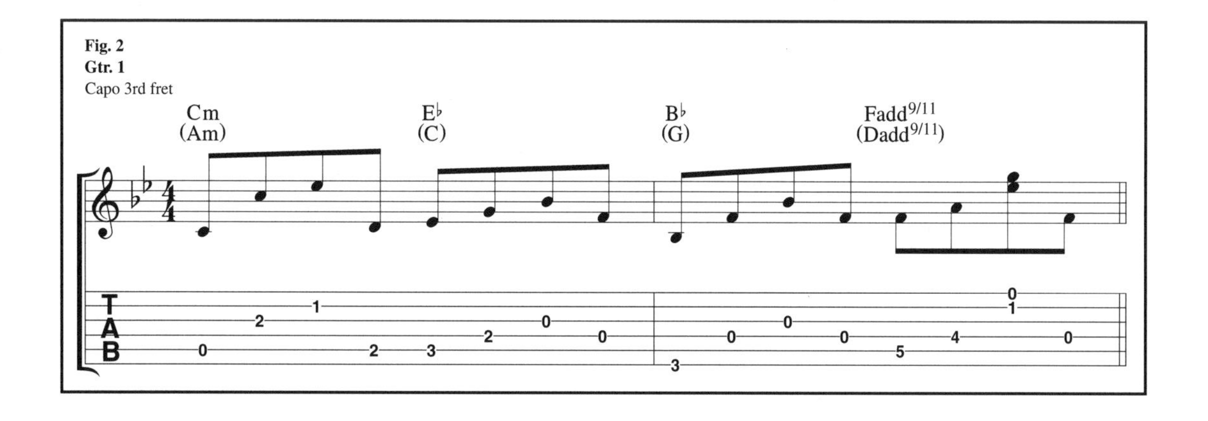

Fig. 2
Gtr. 1
Capo 3rd fret
Cm
(Am)
E♭
(C)
B♭
(G)
Fadd9/11
(Dadd9/11)
TAB

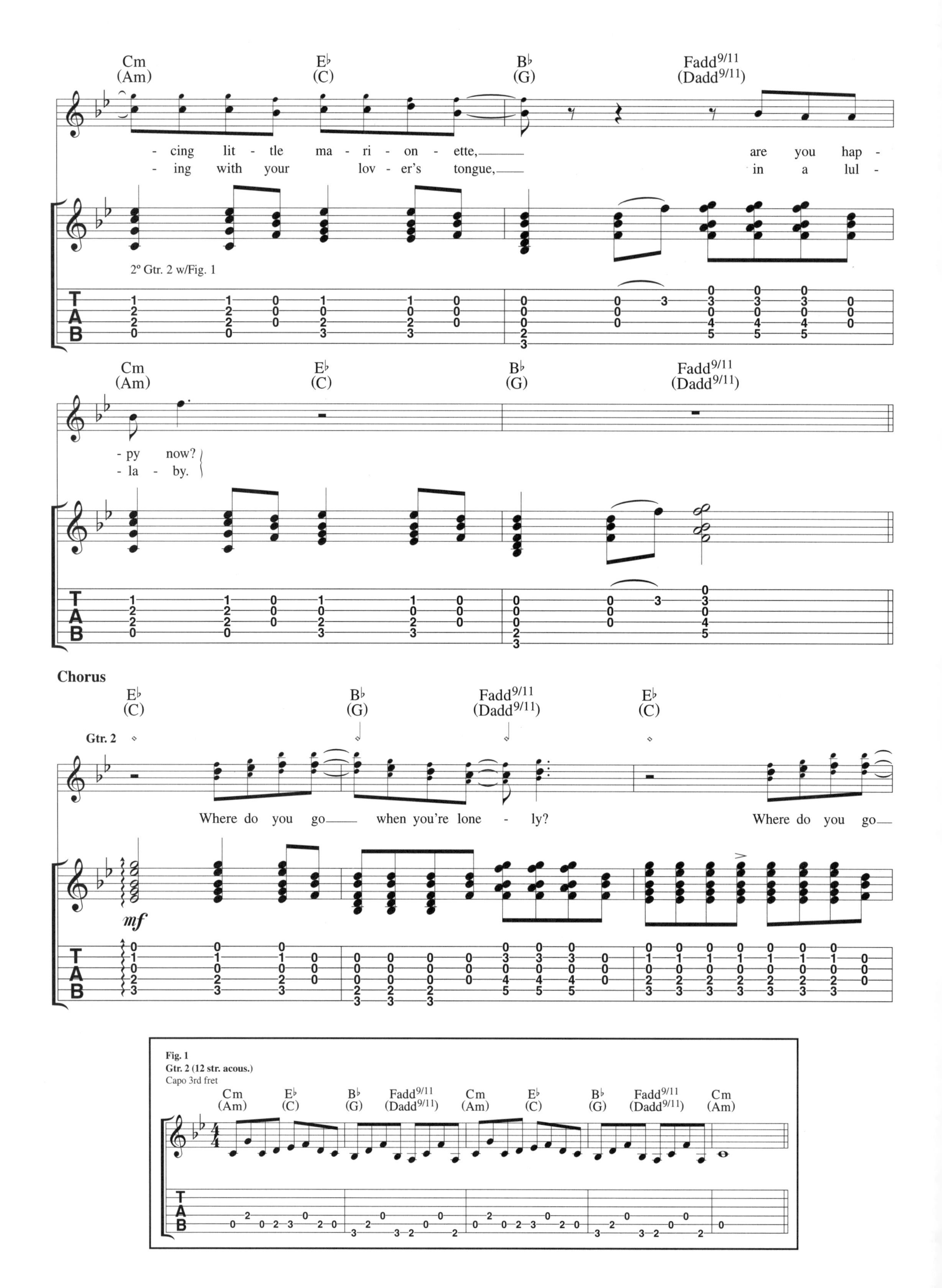
Cm
(Am)
E♭
(C)
B♭
(G)
Fadd9/11
(Dadd9/11)
- cing lit - tle ma - ri - on - ette,
- ing with your lov - er's tongue,
are you hap -
in a lul -
2° Gtr. 2 w/Fig. 1
- py now?
- la - by.
Chorus
Gtr. 2
Where do you go when you're lone - ly?
Where do you go
mf
Fig. 1
Gtr. 2 (12 str. acous.)
Capo 3rd fret

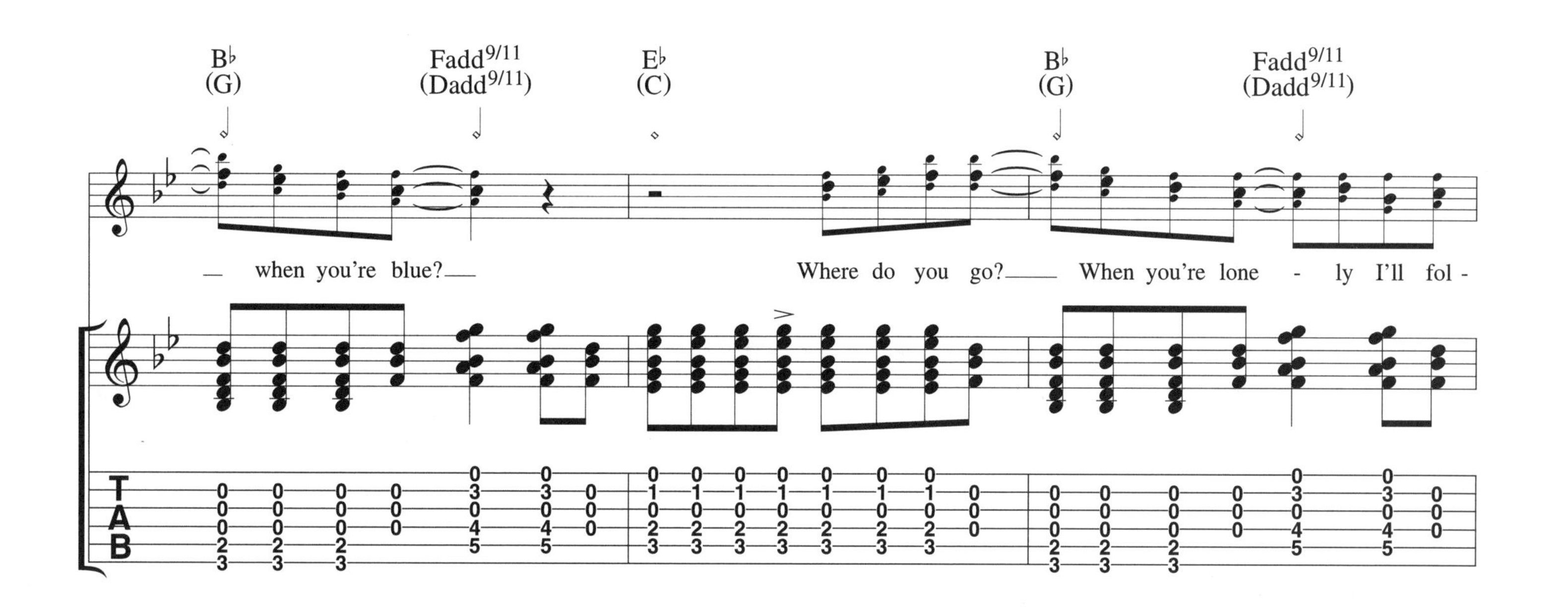
B♭
(G)
Fadd9/11
(Dadd9/11)
E♭
(C)
B♭
(G)
Fadd9/11
(Dadd9/11)
— when you're blue? —
Where do you go? — When you're lone - ly I'll fol -
T
A
B

Cm
(Am)
B♭
(G)
Fadd9/11
(Dadd9/11)
- low you,
when the stars — go
blue,
2° Gtr. 1 + Gtr. 2
T
A
B

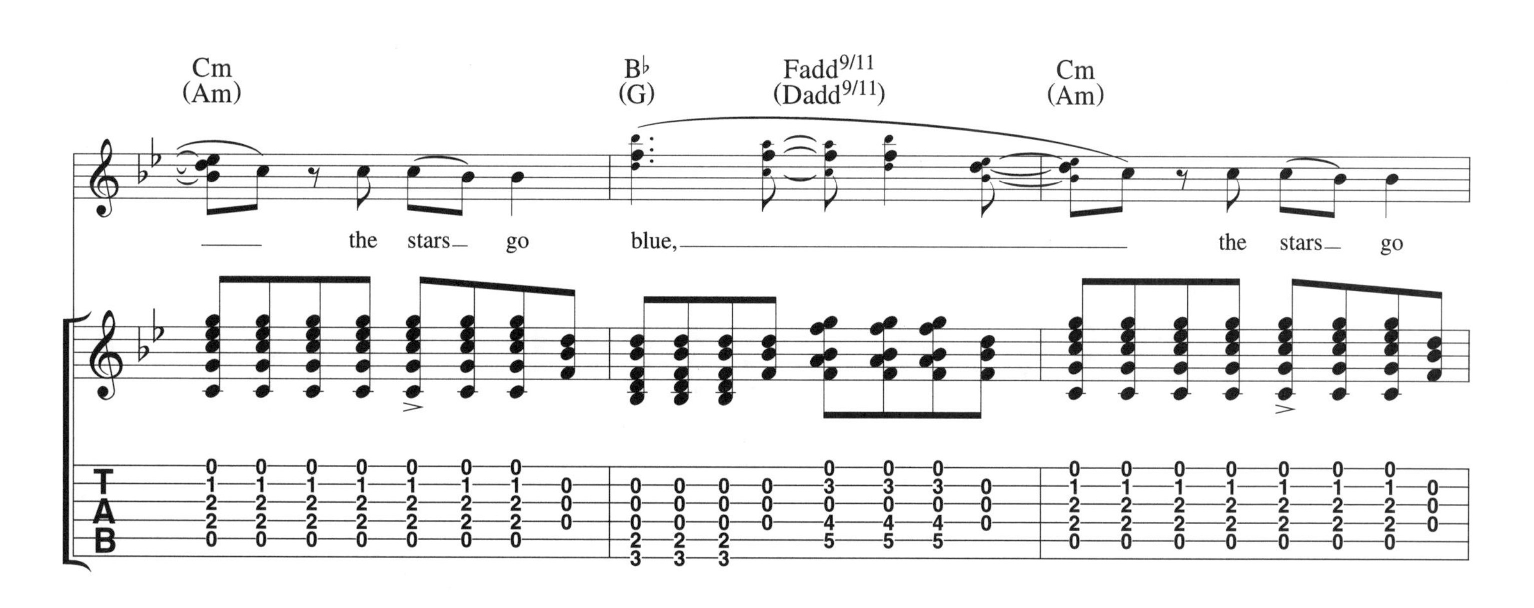
Cm
(Am)
B♭
(G)
Fadd9/11
(Dadd9/11)
Cm
(Am)
the stars — go
blue,
the stars — go
T
A
B

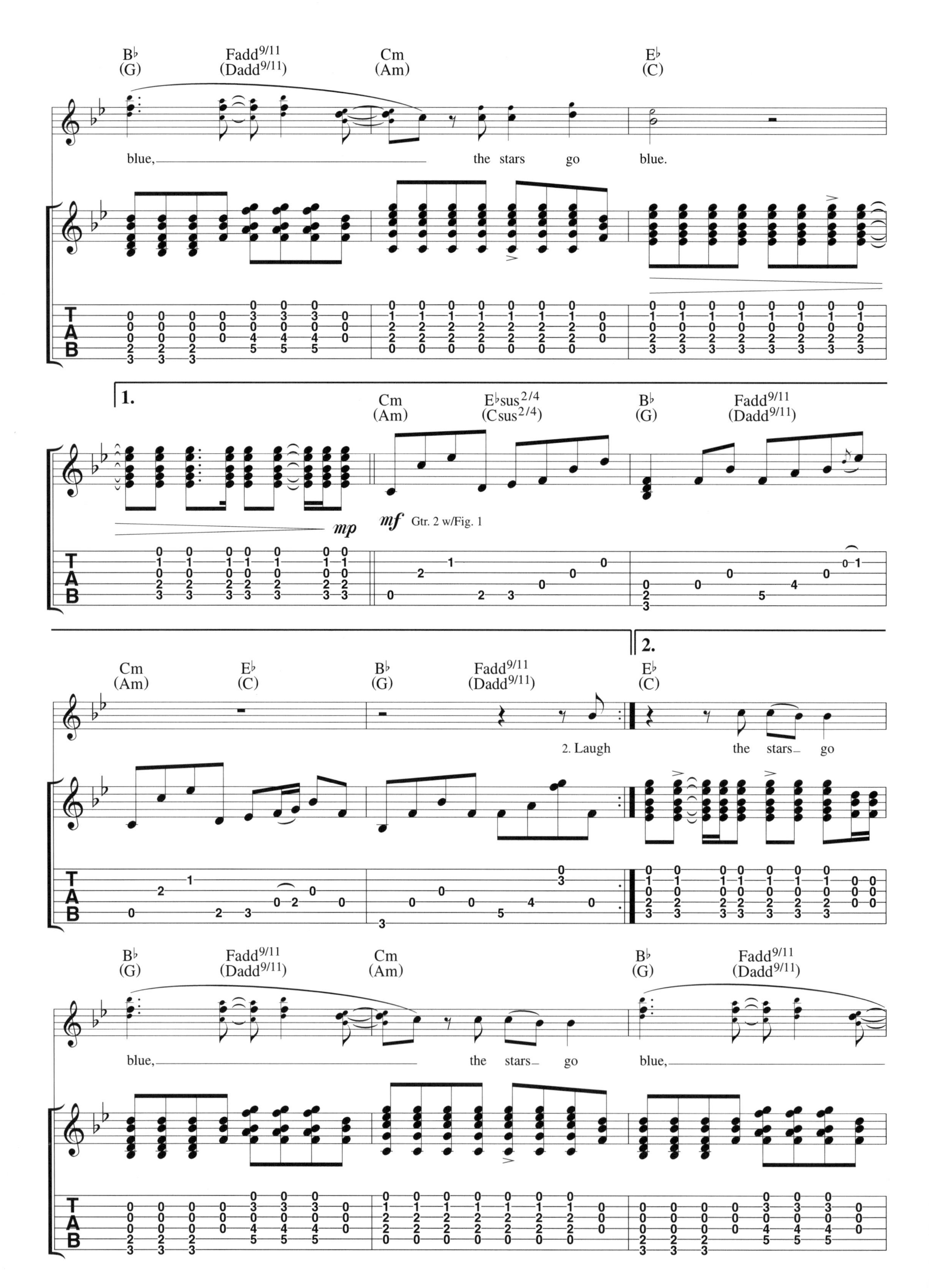
B♭ (G)
Fadd9/11 (Dadd9/11)
Cm (Am)
E♭ (C)
blue,
the stars go
blue.
1.
Cm (Am)
E♭sus2/4 (Csus2/4)
B♭ (G)
Fadd9/11 (Dadd9/11)
mp
mf Gtr. 2 w/Fig. 1
Cm (Am)
E♭ (C)
B♭ (G)
Fadd9/11 (Dadd9/11)
2.
E♭ (C)
2. Laugh
the stars go
B♭ (G)
Fadd9/11 (Dadd9/11)
Cm (Am)
B♭ (G)
Fadd9/11 (Dadd9/11)
blue,
the stars go
blue,

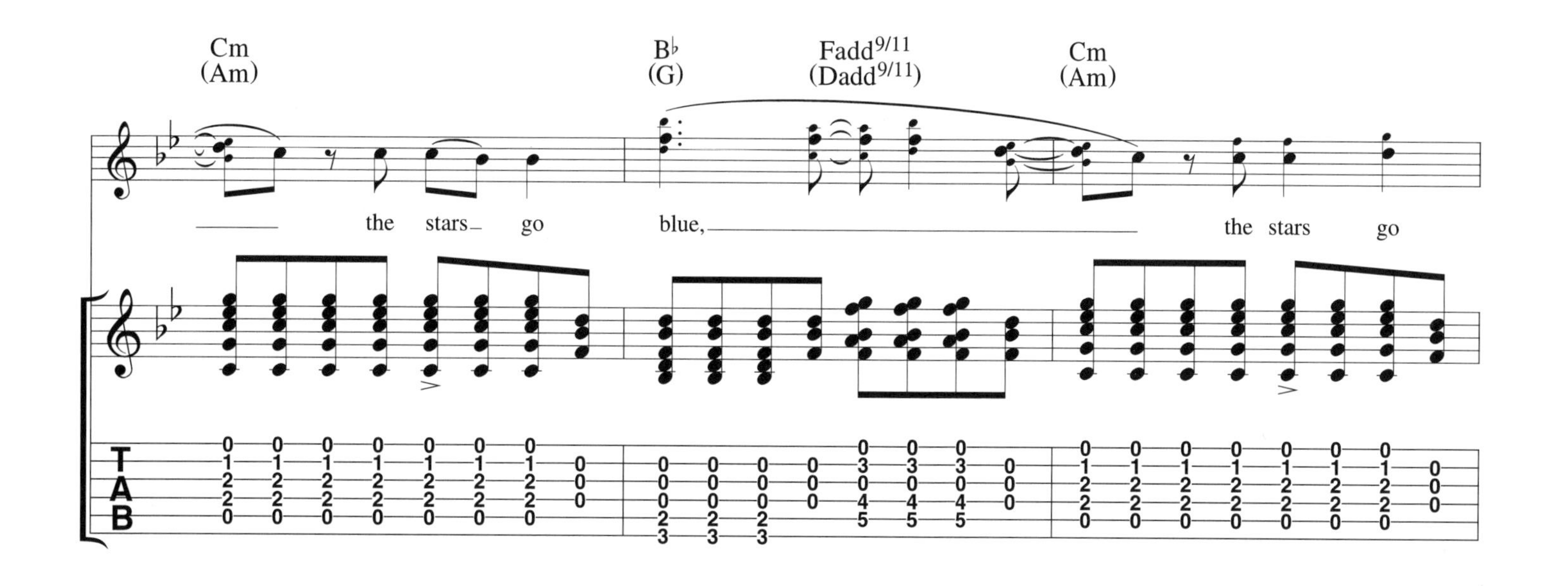
Cm (Am)
B♭ (G)
Fadd9/11 (Dadd9/11)
Cm (Am)
the stars go blue,
the stars go

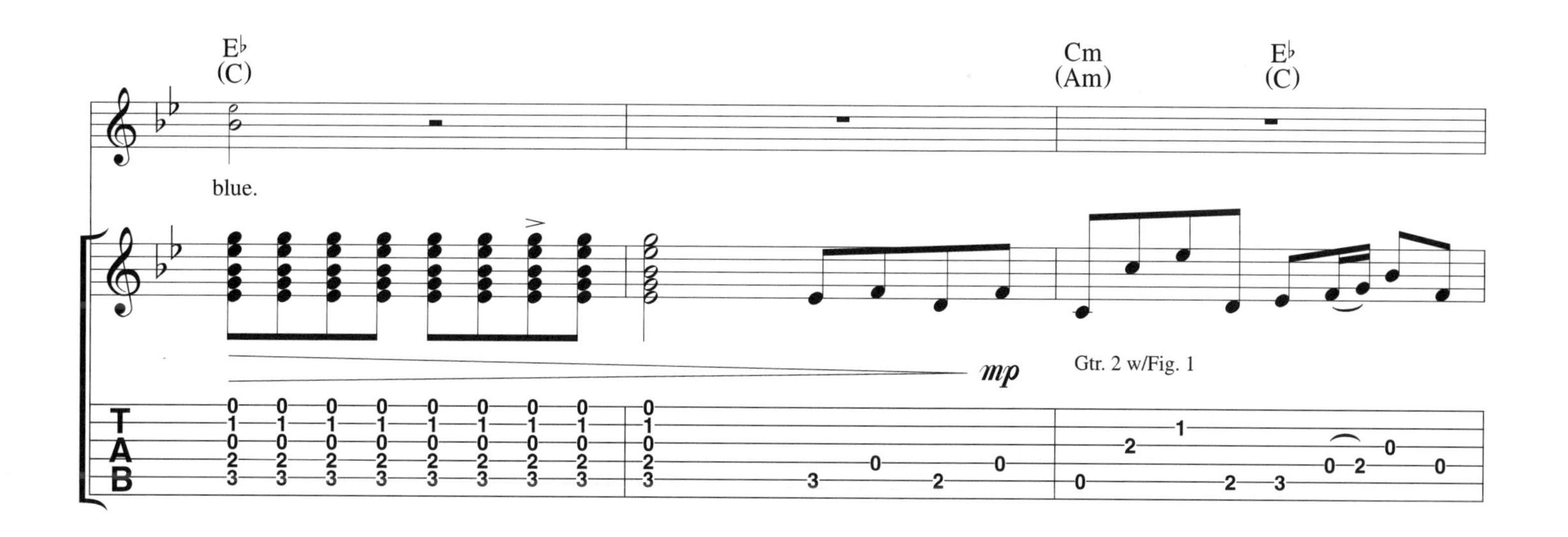
E♭ (C)
Cm (Am)
E♭ (C)
blue.
mp
Gtr. 2 w/Fig. 1

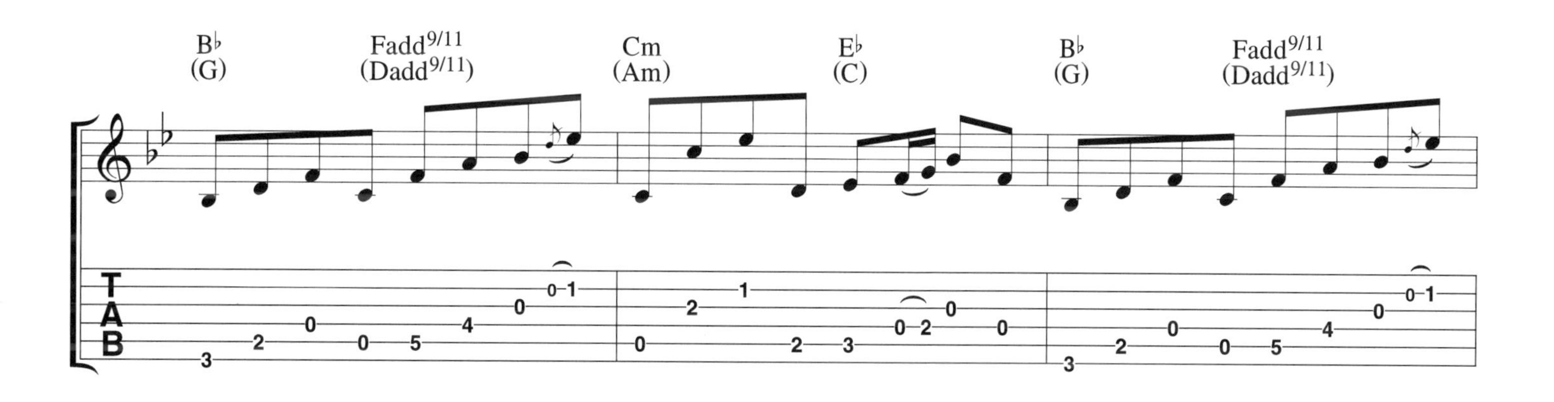
B♭ (G)
Fadd9/11 (Dadd9/11)
Cm (Am)
E♭ (C)
B♭ (G)
Fadd9/11 (Dadd9/11)

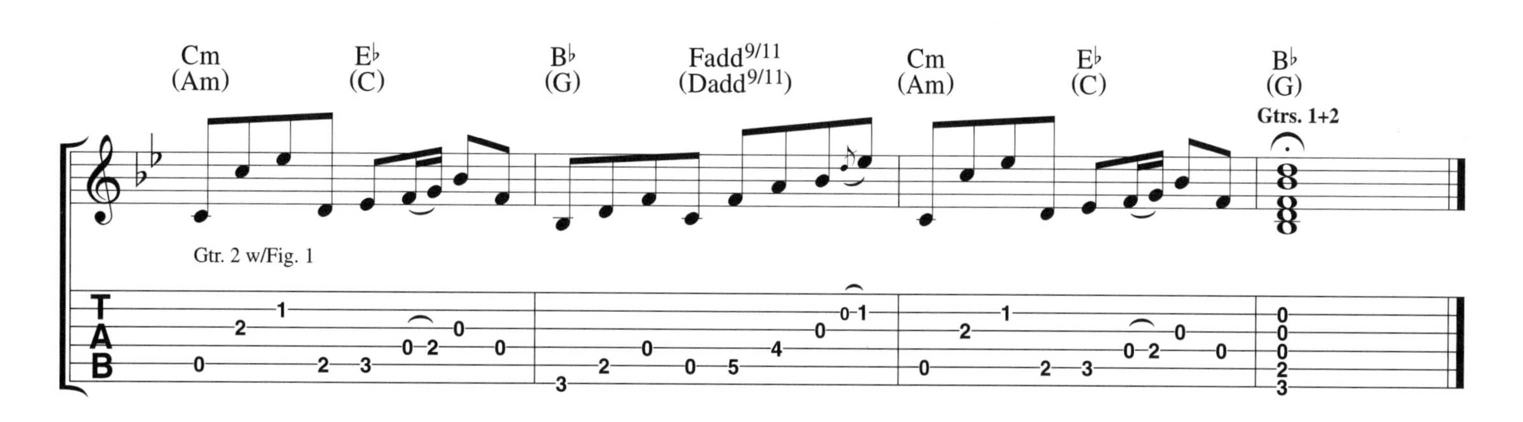
Cm (Am)
E♭ (C)
B♭ (G)
Fadd9/11 (Dadd9/11)
Cm (Am)
E♭ (C)
B♭ (G)
Gtrs. 1+2
Gtr. 2 w/Fig. 1

NOBODY GIRL

Words & Music by Ryan Adams & Ethan Johns

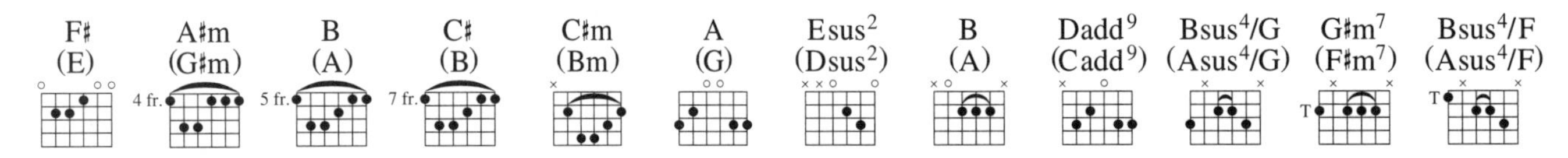

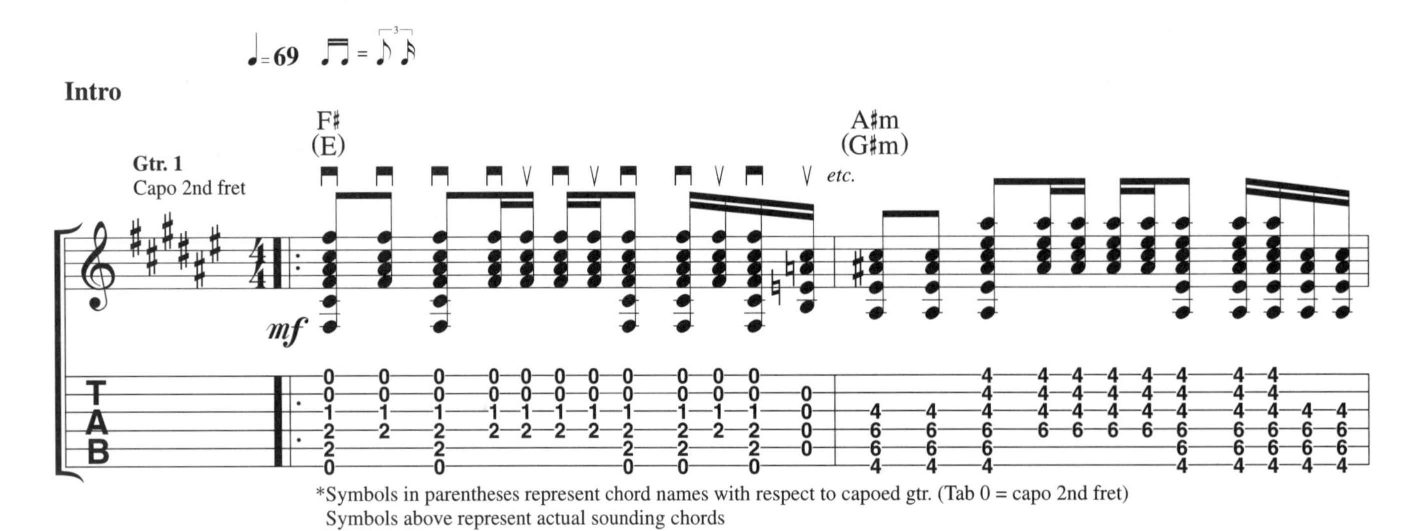

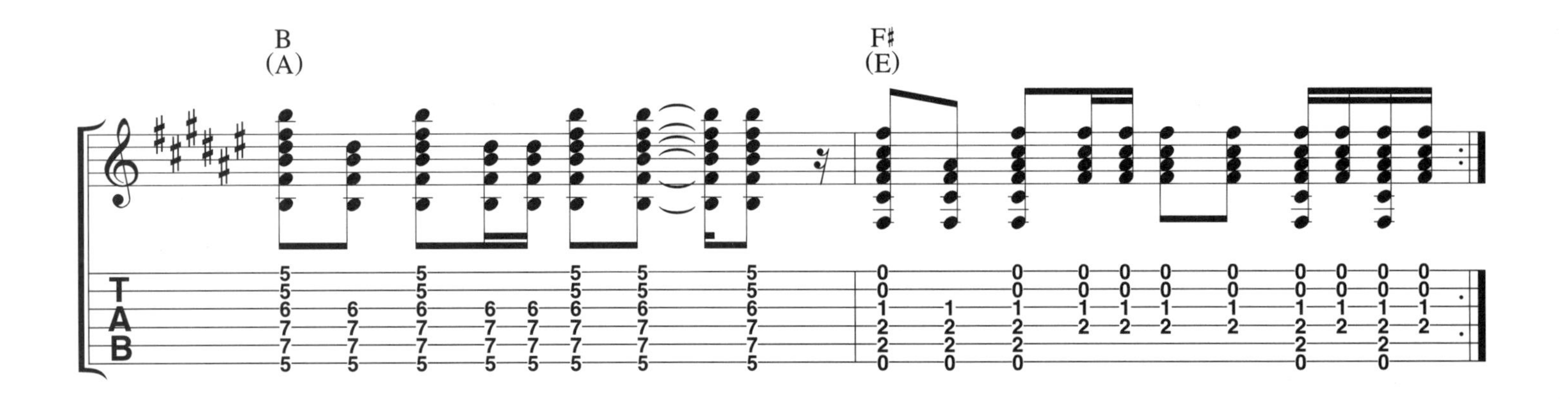

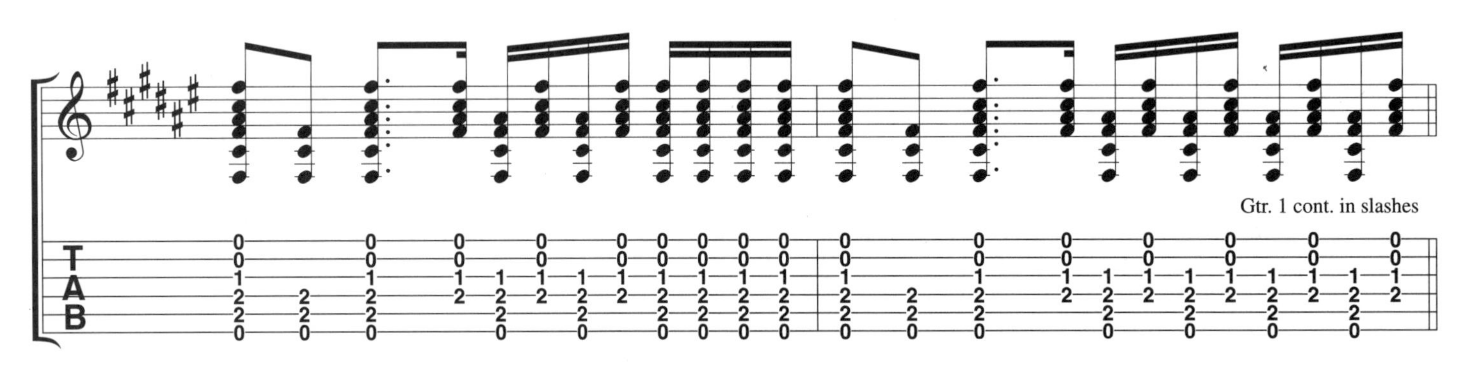

Verse
F♯
(E)
A♯m
(G♯m)
cont. sim.
1. Well, the night makes moves,
2. Just a no - body girl,
(Verse 3 (𝄋) see block lyric)
Gtr. 2 (elec.)
Capo 2nd fret
1° tacet
B
(A)
F♯
(E)
and she shat - ters like bro - ken glass.
with a ra - dar to the scene.
1° Gtr. 1 w/Fig. 1
A♯m
(G♯m)
Bet - ter play it cool,
When the emp - ti - ness finds you,
Fig. 1
Gtr. 2
F♯
(E)

B
(A)
C♯
(B)
bet - ter let it pass.
you find all the num-bers you need.
1º Gtr. 2 w/Fig. 2
F♯
(E)
A♯m
(G♯m)
Have you been screen-ing your smokes and
Say you fol - low your heart, well
B
(A)
F♯
(E)
whis-pers in an all night bar.
ho - ney you're just be - ing lost.
1º Gtr. 2 w/Fig. 3

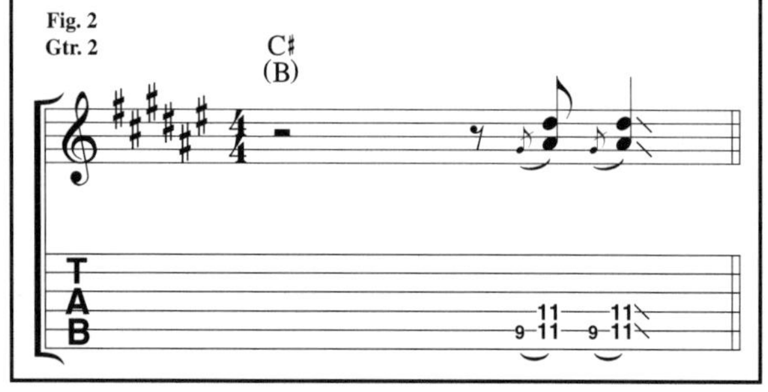
Fig. 2
Gtr. 2
C♯
(B)

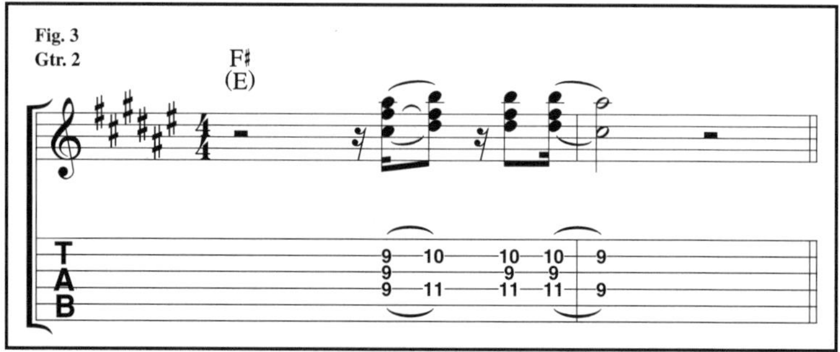
Fig. 3
Gtr. 2
F♯
(E)

A♯m
(G♯m)
Bet - ter off as the fool,
You could fol - low your gut,
B
(A)
F♯
(E)
than the own - er of that kind - a heart.
but how much would it cost.
Pre-Chorus
C♯m
(Bm)
A
(G)
They don't know you an - y - way.
Esus2
(Dsus2)
C♯m
(Bm)
They don't know

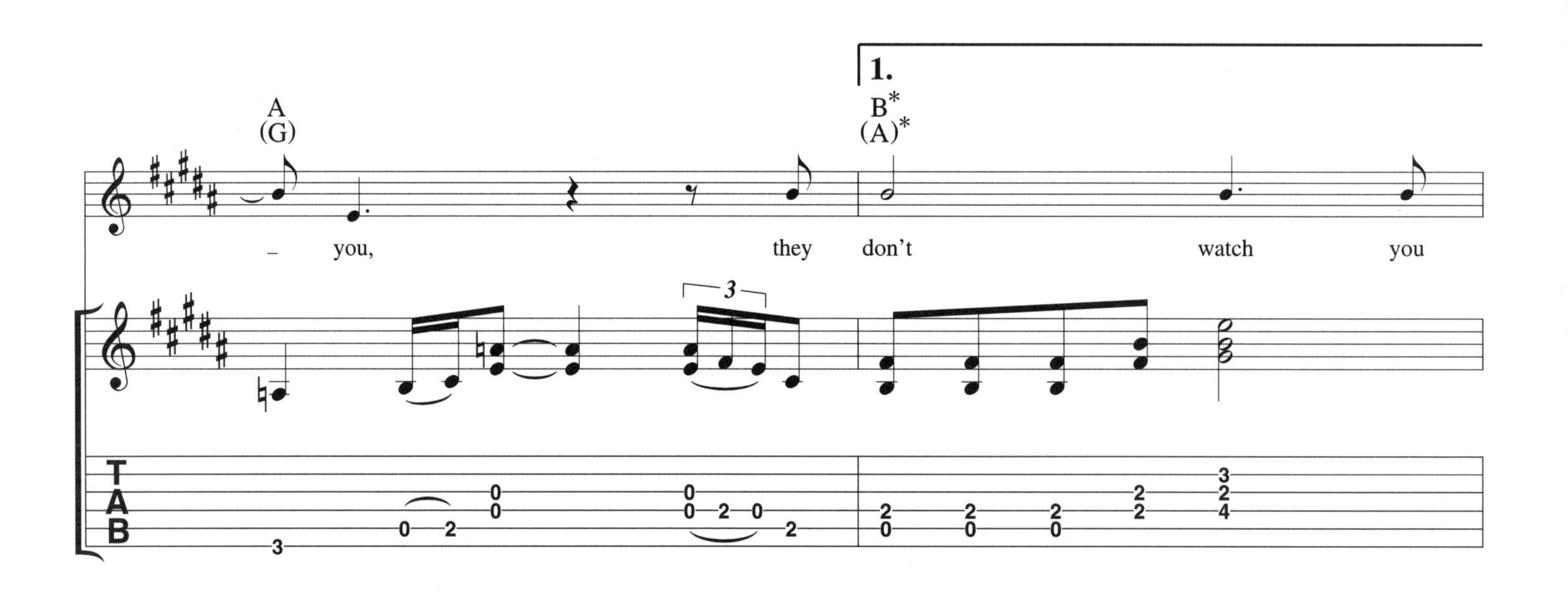
1.
A
(G)
B*
(A)*
you,
they
don't
watch
you

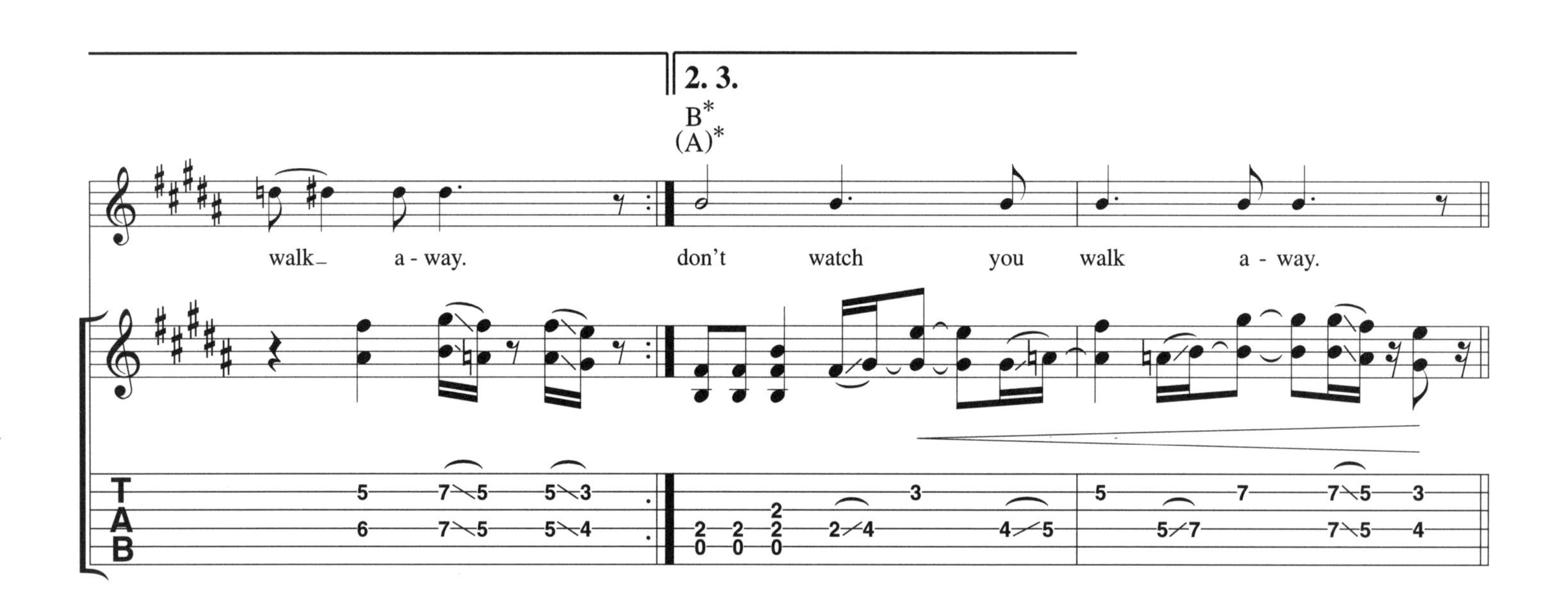
2. 3.
B*
(A)*
walk
a - way.
don't
watch
you
walk
a - way.

Chorus

B*
(A)*
Dadd9
(Cadd9)
Gtr. 3 (elec.)
cont. sim.
You're no - bo-dy girl.
You're no - bo-dy girl.
f Gtr. 3 w/distortion

A
(G)
B*
(A)*
You're no - bo - dy girl.
Full
B
Dadd9
(Cadd9)
You're no - bo - dy girl.
You're no - bo - dy girl.
A
(G)
B*
(A)*
To Coda
You're no - bo - dy girl.
F♯
(E)
mf
D.%. al Coda
take 2º

Coda
B*
(A)*
Dadd9
(Cadd9)
cont. sim.
Gtr. 3
You're a no - bo-dy girl.
No - bo-dy girl.
TAB

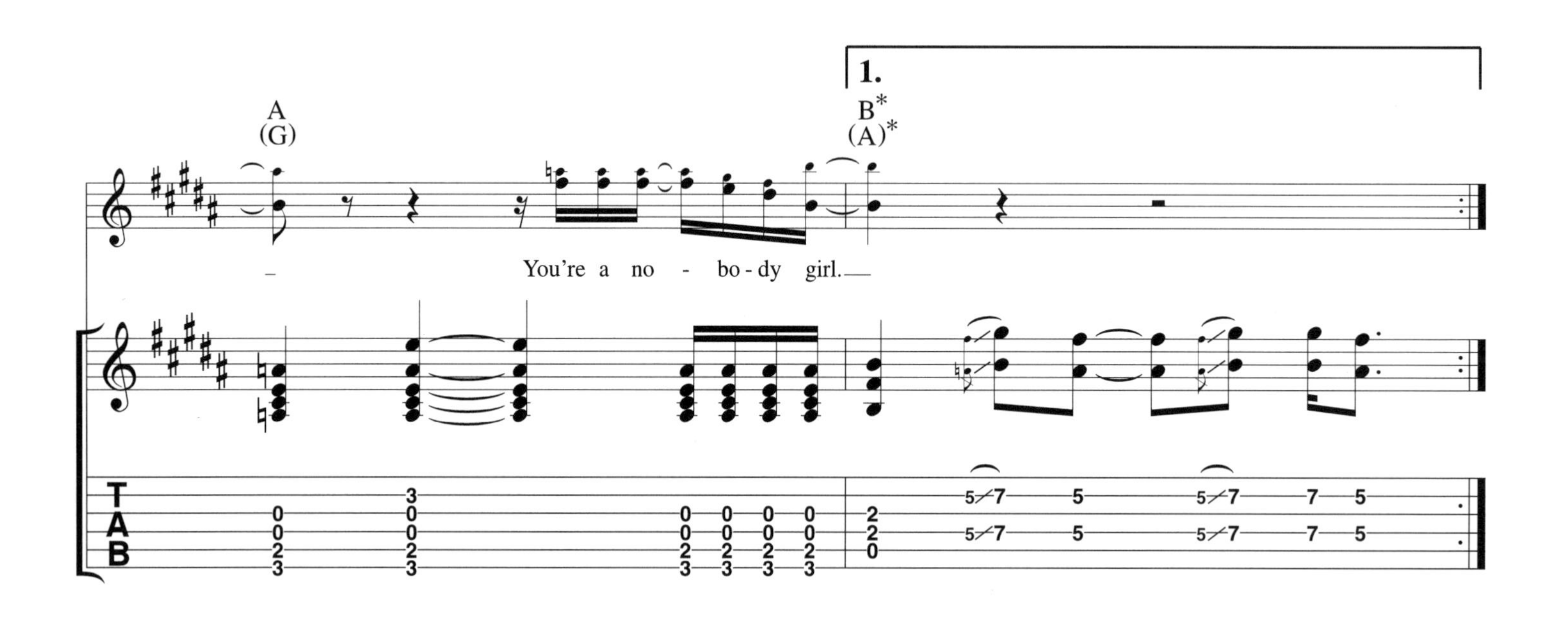
1.
A
(G)
B*
(A)*
You're a no - bo-dy girl.
TAB

2.
B*
(A)*
B
Full
Full
Full
Full
TAB

B*
(A)*
Gtr. 4 (elec.)
f
Full
Dadd9
(Cadd9)
Gtr. 2
ad lib. on rpt.
E
(D)
1.
2.
Gtr. 1
mf Gtrs. 3+4 tacet
Gtr. 2 tacet

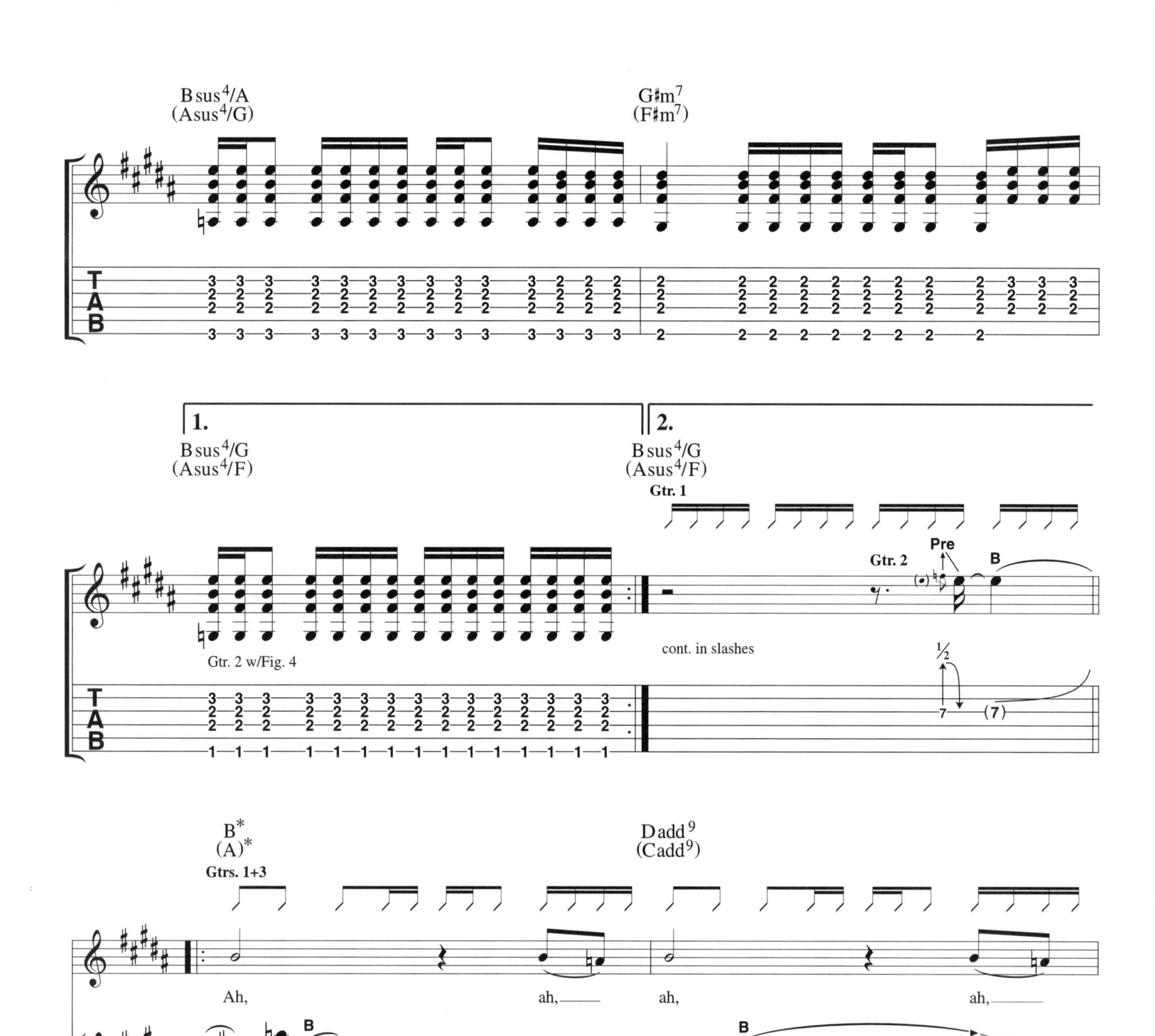

B*
(A)*
Gtrs. 1+3
Dadd9
(Cadd9)
Ah, ah, ah, ah,
Full
Full
Full
B
3

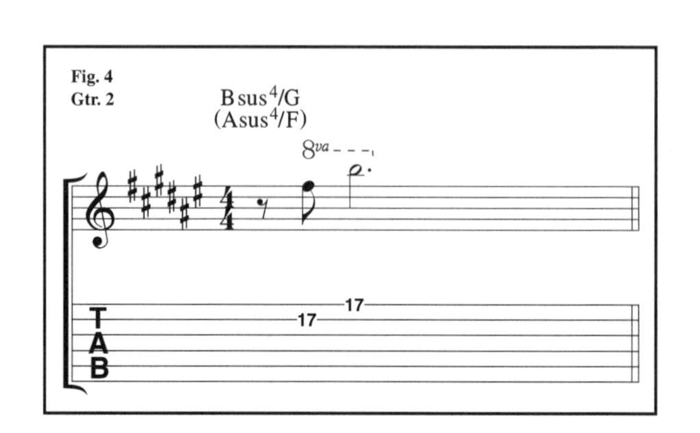

Verse 3:

The night plays games
And the people they come and go
Well, they trade in their pieces
For a late night ride on your rodeo
If your horses could talk
I wonder if they would complain
I know they're rested and ready
They've been going nowhere for days.

They don't know you anyway
They don't know
They don't even mind the weight.

SYLVIA PLATH

Words & Music by Ryan Adams & Richard Causon

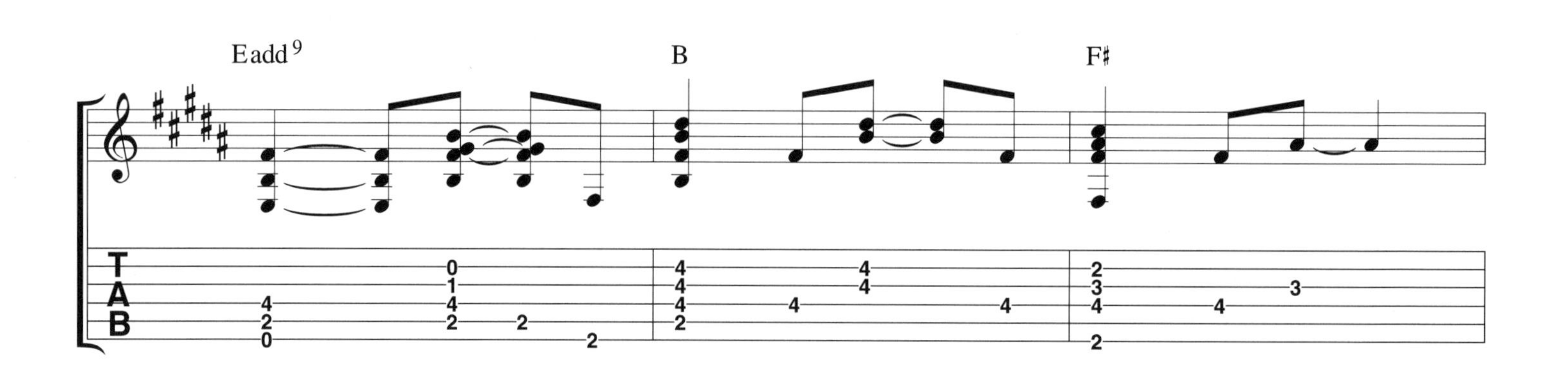

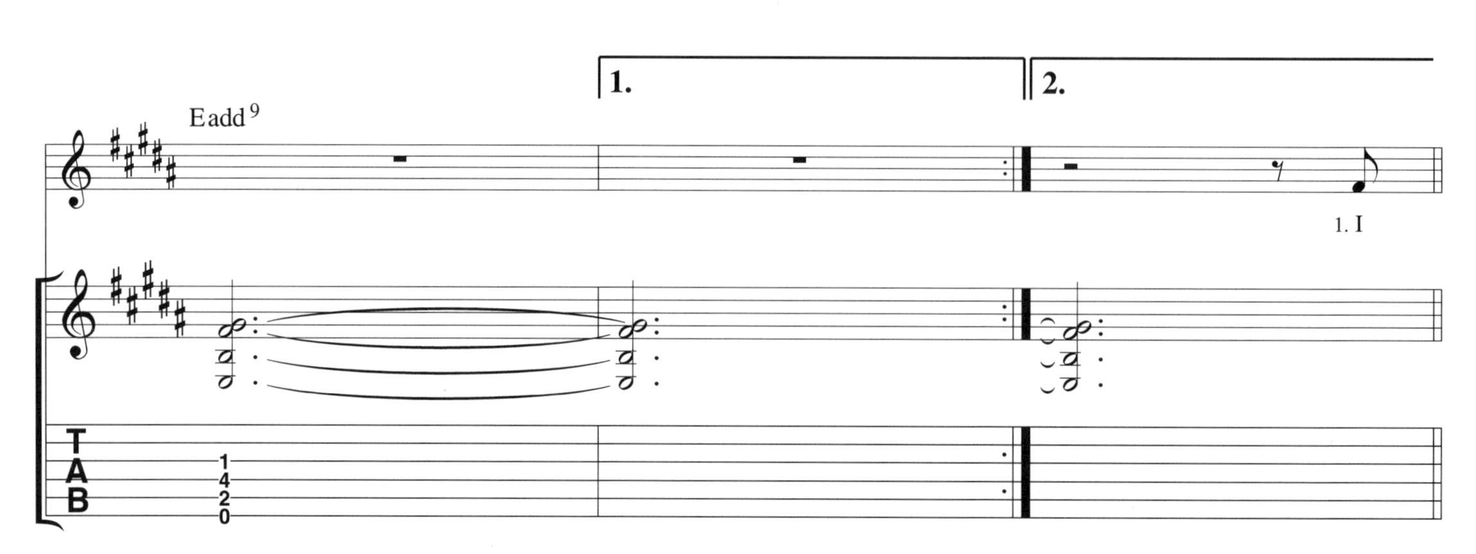

Verse
B F♯ Emaj7/B E
wish I had a Syl - vi - a Plath,
she and I would sleep on a boat and
B F♯ Emaj7/B Eadd9
bust - ed tooth and a smile, and
swim in the sea with - out clothes, with
B F♯ Emaj7/B E
cig - a - rette ash - es in her drink. The
rain fall - ing fast on the sea. While she was
B F♯ Emaj7/B Eadd9
kind that goes out, then sleeps for a week, the
swim - ming a - way she'd be wink - ing at me,

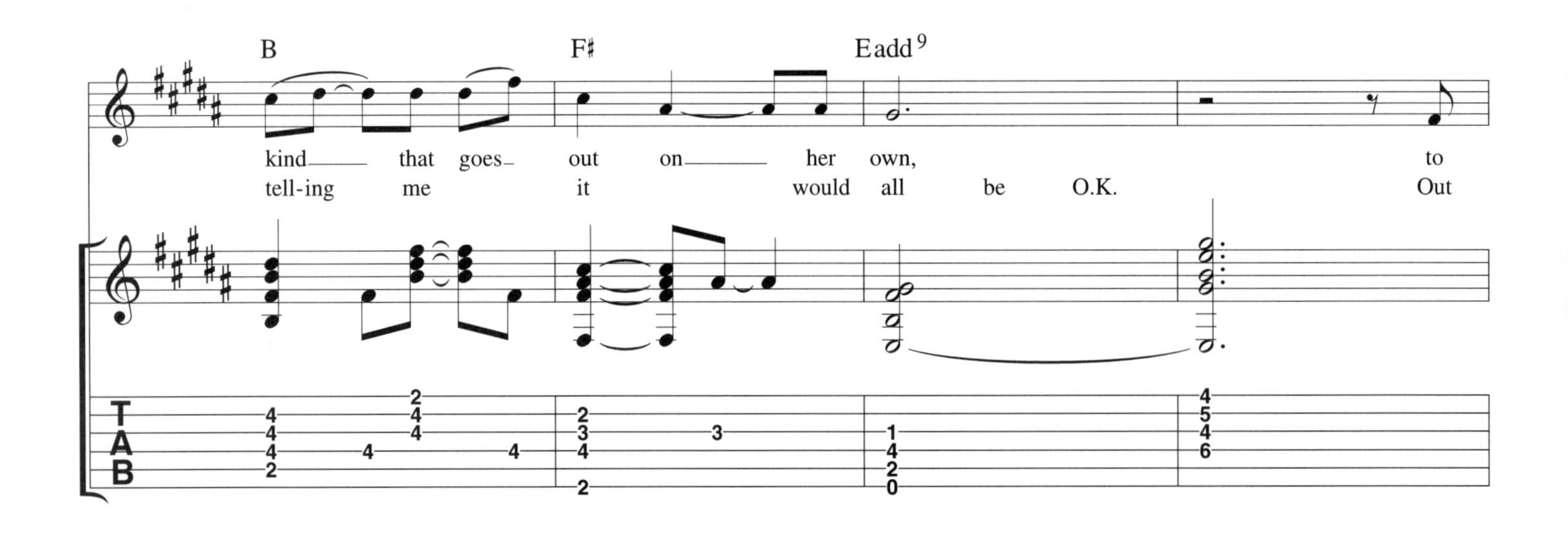
B
F♯
Eadd 9
kind that goes out on her own, to
tell-ing me it would all be O.K. Out
T
A
B

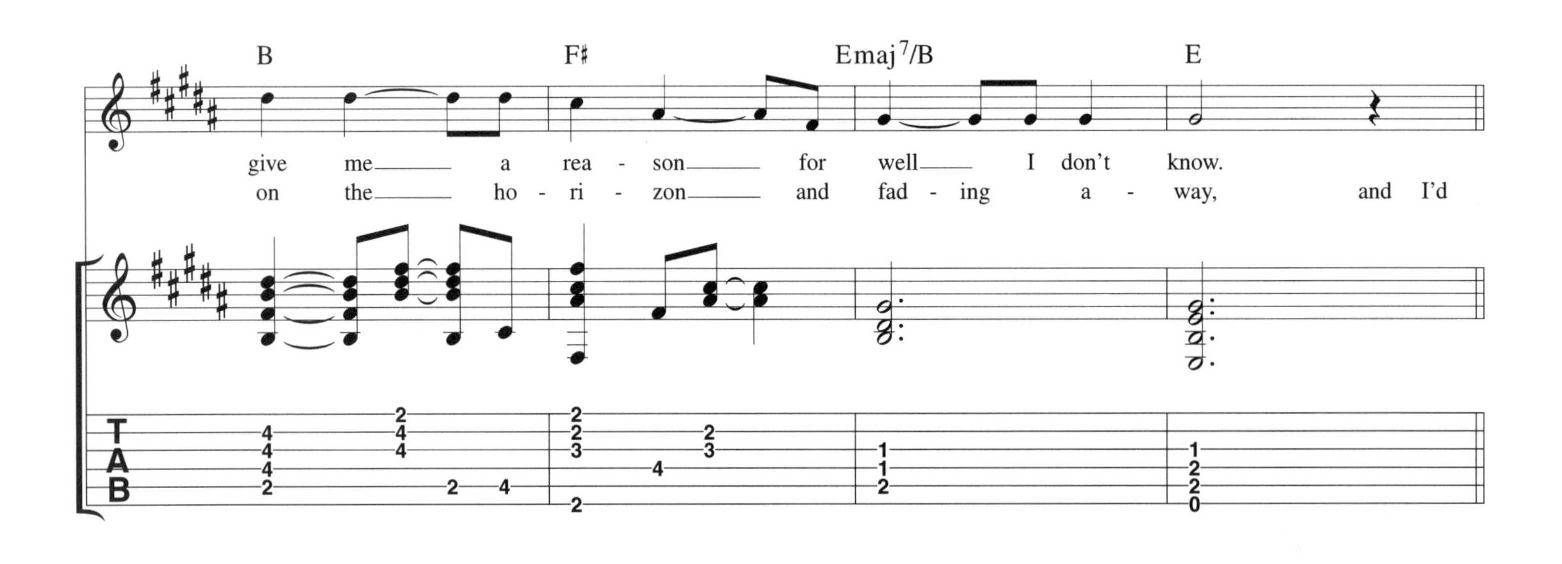
B
F♯
Emaj 7/B
E
give me a rea - son for well I don't know.
on the ho - ri - zon and fad - ing a - way, and I'd
T
A
B

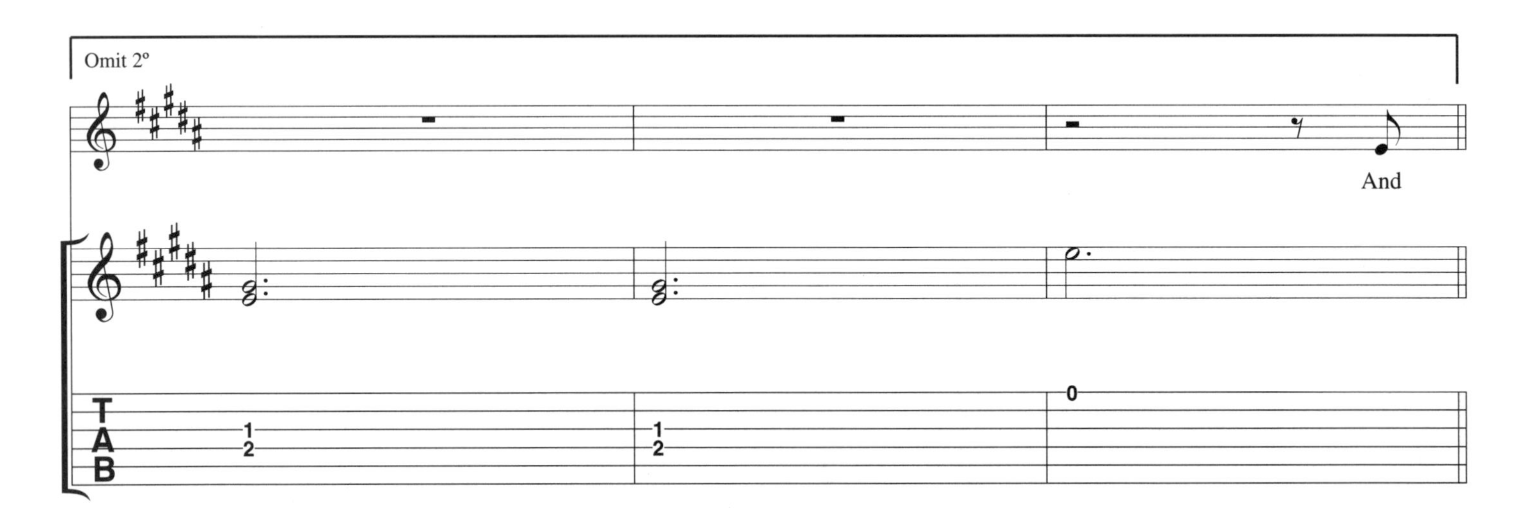
Omit 2º
And
T
A
B

Omit 1°
B
F♯
Emaj7/B
Eadd9
swim to the boat and I'd laugh. I got - ta
G♯
C♯7sus2
F♯
get me a Syl - vi - a Plath. And
Chorus
A/C♯
E
may - be she'd take me to France, or
F♯sus4
F♯7sus4
B
may - be to Spain, she'd ask me to dance in a

A/C♯
E
man - sion on the top of a hill. She'd
F♯sus4
B
ash on the car - pets and slip me a pill and she'd
A/C♯
E
get me pret - ty load - ed on gin. And
C♯7sus4
B
may - be she'd give me a bath, how I

1.
G♯
C♯sus4
F♯
wish I had a Syl - vi - a Plath.
B
F♯
Emaj7/B
E
B
F♯
E
Eadd9
2. And
2.
F♯
G♯
C♯sus4
F♯
I wish I had a Syl - vi - a Plath.

SOMEHOW, SOMEDAY

Words & Music by Ryan Adams

Gtr. 1 (no capo)

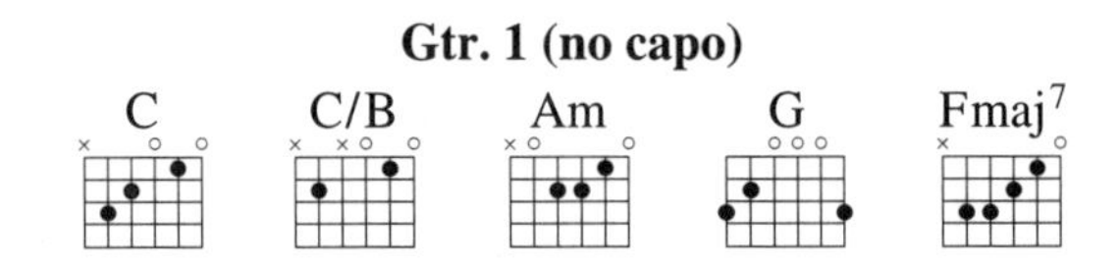

C
long — a - go.
like lit - tle kids.
2º Gtr. 2 w/Fig. 2
G
I wish that you and I —
I'll ne - ver know just how —
– had those kids, may - be bought us that home.
– bad it hurt, or what I did.
2º Gtr. 2 w/Fig. 2

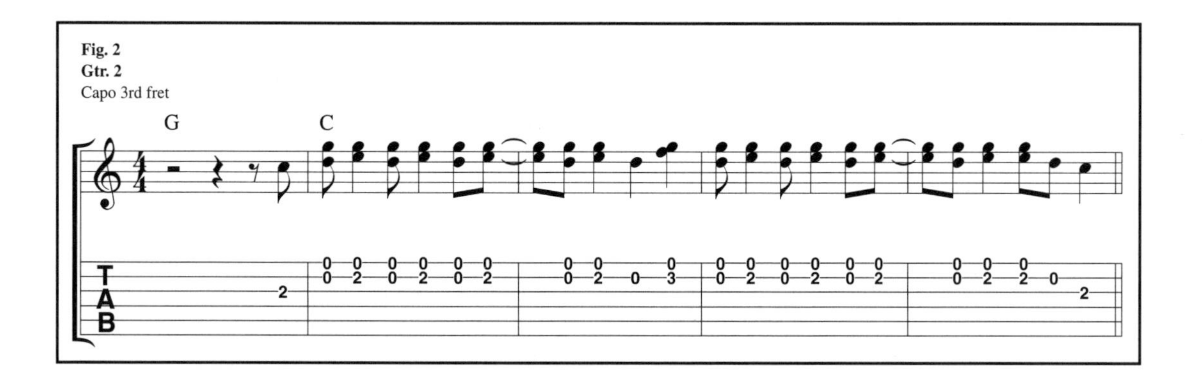
Fig. 2
Gtr. 2
Capo 3rd fret
G
C

C
Fmaj7
I wish that we were stum - bl - ing fast
I wish that we were stum - bl - ing fast
down on Irv - ing Four - teenth street.
down on Irv - ing and Sixth.
G
C

Fmaj7
I wish that we were still in your room, in your bed and you were
I wish that we were still ma - king plans, but now there's
2º Gtr. 2 w/Fig. 3
G
hold - ing me.
no - thing to fix.
'Cause there
C C/B Am G Fmaj7
cont. sim.
ain't no way I'll ev - er stop from lov-in' you now.
There

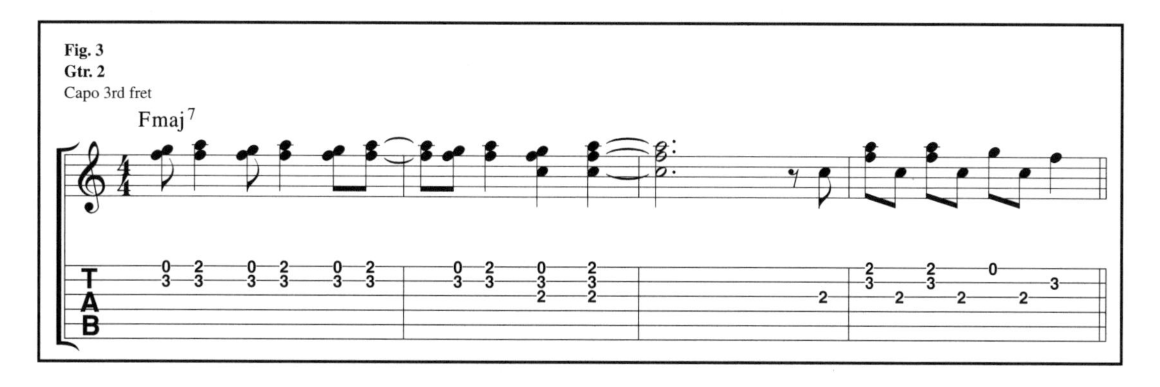
Fig. 3
Gtr. 2
Capo 3rd fret
Fmaj7

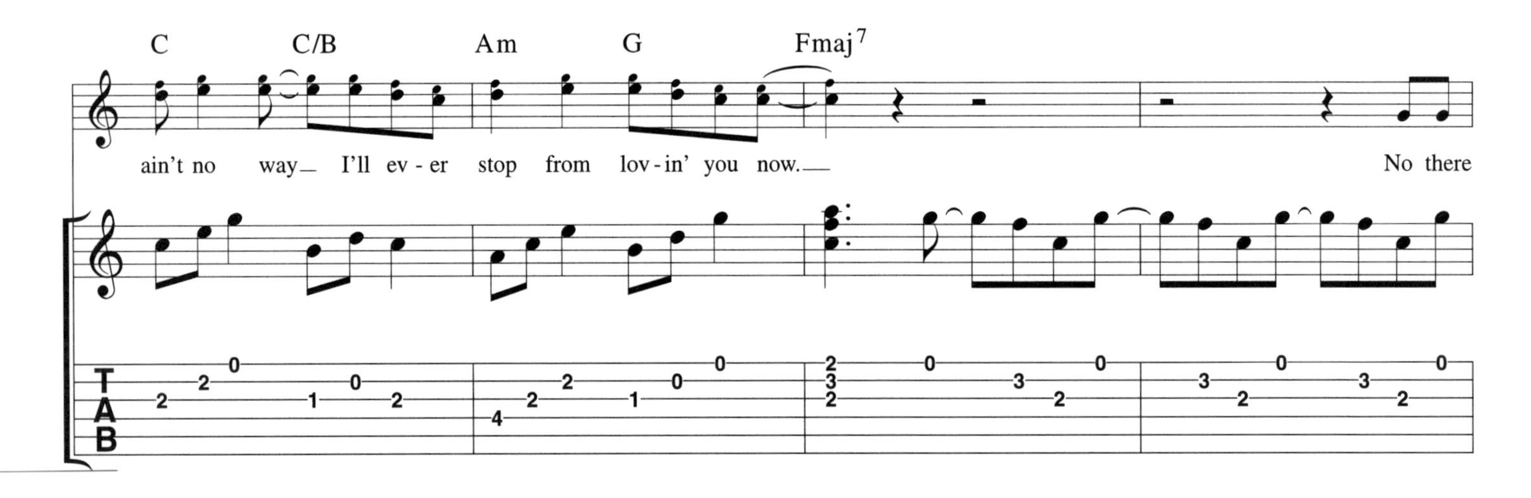
C
C/B
Am
G
Fmaj7
ain't no way I'll ev - er stop from lov - in' you now.
No there
T
A
B

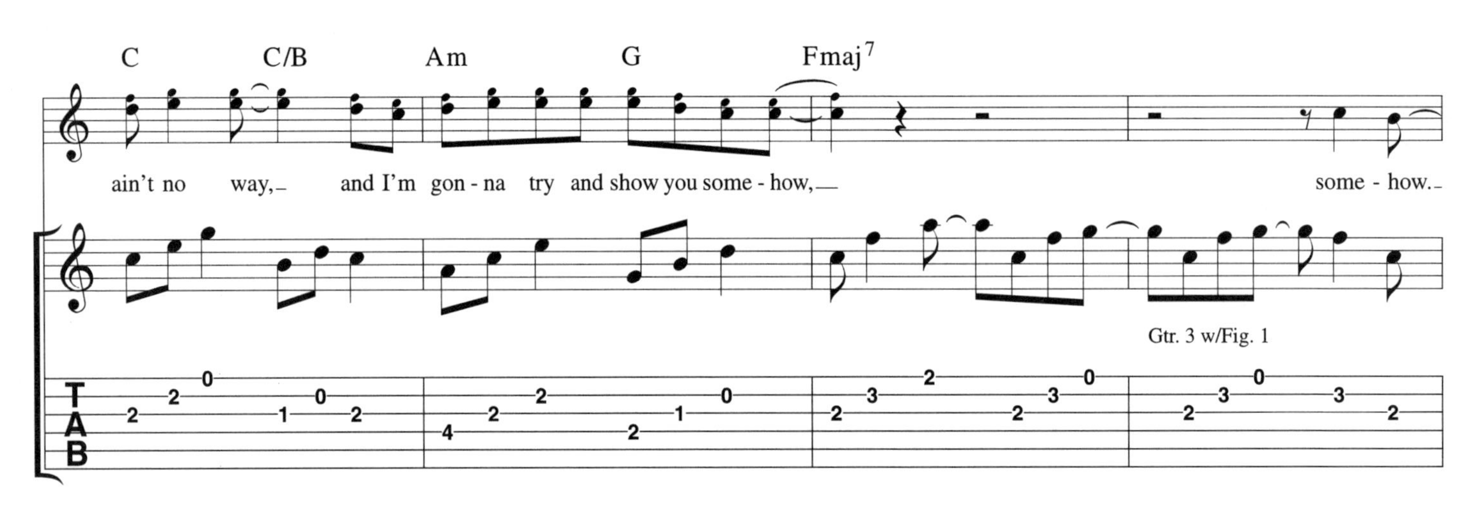
C
C/B
Am
G
Fmaj7
ain't no way, and I'm gon - na try and show you some - how,
some - how.
Gtr. 3 w/Fig. 1
T
A
B

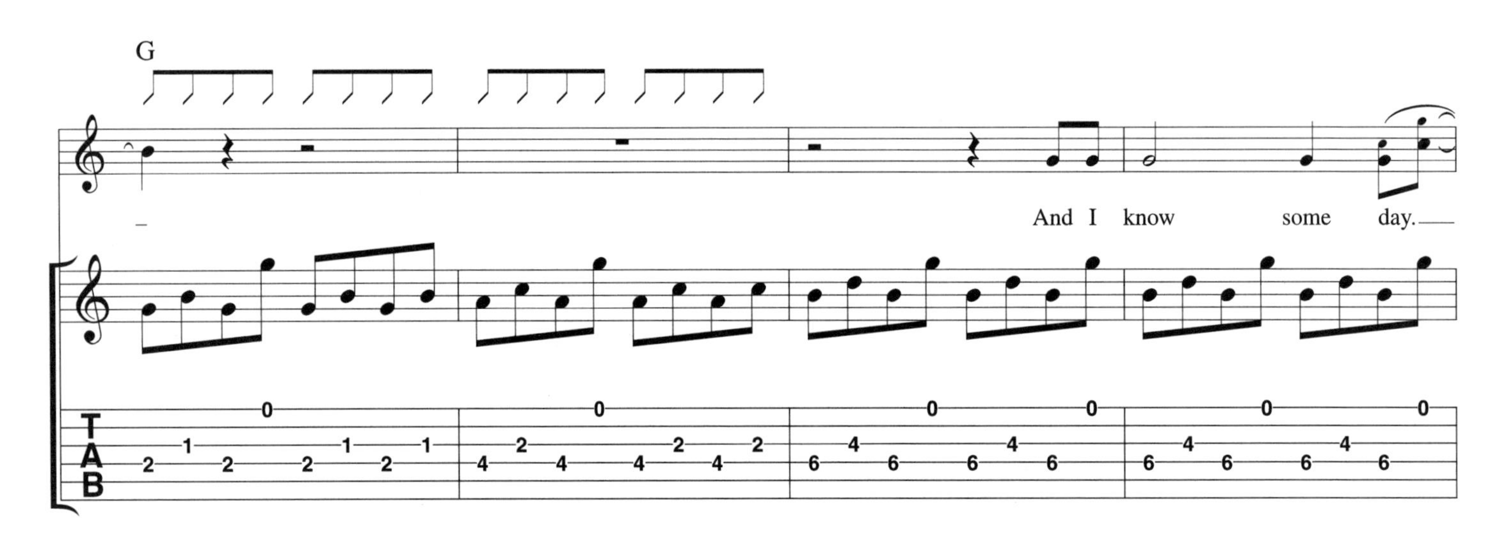
G
And I know some day.
T
A
B

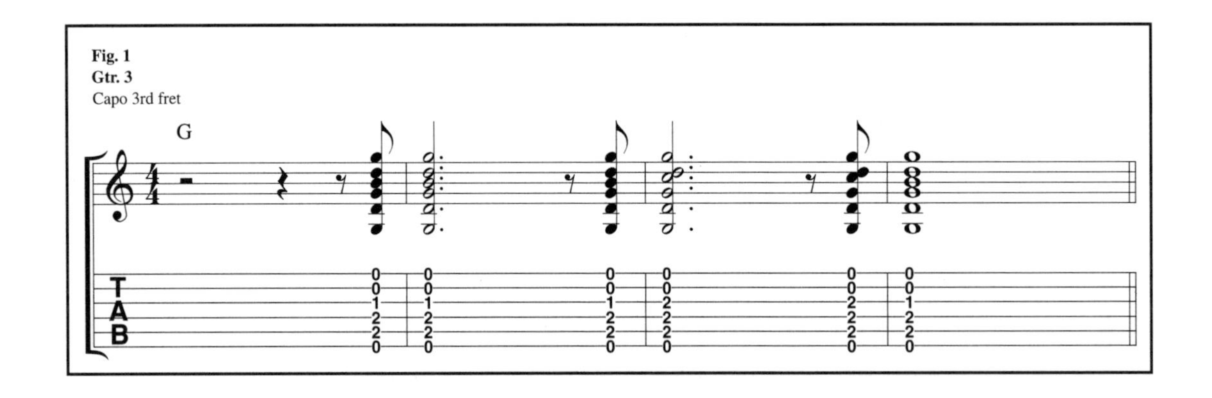
Fig. 1
Gtr. 3
Capo 3rd fret
G
T
A
B

C
C/B
Am
G
Fmaj7
Some
day.
C
C/B
Am
G
Fmaj7
1.
Some
day.
C
2.
Fmaj7
C
C/B
Am
G
Some
day.

Fmaj7
C
C/B
Some
day.
Am
G
Fmaj7
C
C/B
Oh
ho - ney.
Some_ day.
Am
G
Fmaj7
C
C/B
cont. sim.
Some_ day.
Ah.
Am
G
Fmaj7
C
rit.

ENEMY FIRE

Words & Music by Ryan Adams & Gillian Welch

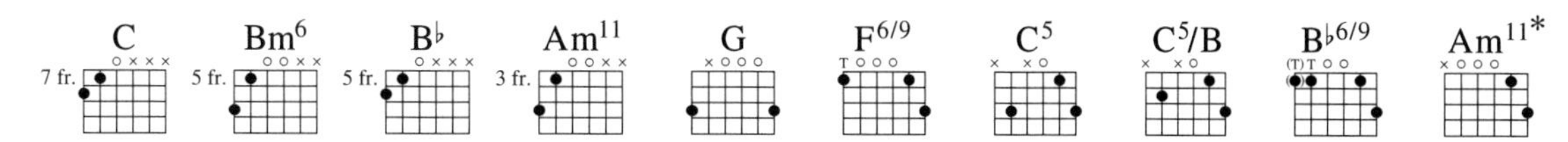

♩= 80

Intro

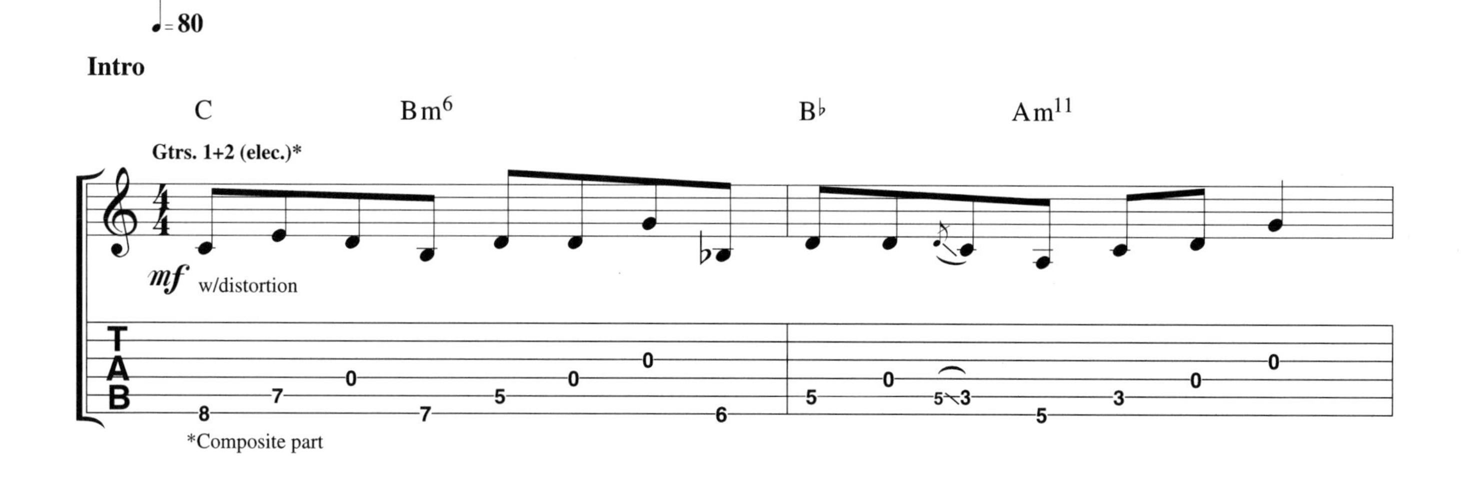

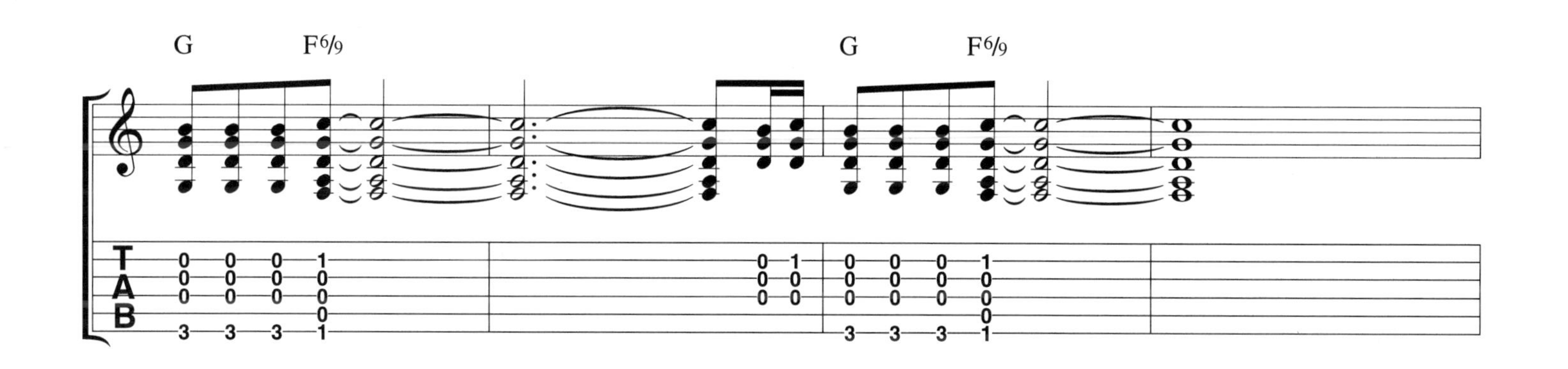

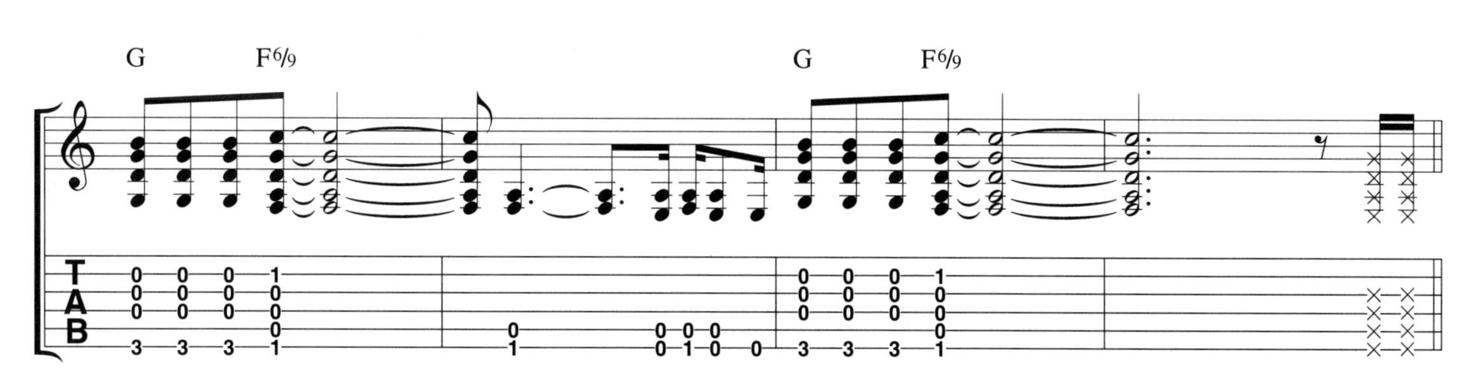

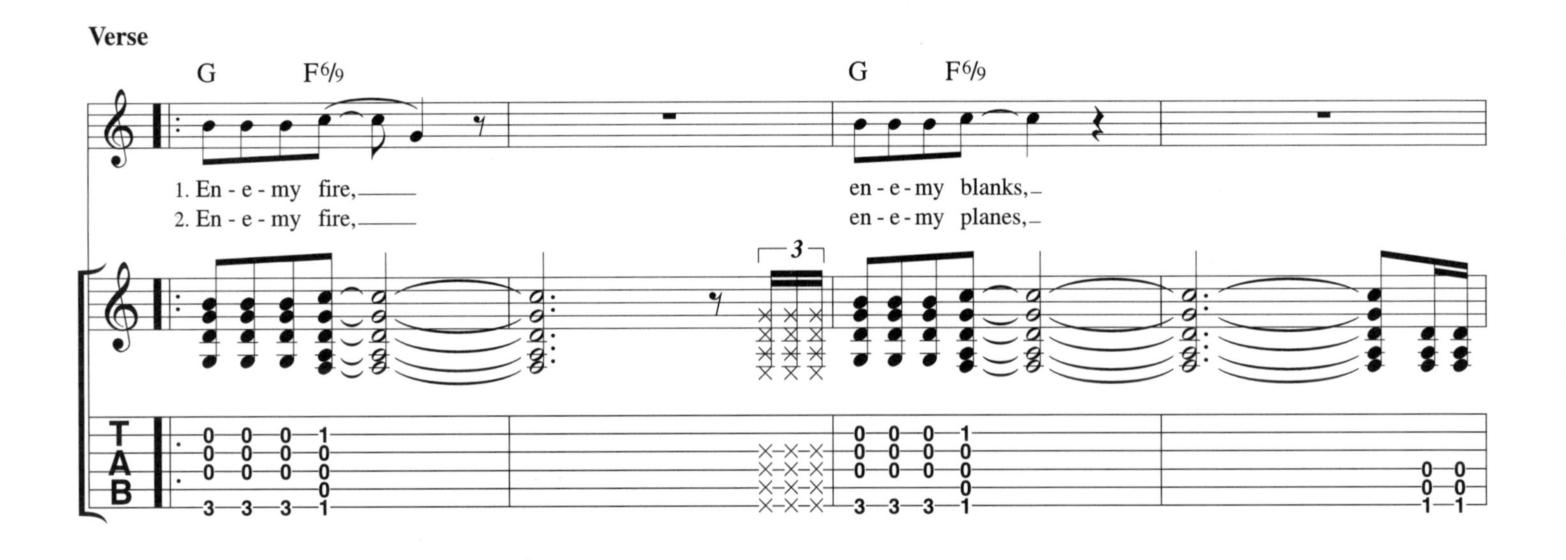
Verse
G
F6/9
G
F6/9
1. En - e - my fire,
2. En - e - my fire,
en - e - my blanks,
en - e - my planes,

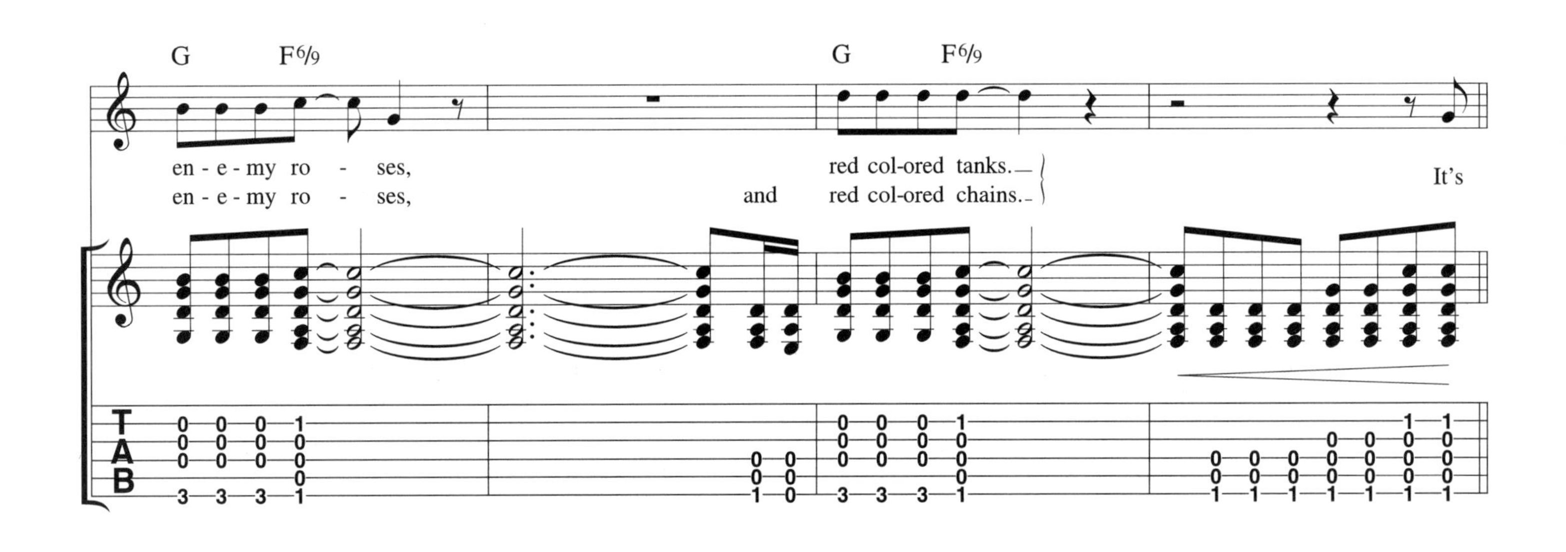
G
F6/9
G
F6/9
en - e - my ro - ses,
en - e - my ro - ses,
red col-ored tanks.
and red col-ored chains.
It's

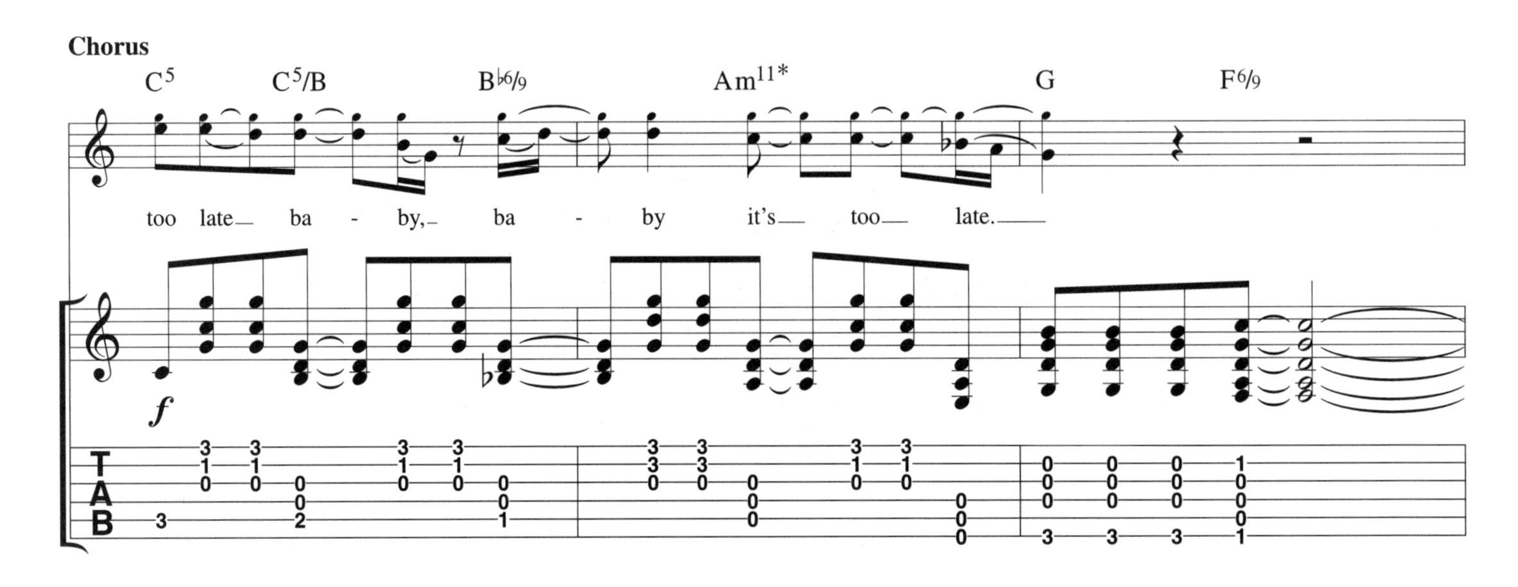
Chorus
C5
C5/B
B♭6/9
Am11*
G
F6/9
too late ba - by, ba - by it's too late.

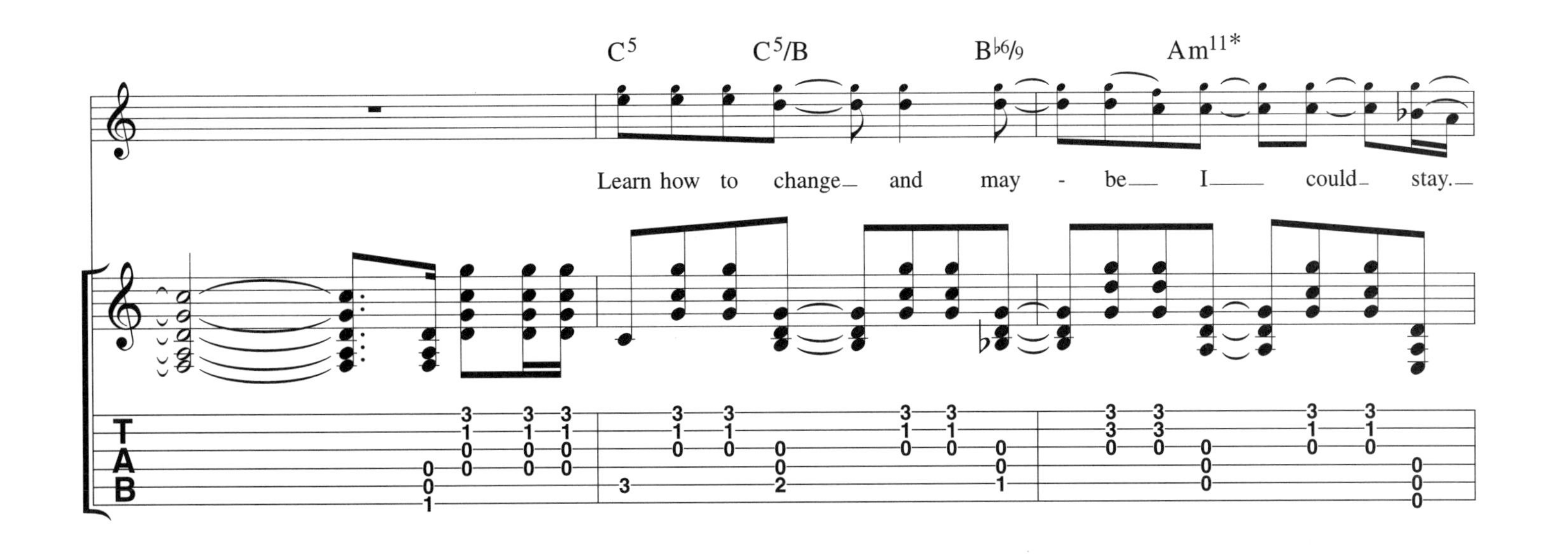
C5 C5/B B♭6/9 Am11*
Learn how to change and may - be I could stay.
T
A
B

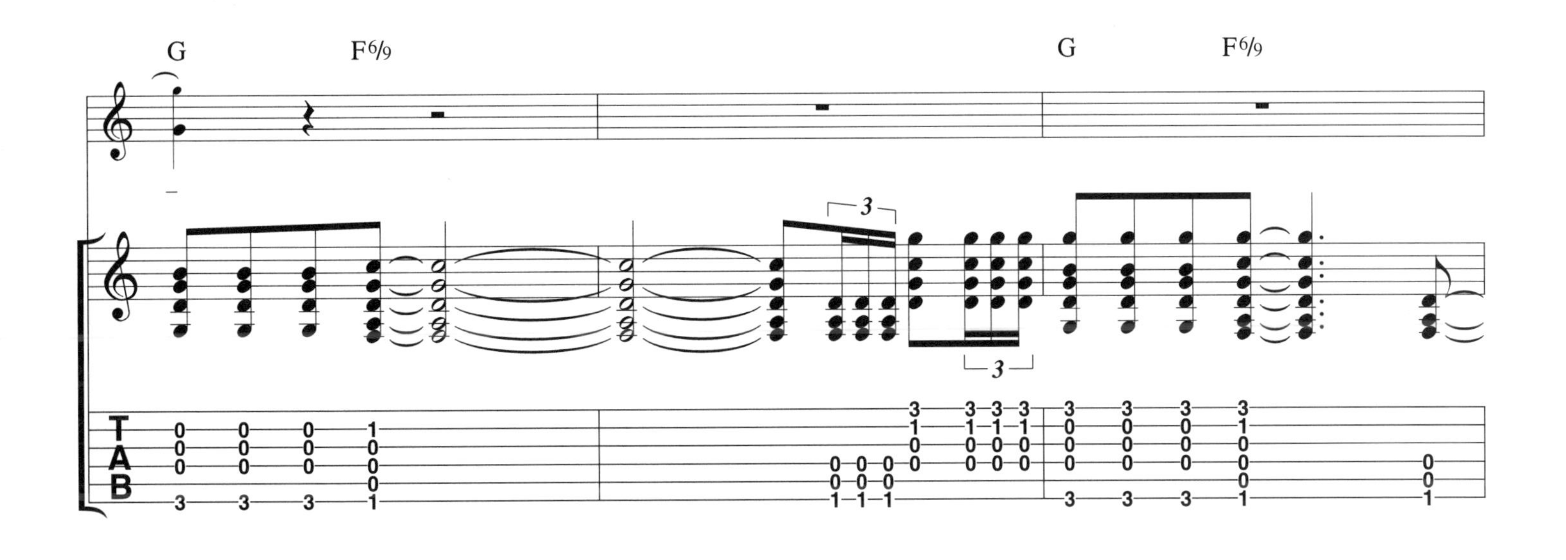
G F6/9 G F6/9
3
T
A
B

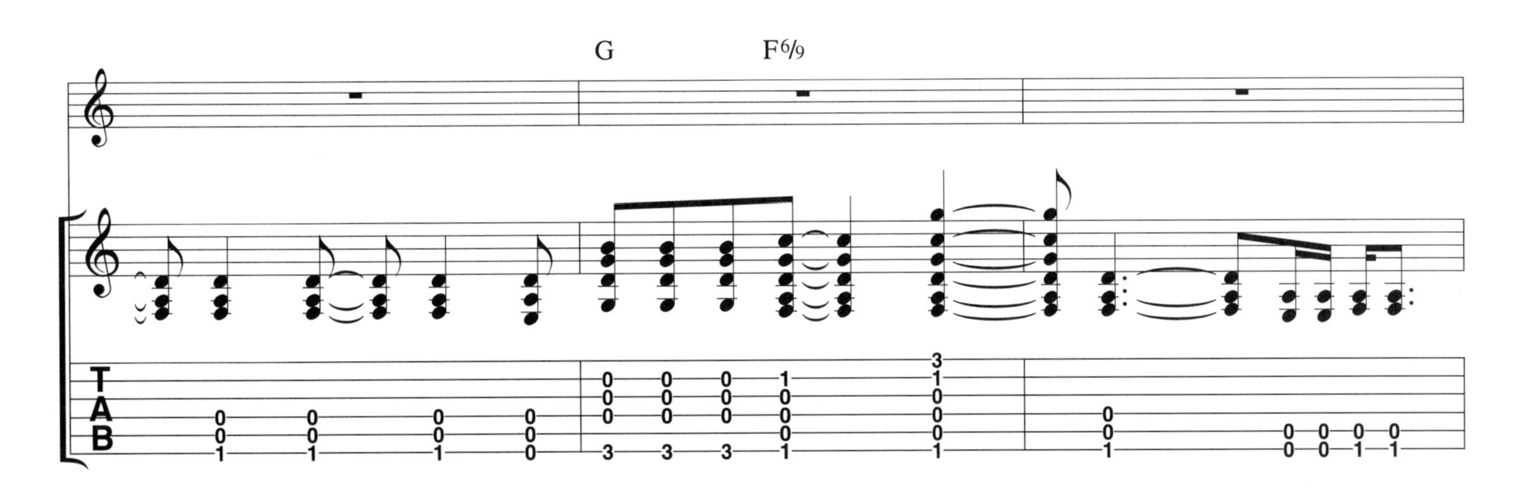
G F6/9
T
A
B

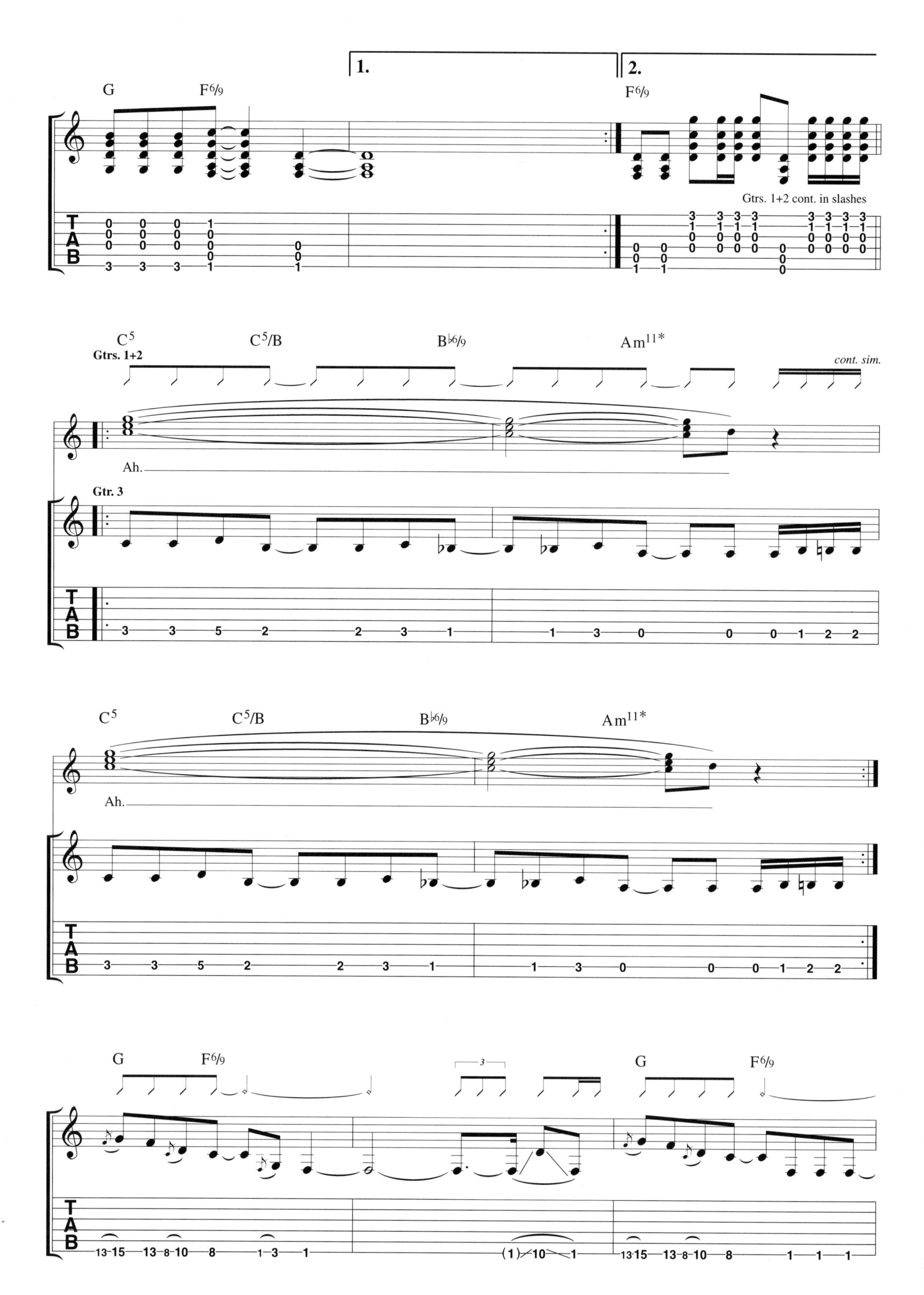

1.
2.
G
F6/9
Gtrs. 1+2 cont. in slashes
C5
C5/B
B♭6/9
Am11*
Gtrs. 1+2
cont. sim.
Ah.
Gtr. 3

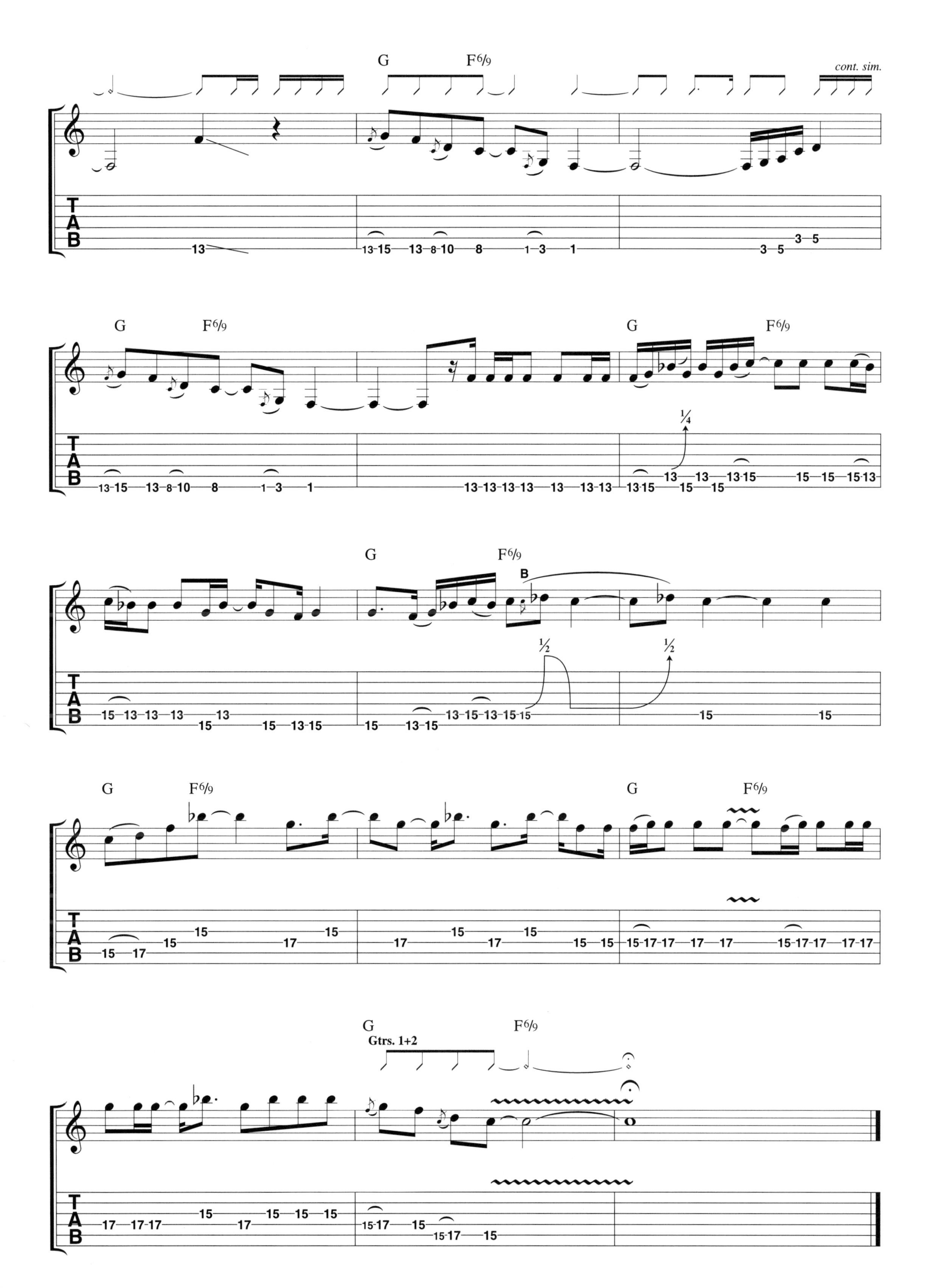

G
F6/9
cont. sim.
B
Gtrs. 1+2

GONNA MAKE YOU LOVE ME

Words & Music by Ryan Adams

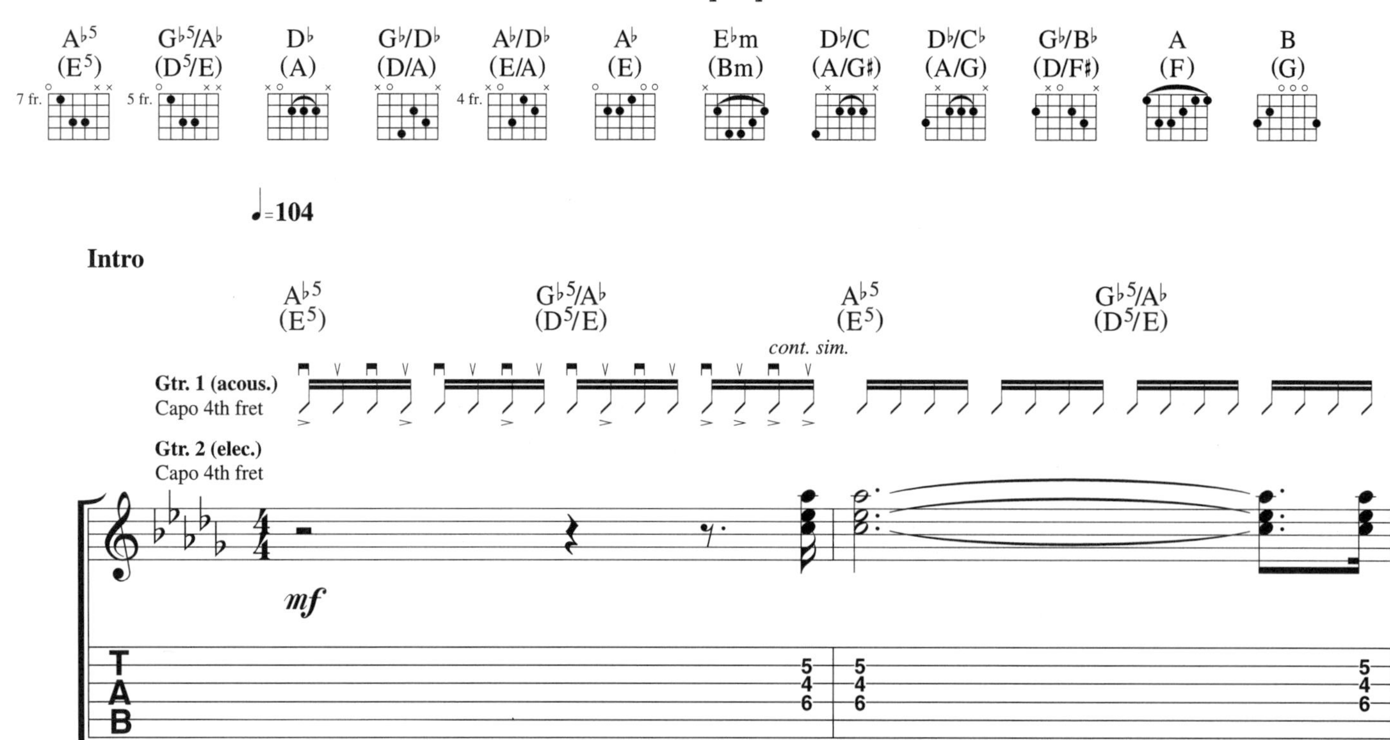

*Symbols in parentheses represent chord names with respect to capoed gtr. (Tab 0 = capo 4th fret)
Symbols above represent actual sounding chords

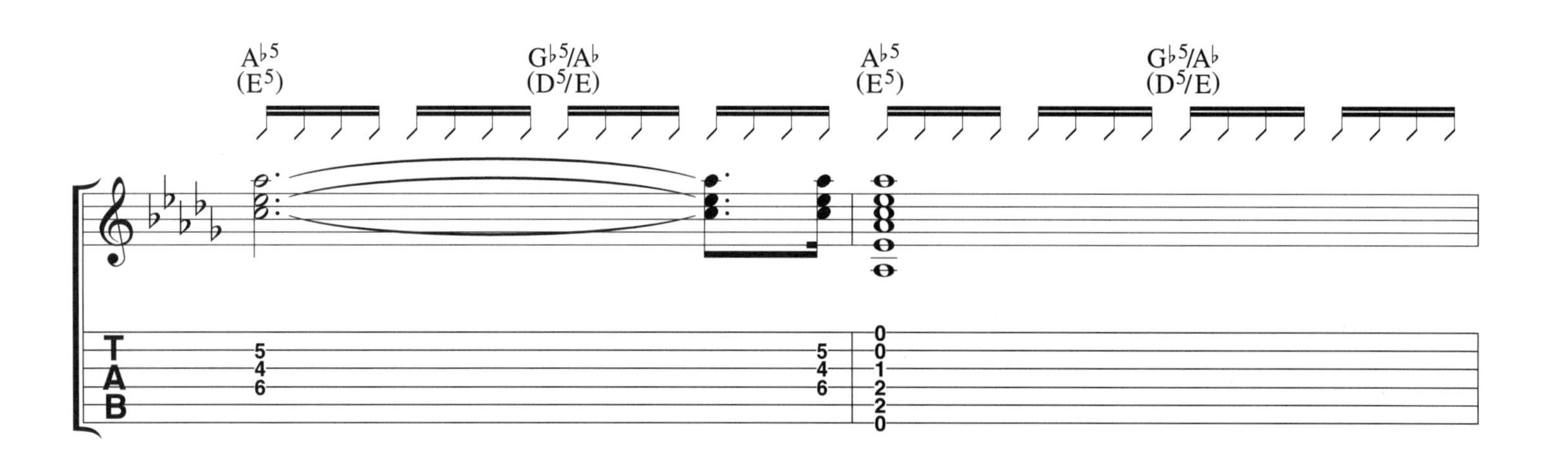

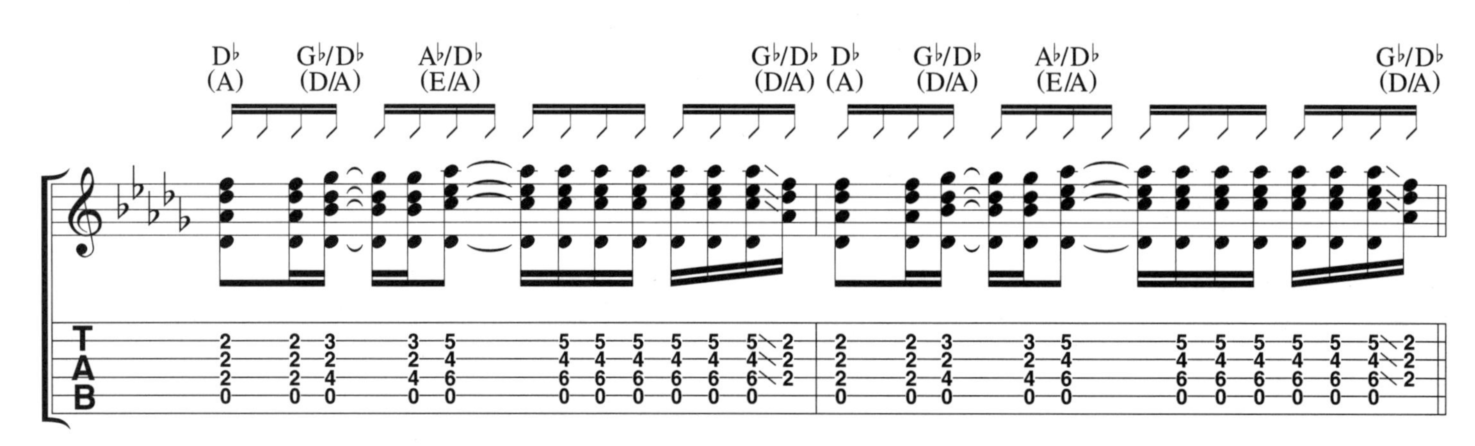

Verse

D♭
(A)
G♭/D♭ D♭
(D/A) (A)
G♭/D♭ D♭
(D/A) (A)
1. Ri - ot in the streets, the touch be - neath the sheets, it's
2. Moon - light on the beach, sweet am - phet - a - mines, it's
(Verse 3 (𝄋) see block lyric)
TAB

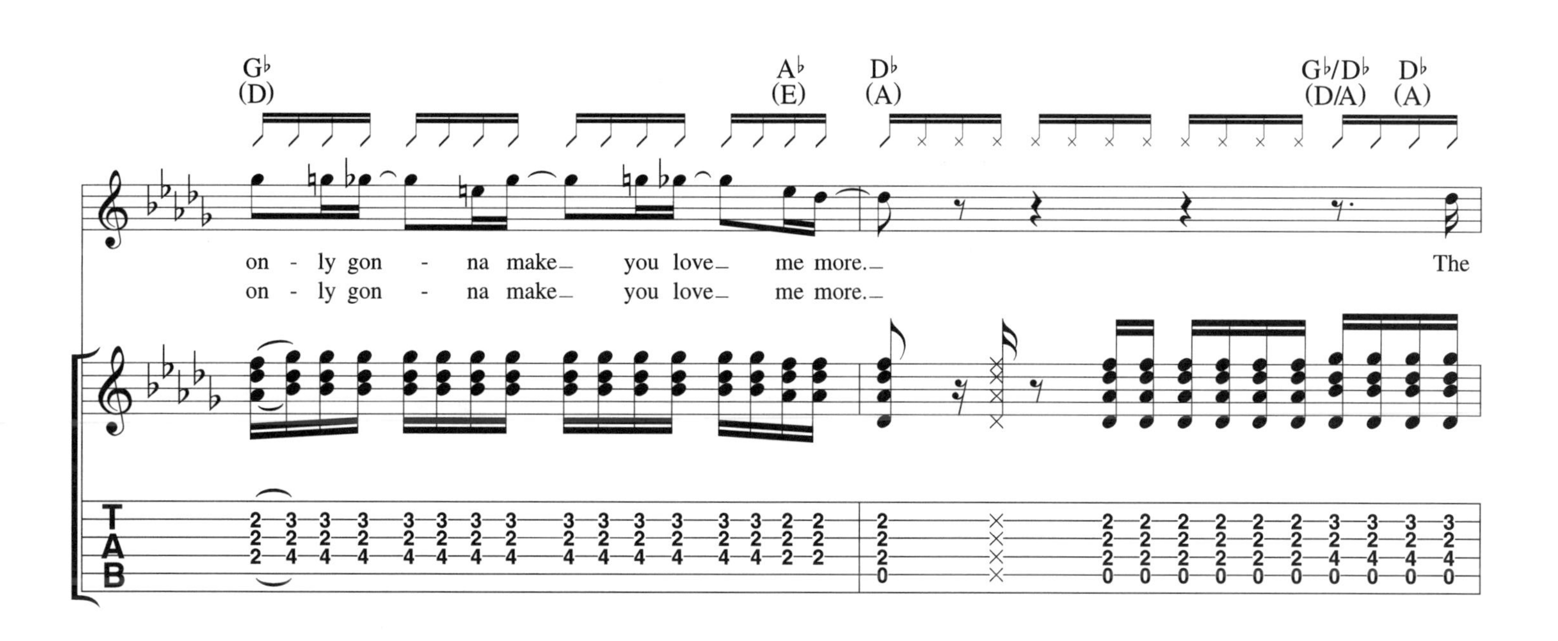
G♭
(D)
A♭
(E)
D♭
(A)
G♭/D♭ D♭
(D/A) (A)
on - ly gon - na make you love me more. The
on - ly gon - na make you love me more.
TAB

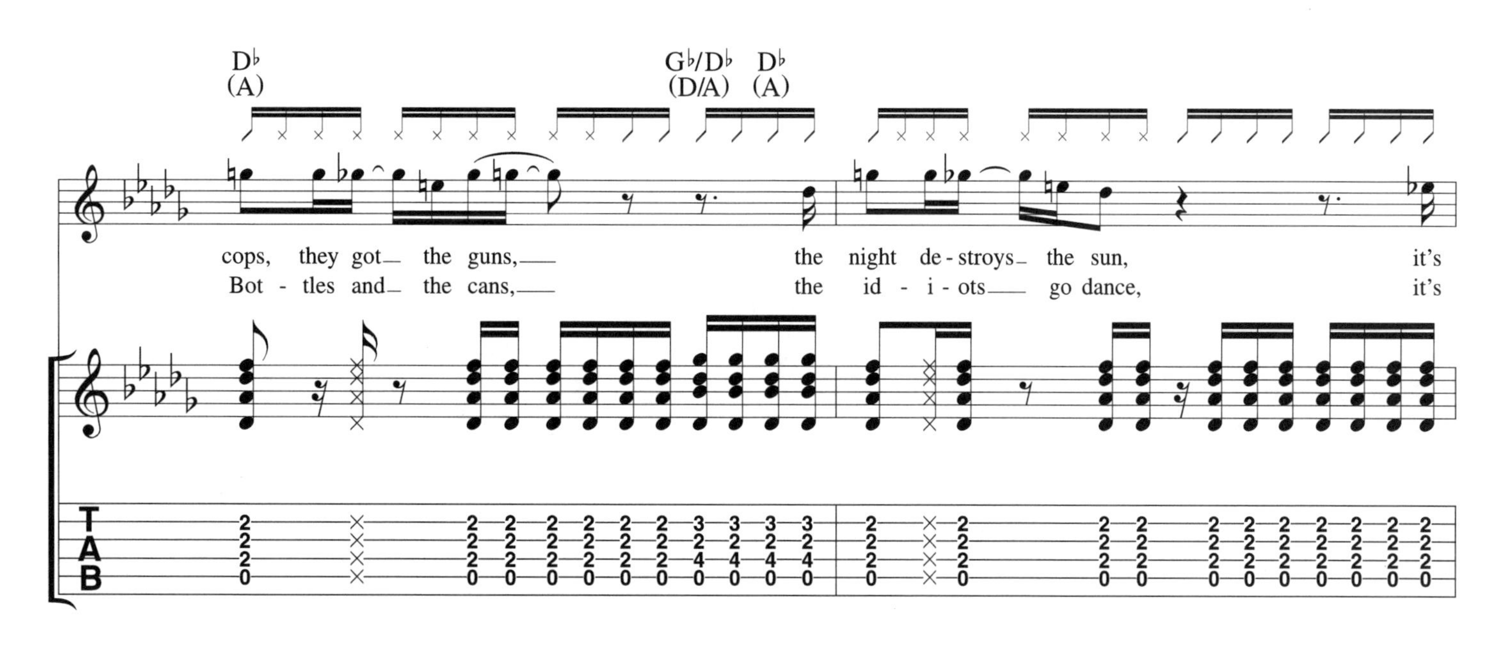
D♭
(A)
G♭/D♭ D♭
(D/A) (A)
cops, they got the guns, the night de - stroys the sun, it's
Bot - tles and the cans, the id - i - ots go dance, it's
TAB

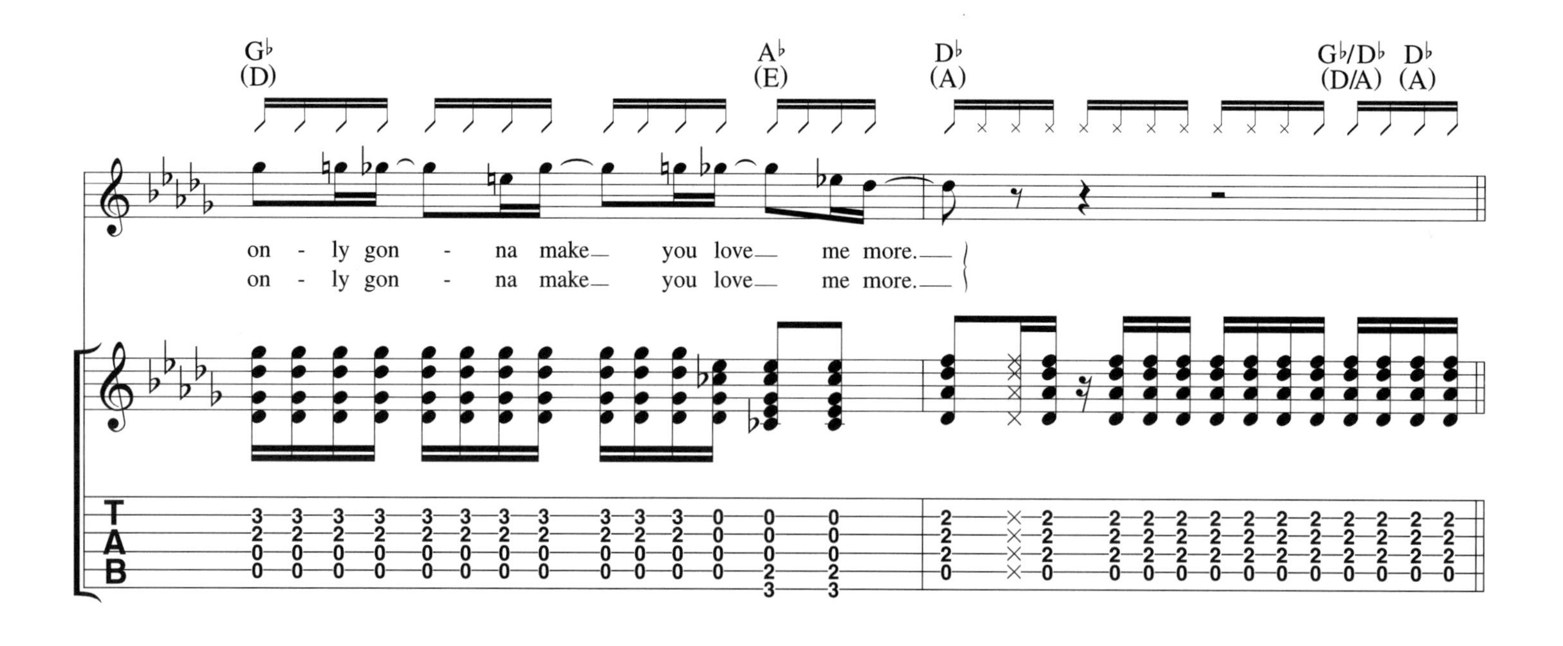

G♭ (D)
A♭ (E)
D♭ (A)
G♭/D♭ (D/A) D♭ (A)
on - ly gon - na make you love me more.
on - ly gon - na make you love me more.

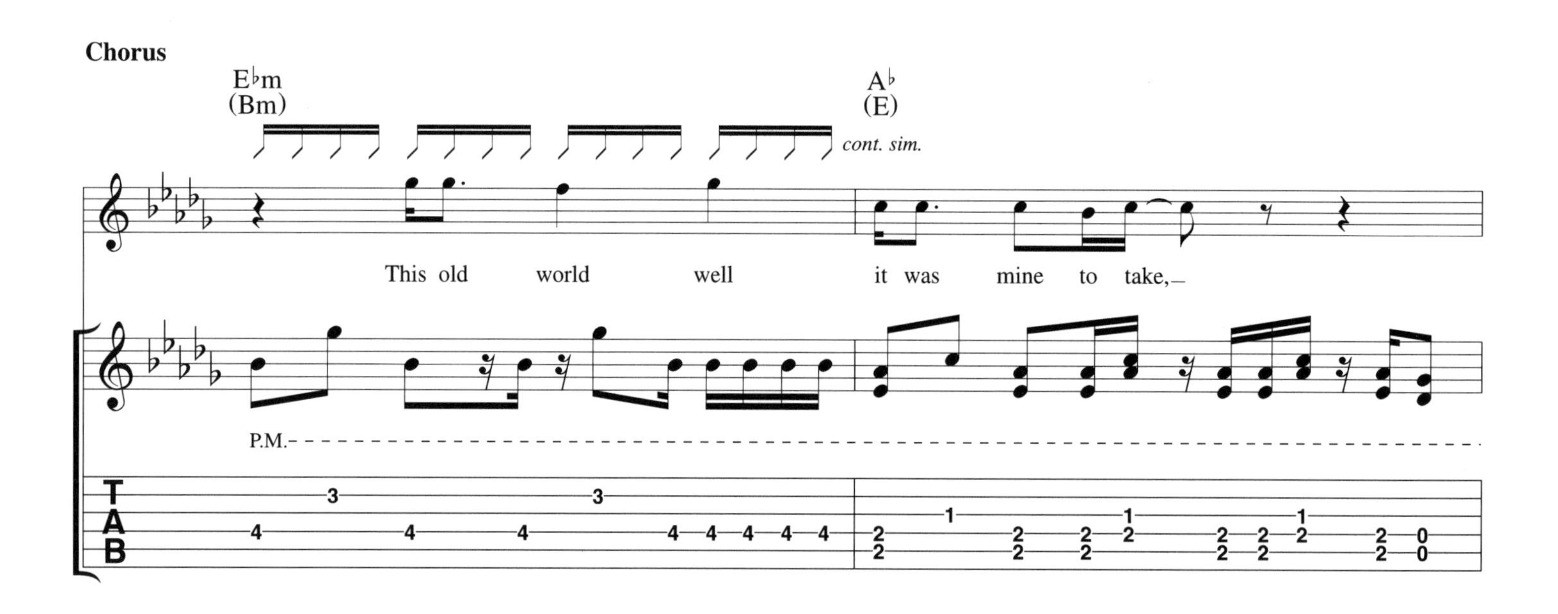

Chorus
E♭m (Bm)
A♭ (E)
cont. sim.
This old world well it was mine to take,
P.M.

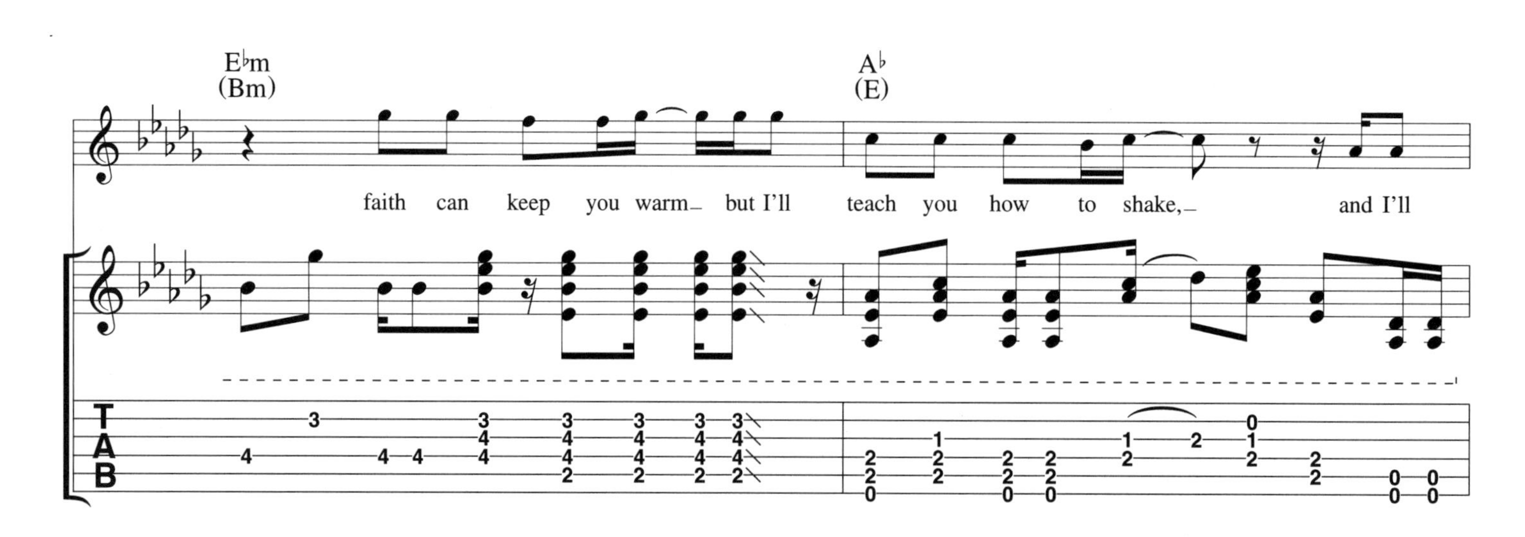

E♭m (Bm)
A♭ (E)
faith can keep you warm but I'll teach you how to shake, and I'll

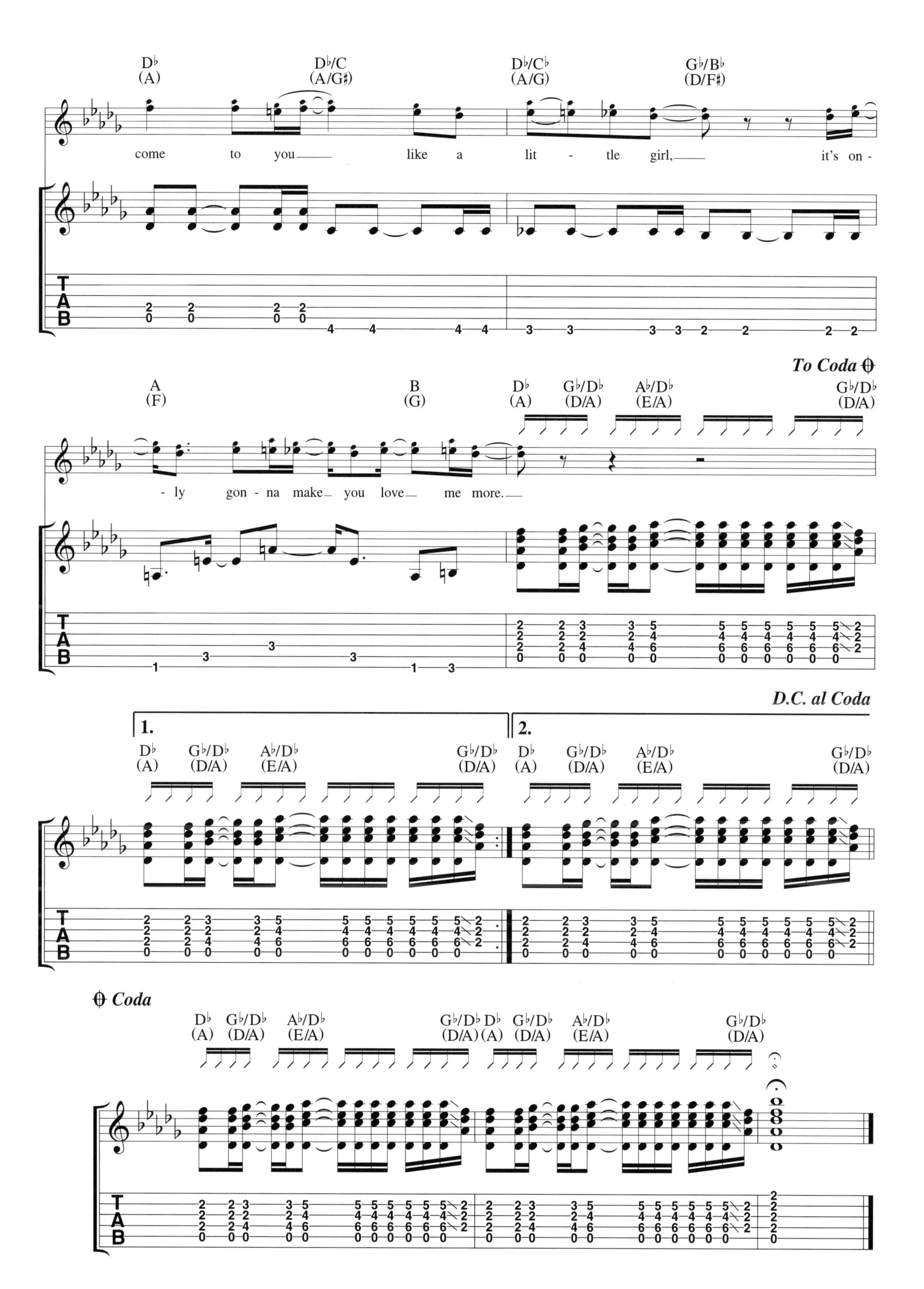
D♭ (A)
D♭/C (A/G♯)
D♭/C♭ (A/G)
G♭/B♭ (D/F♯)
come to you like a lit - tle girl, it's on -
To Coda
A (F)
B (G)
D♭ (A)
G♭/D♭ (D/A)
A♭/D♭ (E/A)
G♭/D♭ (D/A)
- ly gon - na make you love me more.
D.C. al Coda
1.
2.
Coda

WILD FLOWERS

Words & Music by Ryan Adams

D6 Gmaj7 G6
but a rough dia - mond,
Gm D Dsus2
sleep now and your an - gels will come dear.
D Dsus2
2. Poor Ma - til - da,
Dmaj9 D6 Gmaj7 G6
hand - cuffed hard to the wheel and steer - ing wild -

Gm
ly through loves fields so blind
D
Dsus2
ly. For
Chorus
Dm
C
G
ever only takes its toll on some. Ah.
† Tap body of gtr.
F♯
Omit 1°
G
A
But tonight

Bm A Gmaj7 G6 A
– you're sleep-ing a - lone, with - out him to - night
Bm A Gmaj7 G6
– you're sleep-ing a - lone with - out him, and
Esus4 D/F♯ 1. G
ev - 'ry - thing went up in smoke like
A D/F♯ G6/9
wild flow - ers.
Gtr. 1 +
Gtr. 2 (acous. 12 str.)*
mf
* Composite part

A
D/F♯
Gmaj7
N.C.
wild flow - ers, dear.

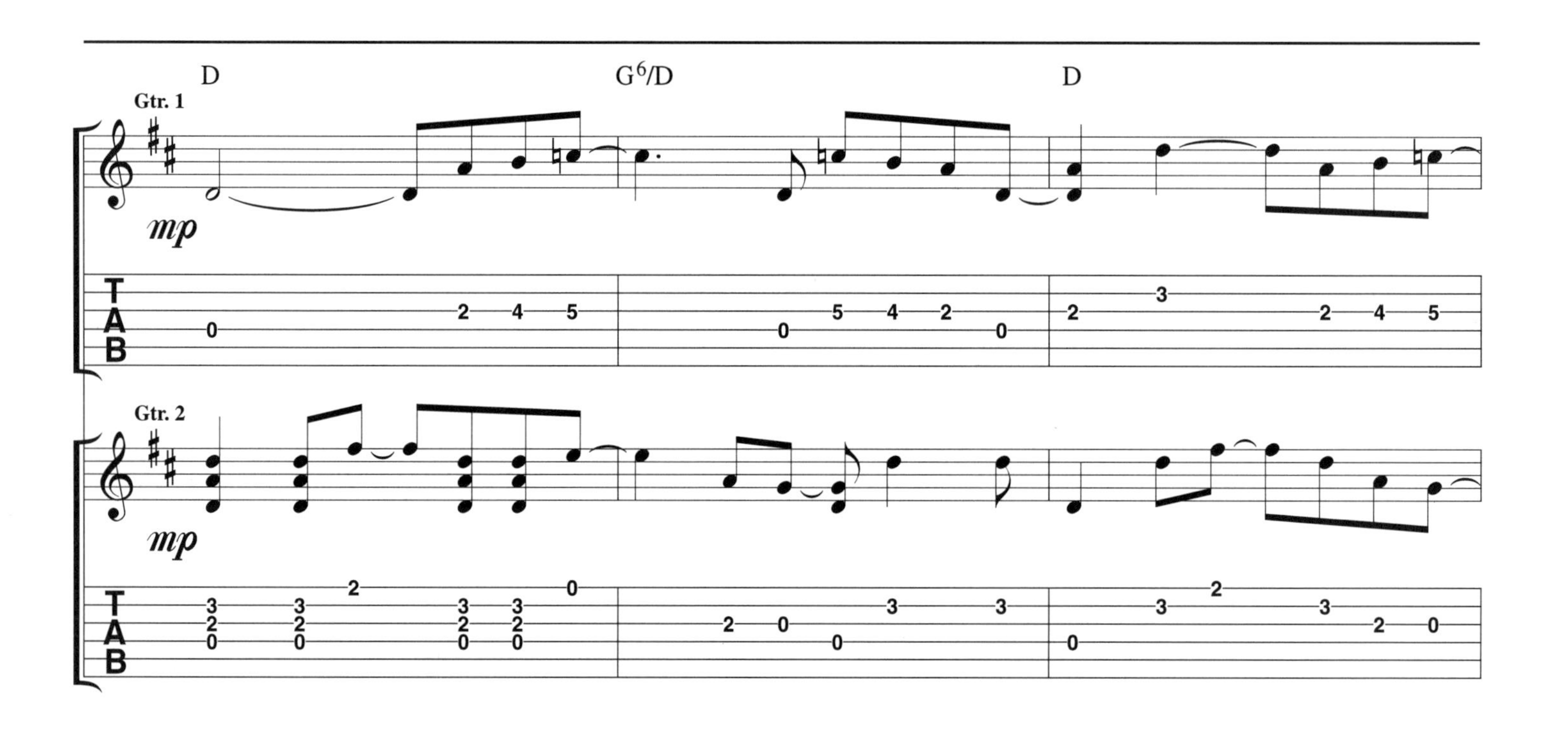
D
G6/D
D
Gtr. 1
mp
Gtr. 2
mp

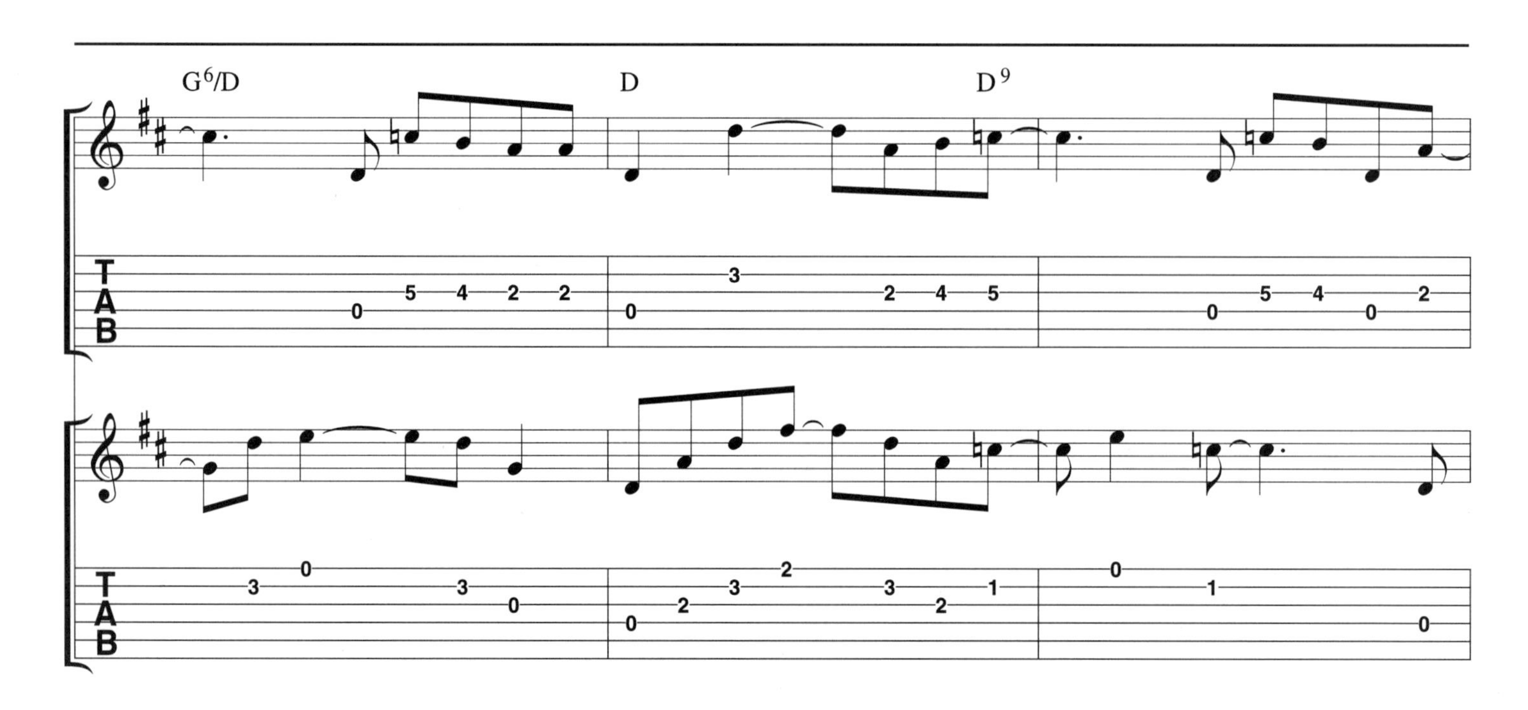
G6/D
D
D9

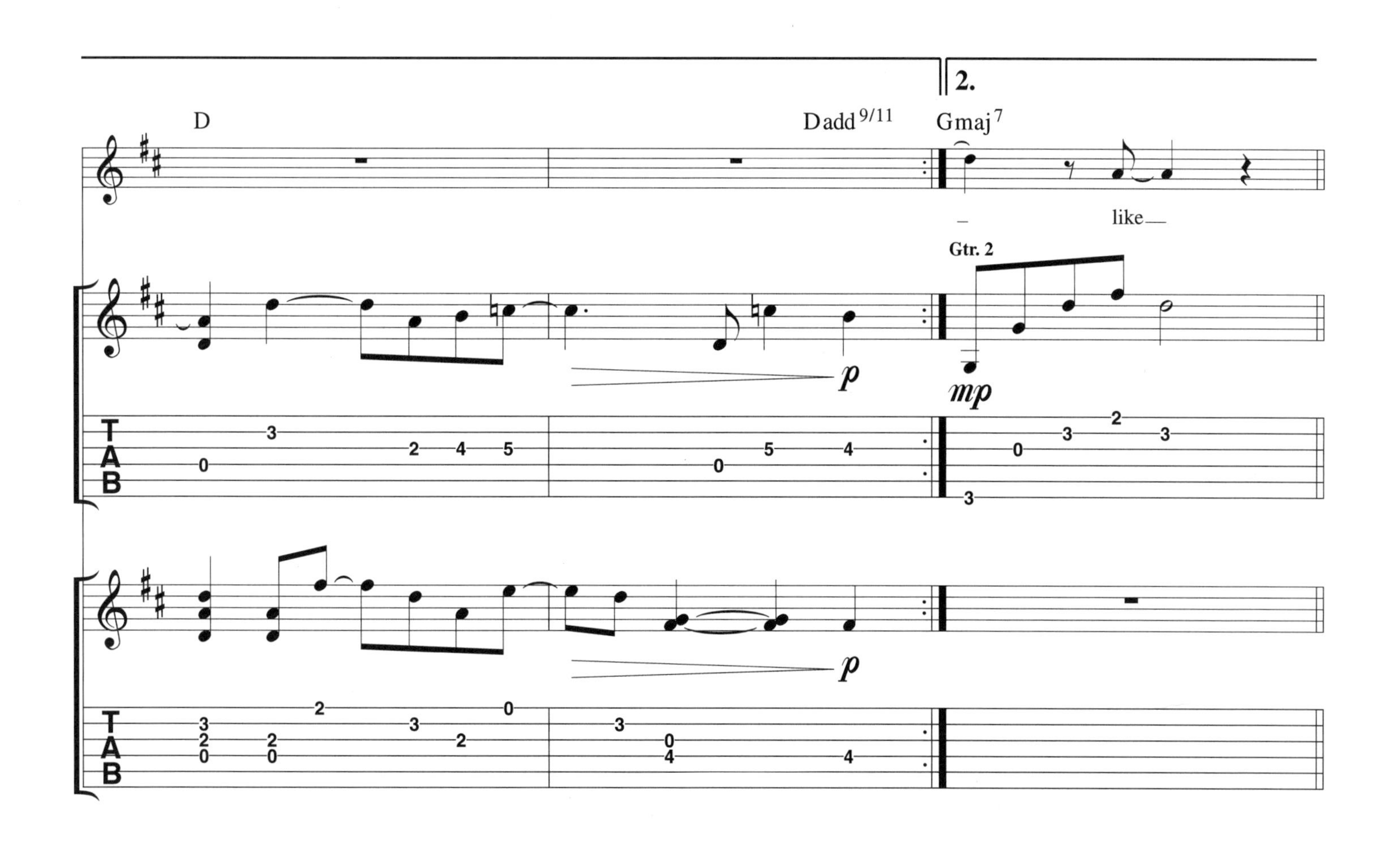
2.
D
Dadd 9/11
Gmaj 7
like
Gtr. 2
p
mp
p

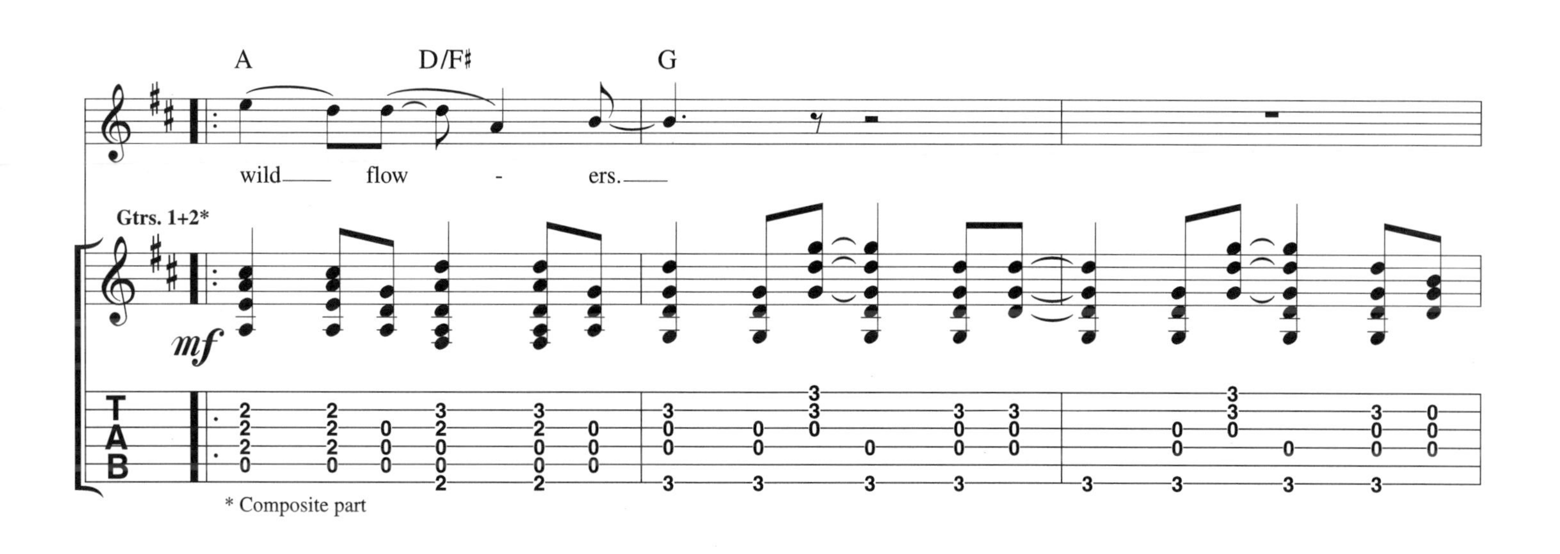
A
D/F♯
G
wild
flow
-
ers.
Gtrs. 1+2*
mf
* Composite part

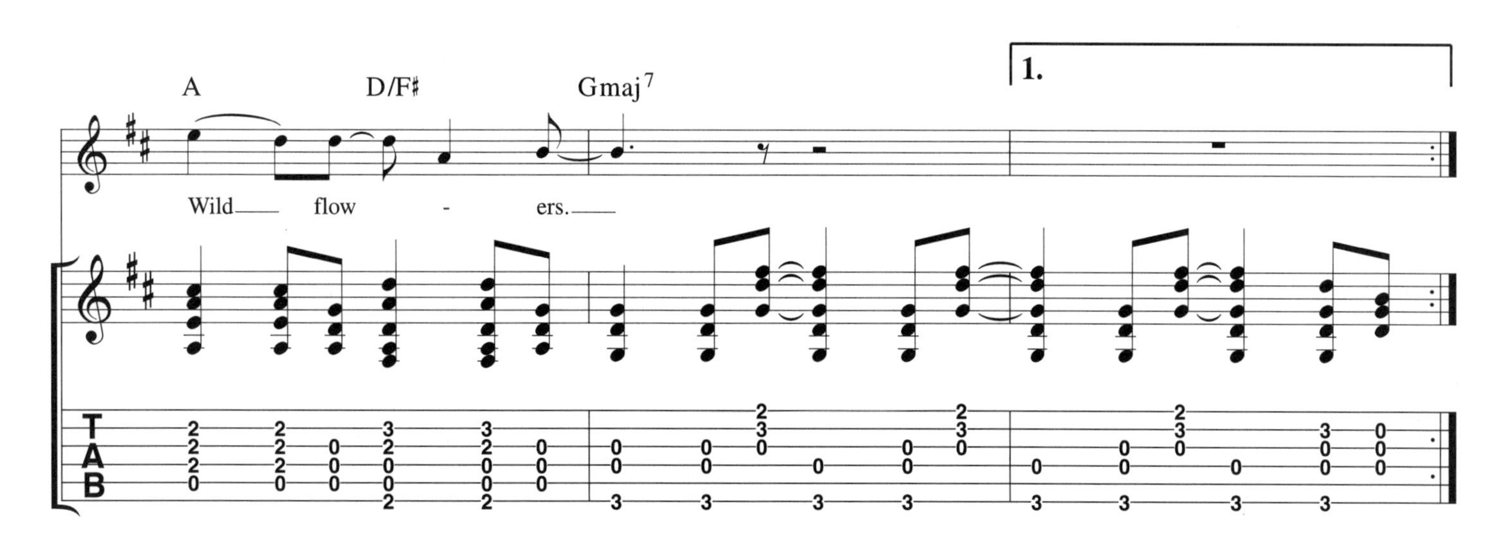
1.
A
D/F♯
Gmaj 7
Wild
flow
-
ers.

2.
Gmaj7
G6
A
D/F♯
G
Oh.
mf
1.
2.
N.C.
Gtr. 2 tacet
mp
D
G6/D

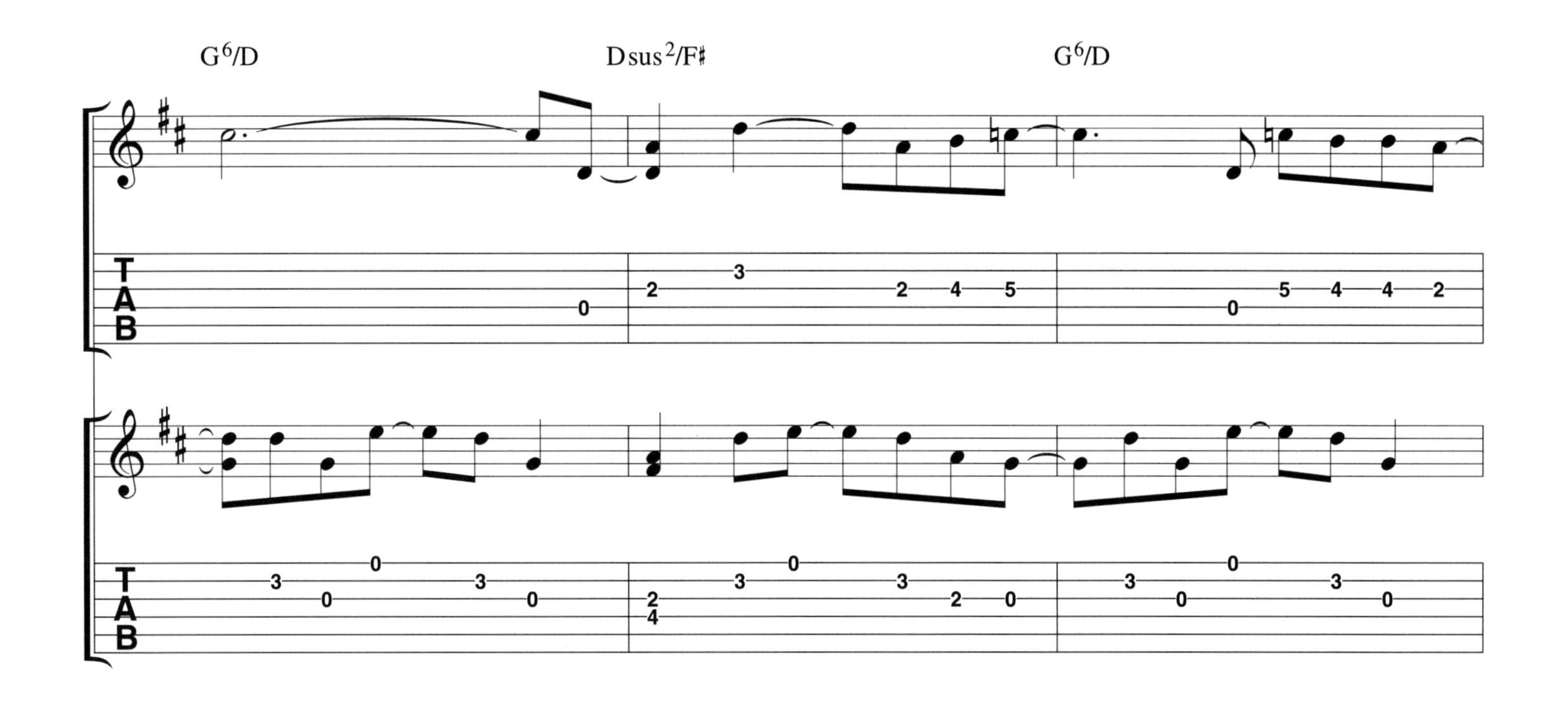

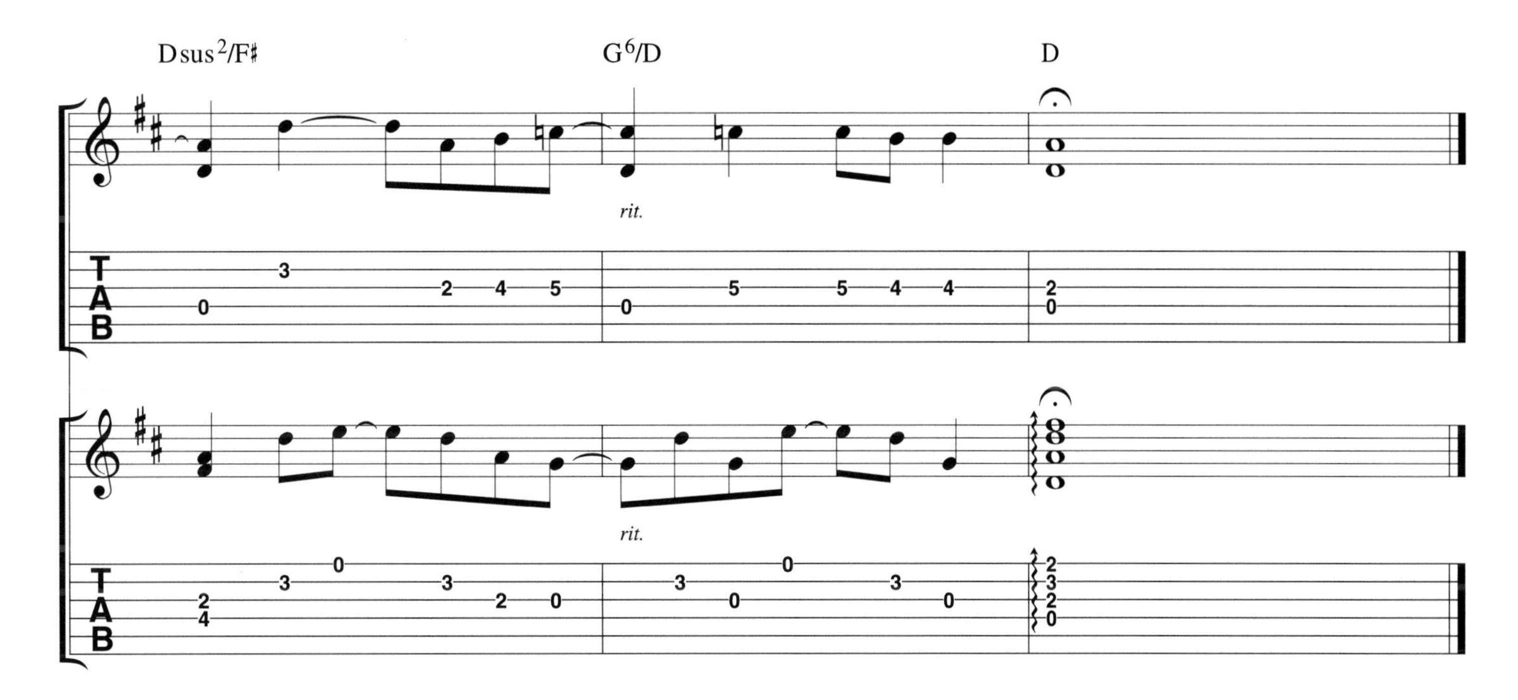

Verse 2:

Poor girl
Lonely, shuffles through the parade
Of a sleepless circus promenade
Hold on dear.

Poor girl, no Ma
Sister steals her a coat
For the windless breezes
Sleep now and Jesus will come, dear.

HARDER NOW THAT IT'S OVER

Words & Music by Ryan Adams & Chris Stills

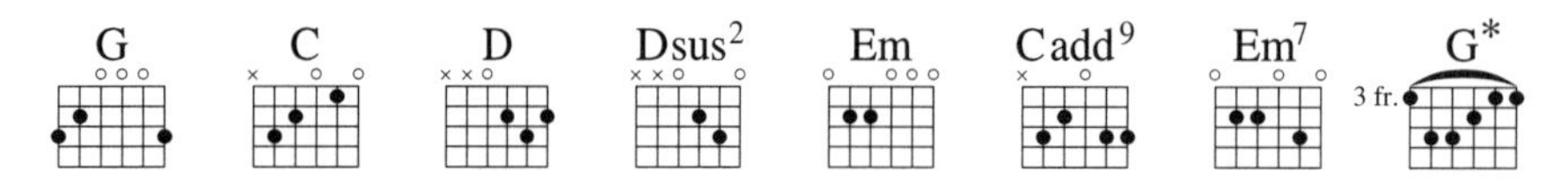

♩= 63

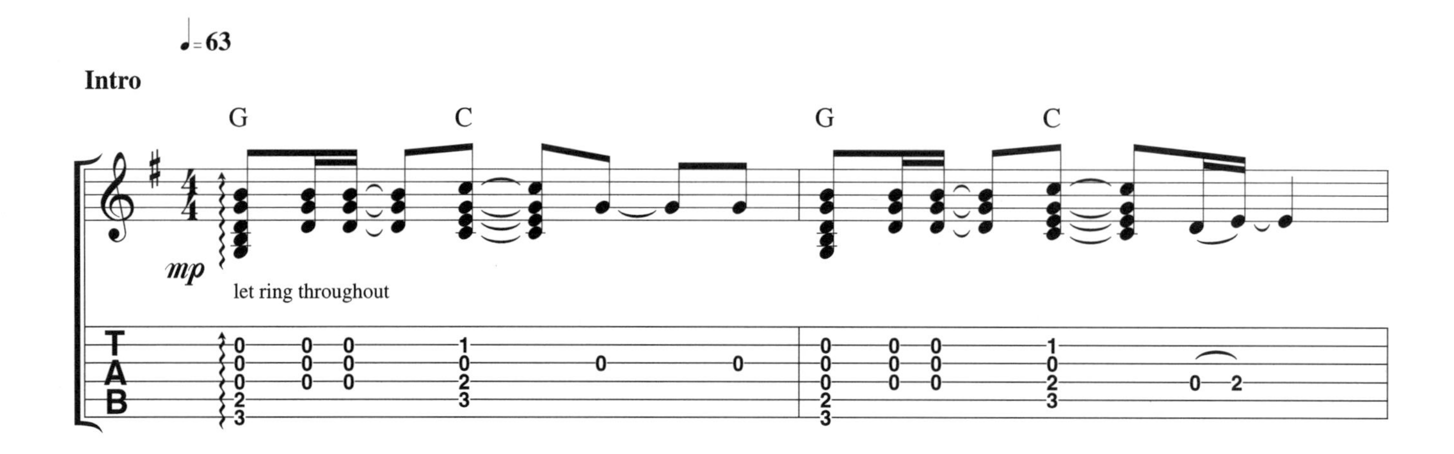

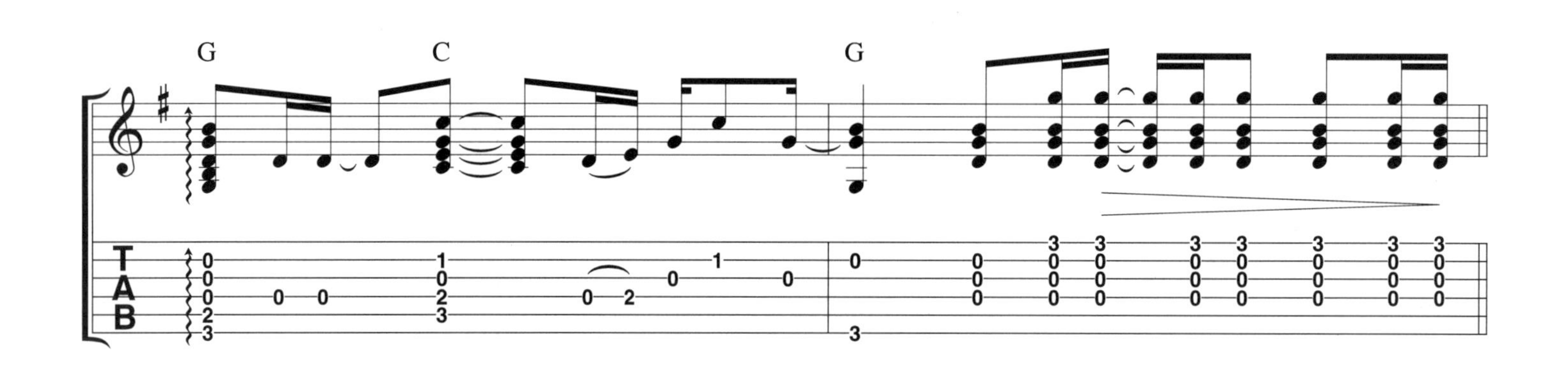

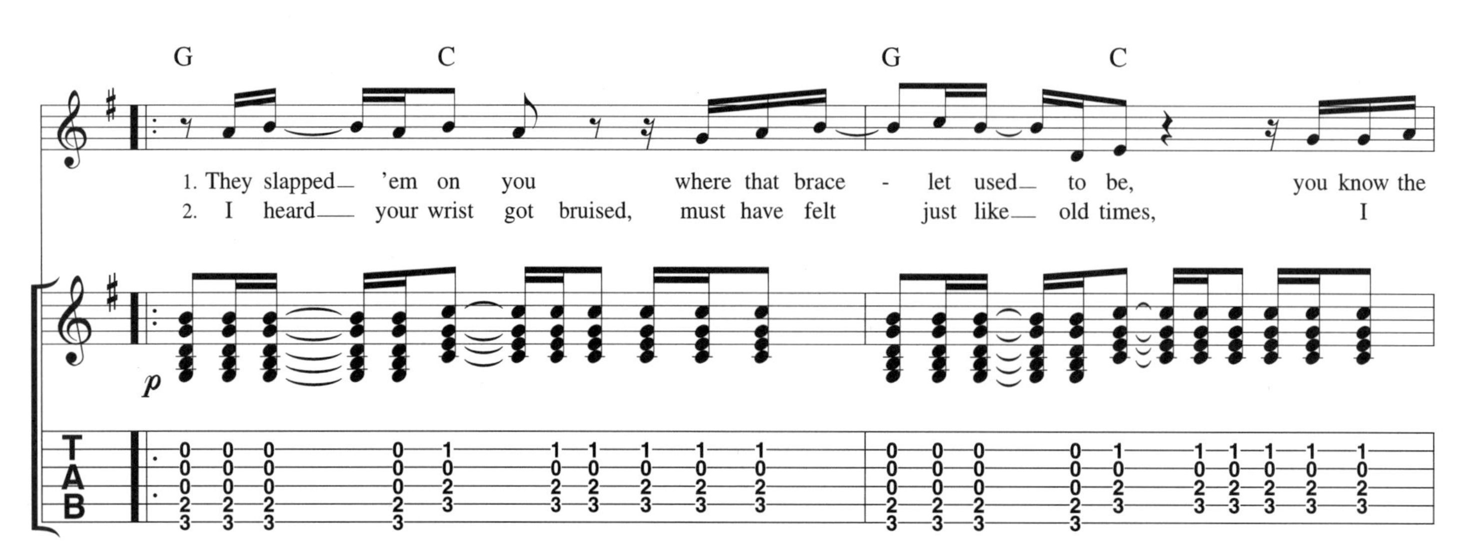

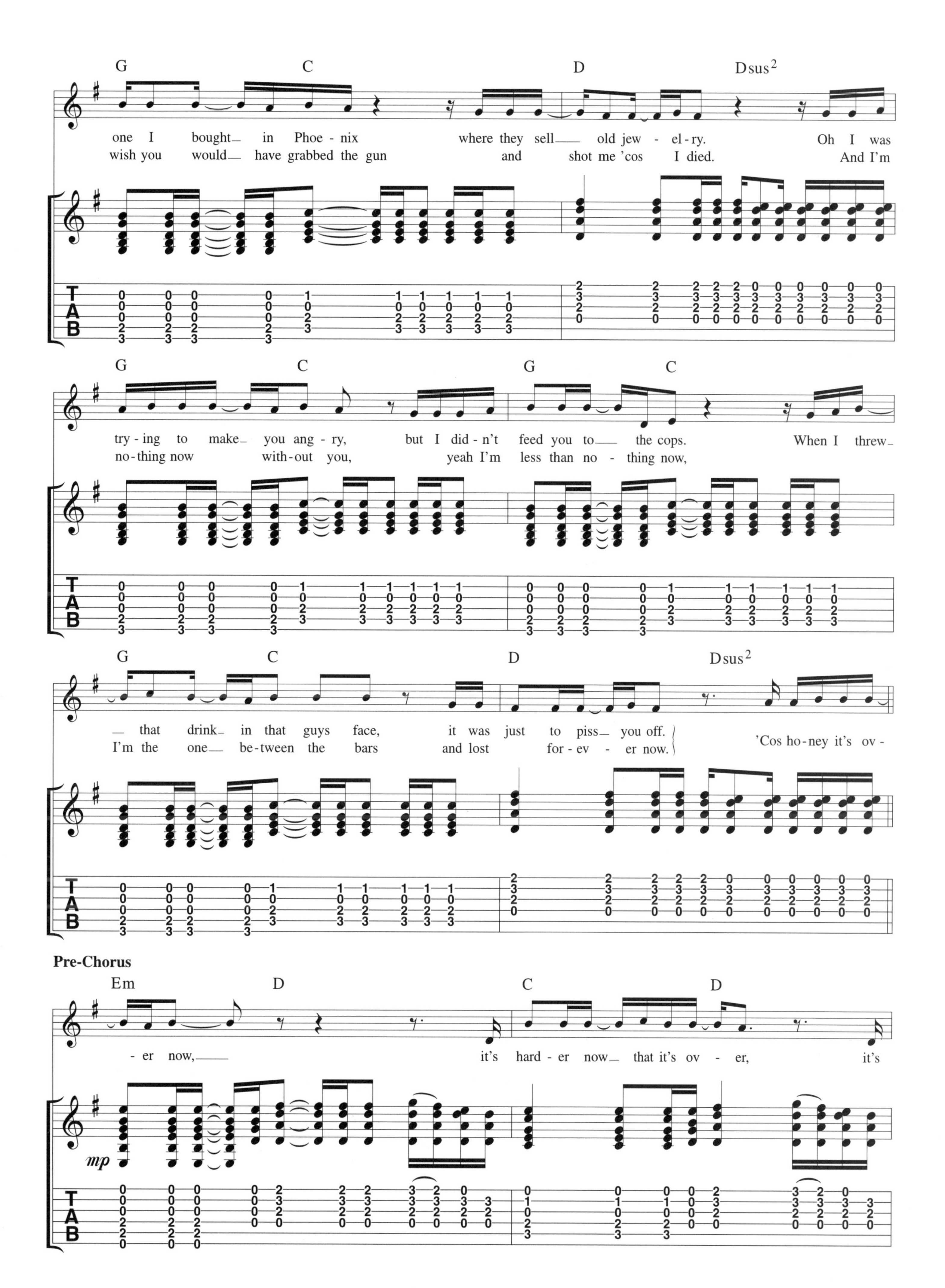
G C D Dsus2
one I bought in Phoe - nix where they sell old jew - el - ry. Oh I was
wish you would have grabbed the gun and shot me 'cos I died. And I'm
G C G C
try - ing to make you ang - ry, but I did - n't feed you to the cops. When I threw
no - thing now with - out you, yeah I'm less than no - thing now,
G C D Dsus2
that drink in that guys face, it was just to piss you off.
I'm the one be - tween the bars and lost for - ev - er now.
'Cos ho - ney it's ov -
Pre-Chorus
Em D C D
- er now, it's hard - er now that it's ov - er, it's
mp
TAB

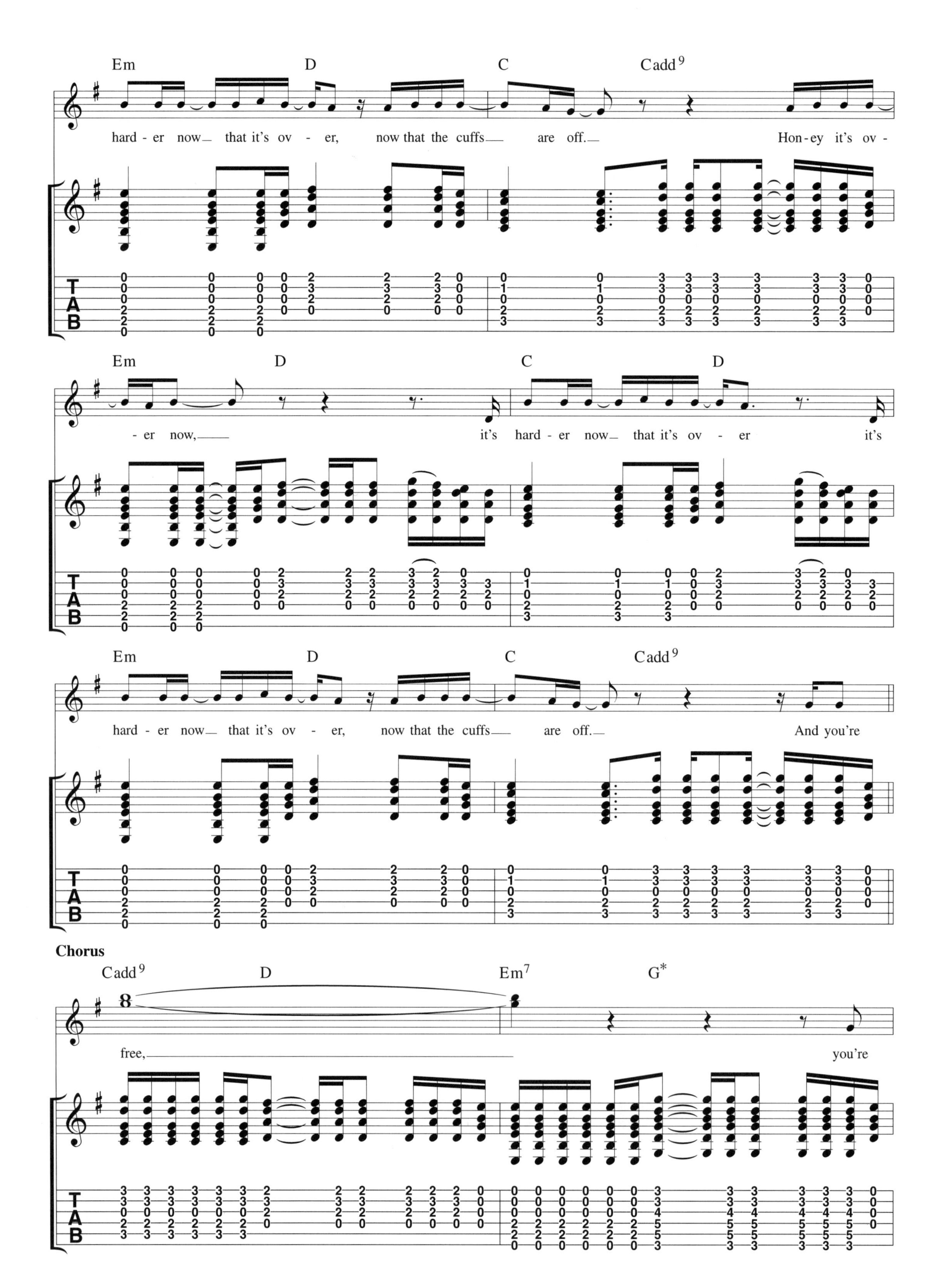
Em
D
C
Cadd9
hard - er now that it's ov - er, now that the cuffs are off.
Hon-ey it's ov -
- er now,
it's hard - er now that it's ov - er it's
hard - er now that it's ov - er, now that the cuffs are off.
And you're
Chorus
Cadd9
D
Em7
G*
free,
you're

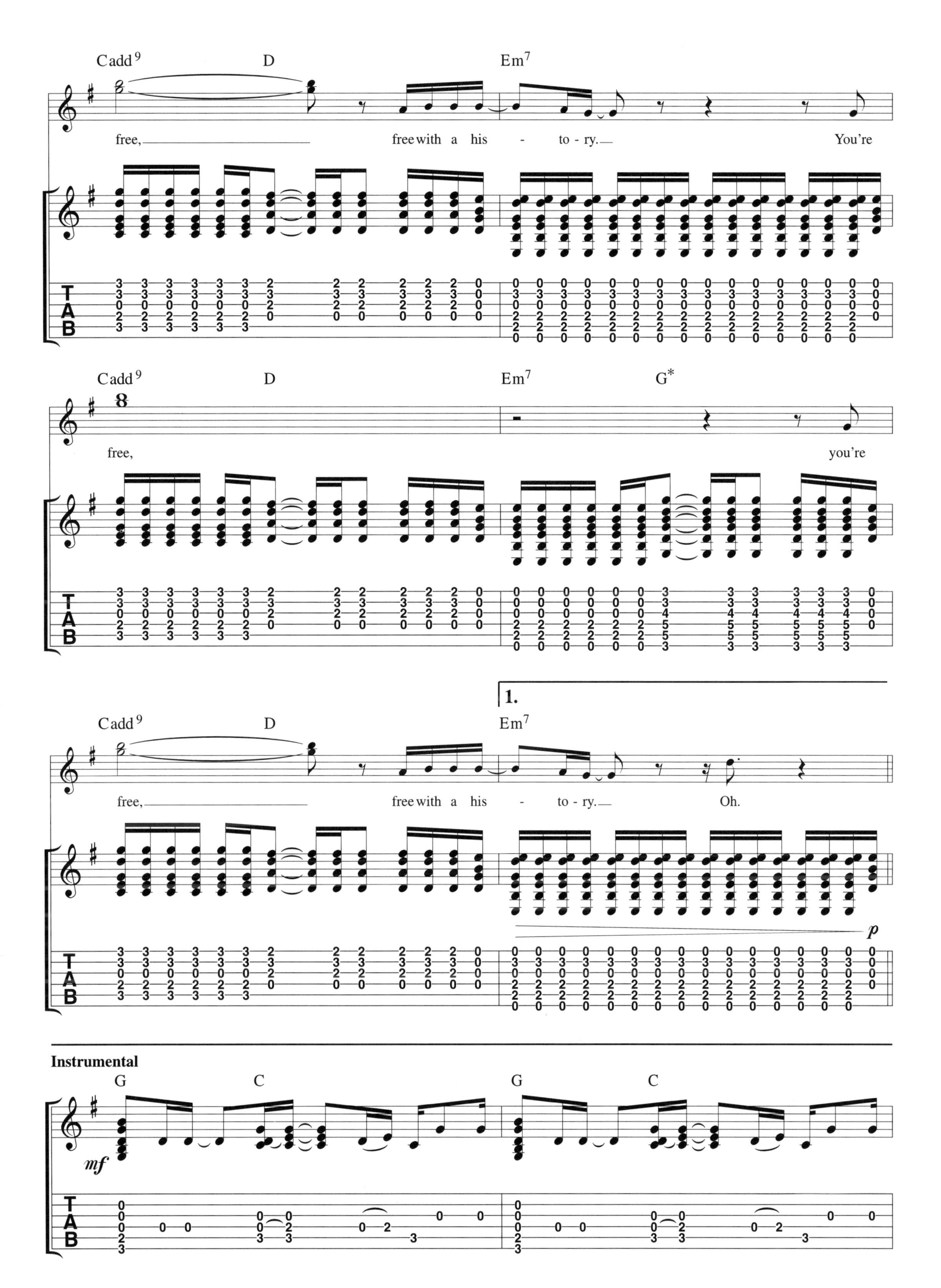

Cadd9
D
Em7
free, free with a his - to - ry. You're
Cadd9
D
Em7
G*
free, you're
1.
Cadd9
D
Em7
free, free with a his - to - ry. Oh.
p
Instrumental
G
C
G
C
mf

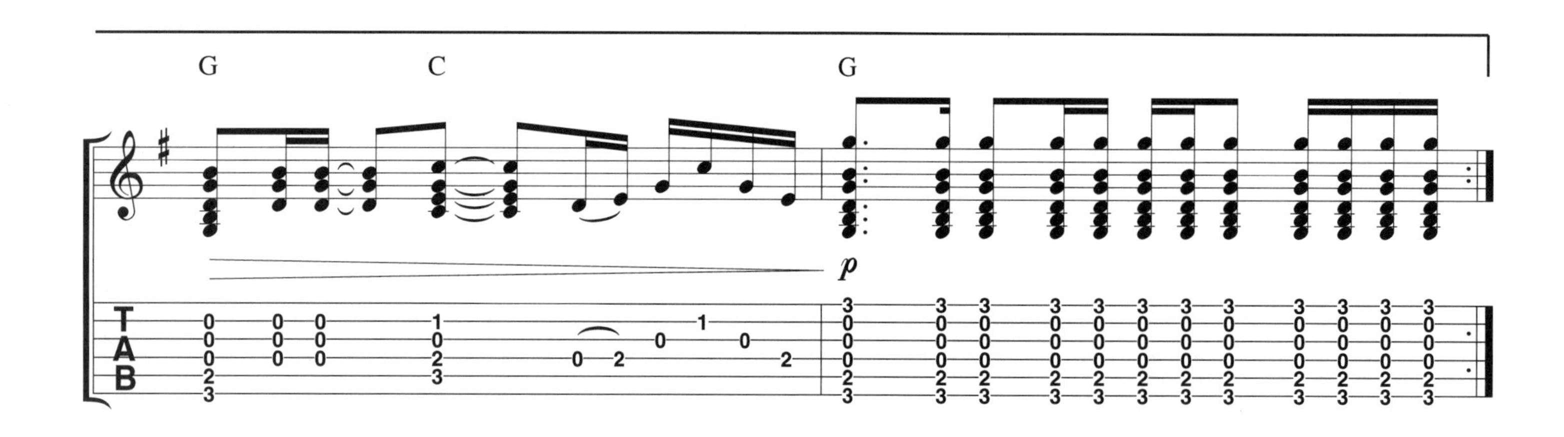
G
C
G
p
TAB

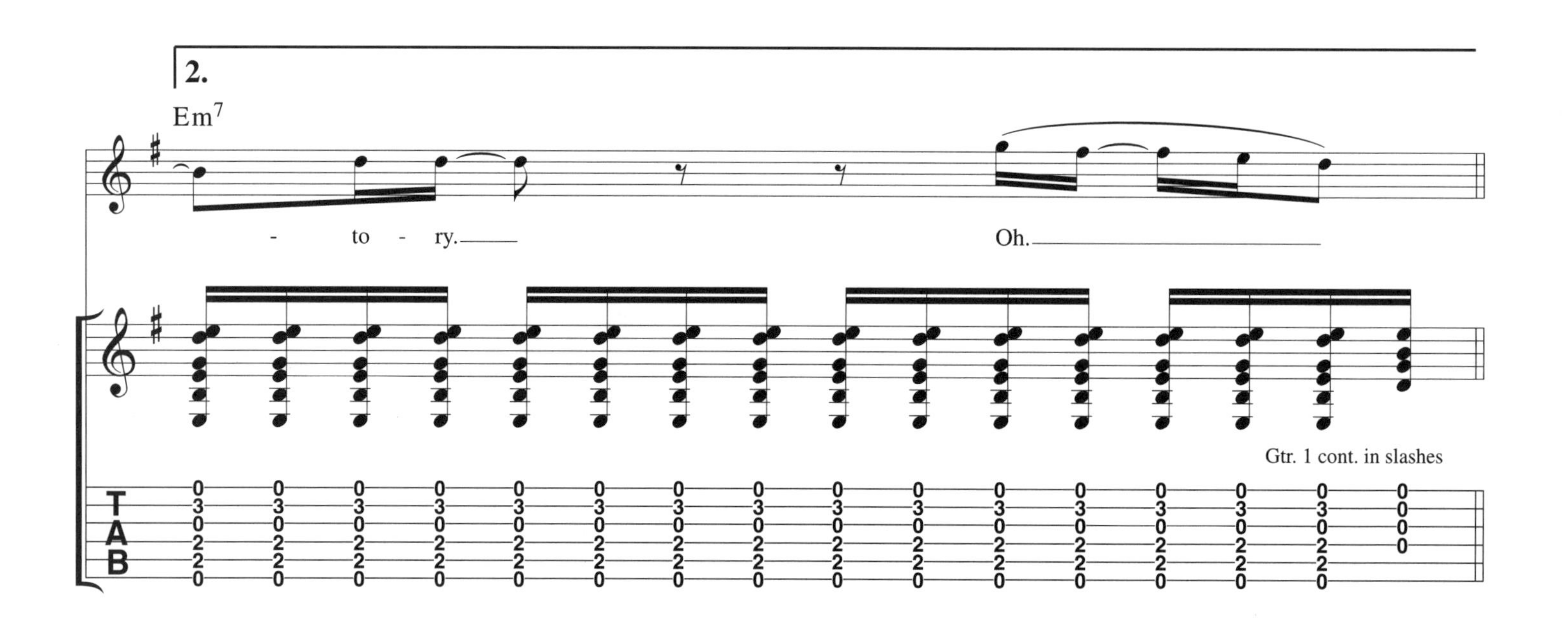
2.
Em7
- to - ry.
Oh.
Gtr. 1 cont. in slashes
TAB

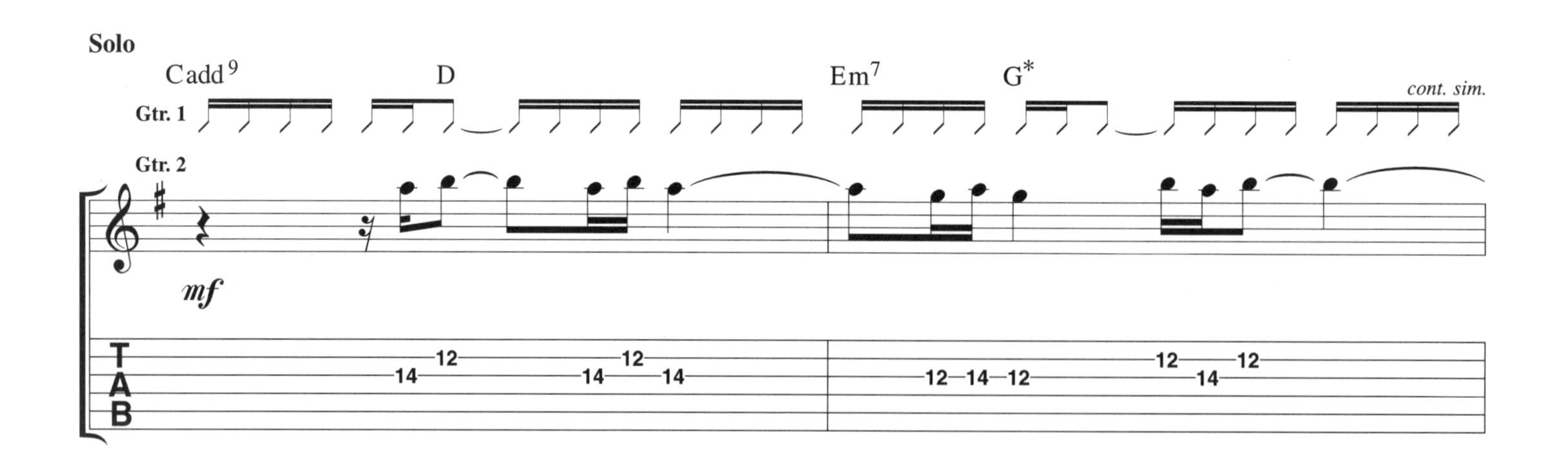
Solo
Cadd9
D
Em7
G*
cont. sim.
Gtr. 1
Gtr. 2
mf
TAB

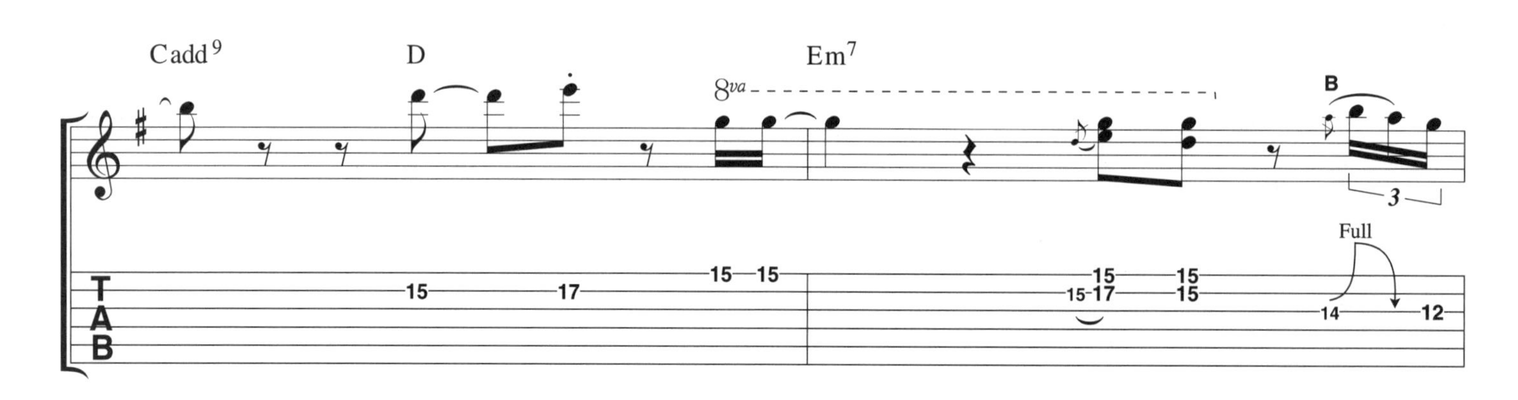
Cadd9
D
Em7
8va
B
3
Full
TAB

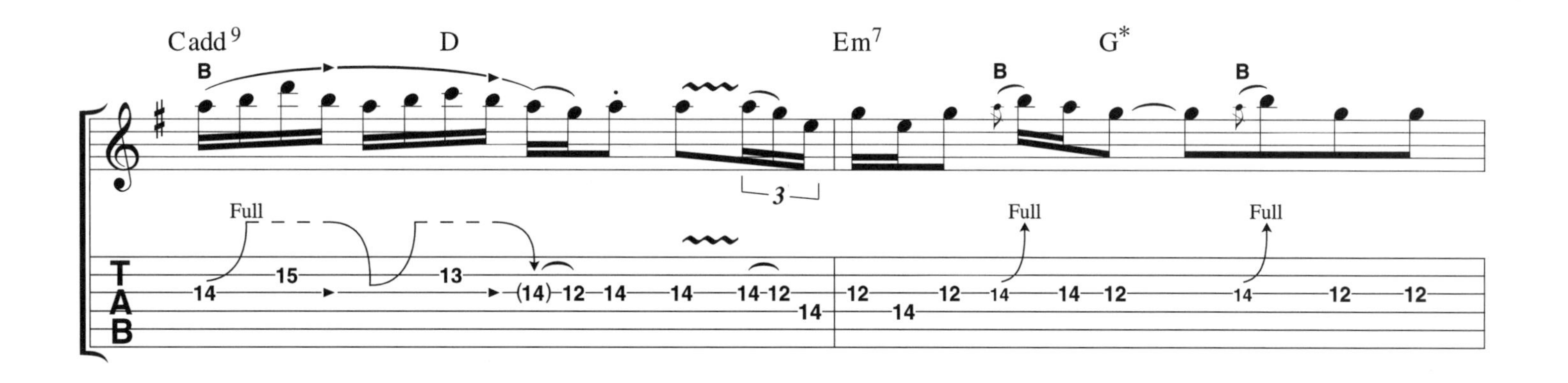
Cadd9
D
Em7
G*
B
Full
Full
Full

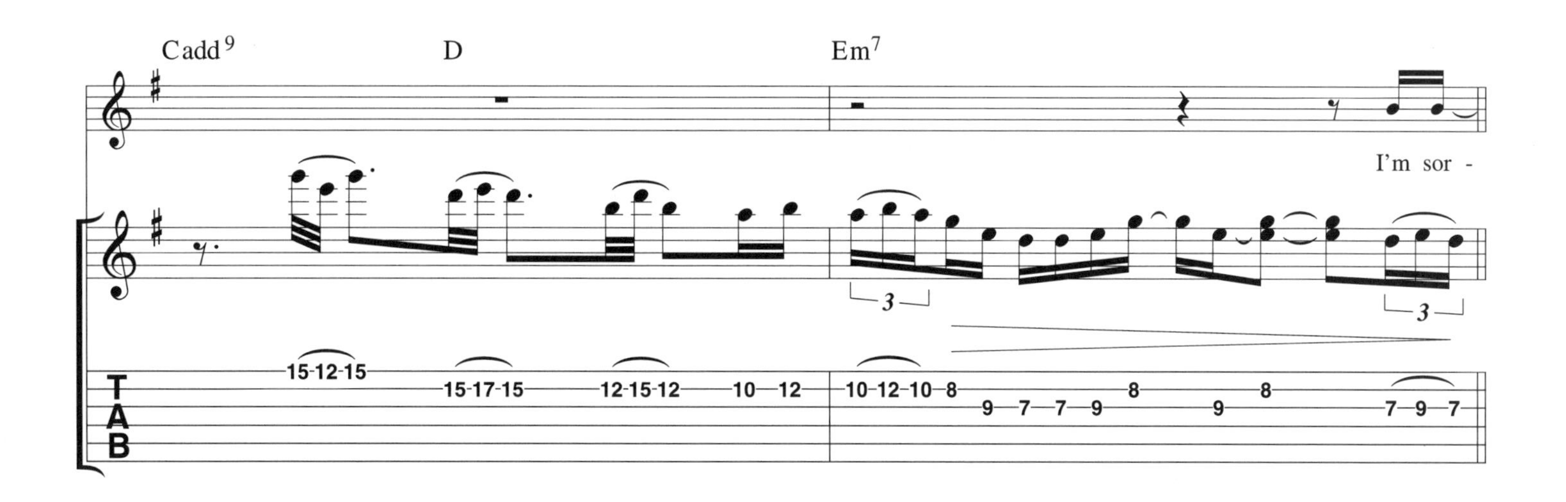
Cadd9
D
Em7
I'm sor -

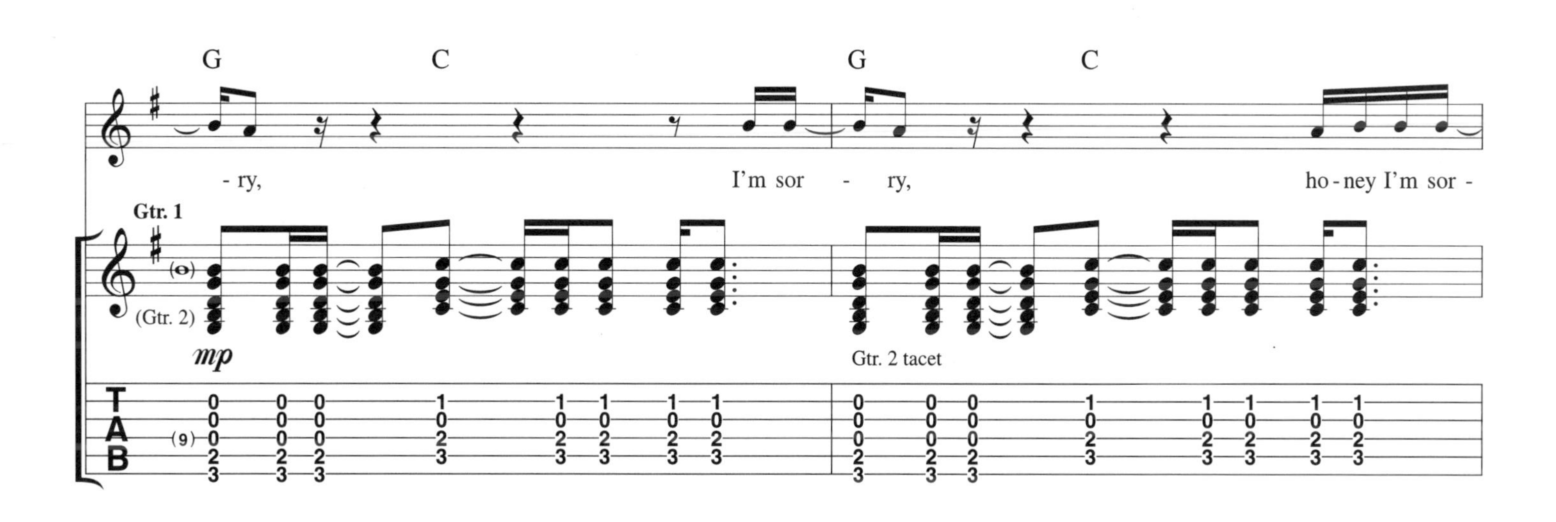
G
C
G
C
- ry,
I'm sor - ry,
ho - ney I'm sor -
Gtr. 1
(Gtr. 2)
mp
Gtr. 2 tacet

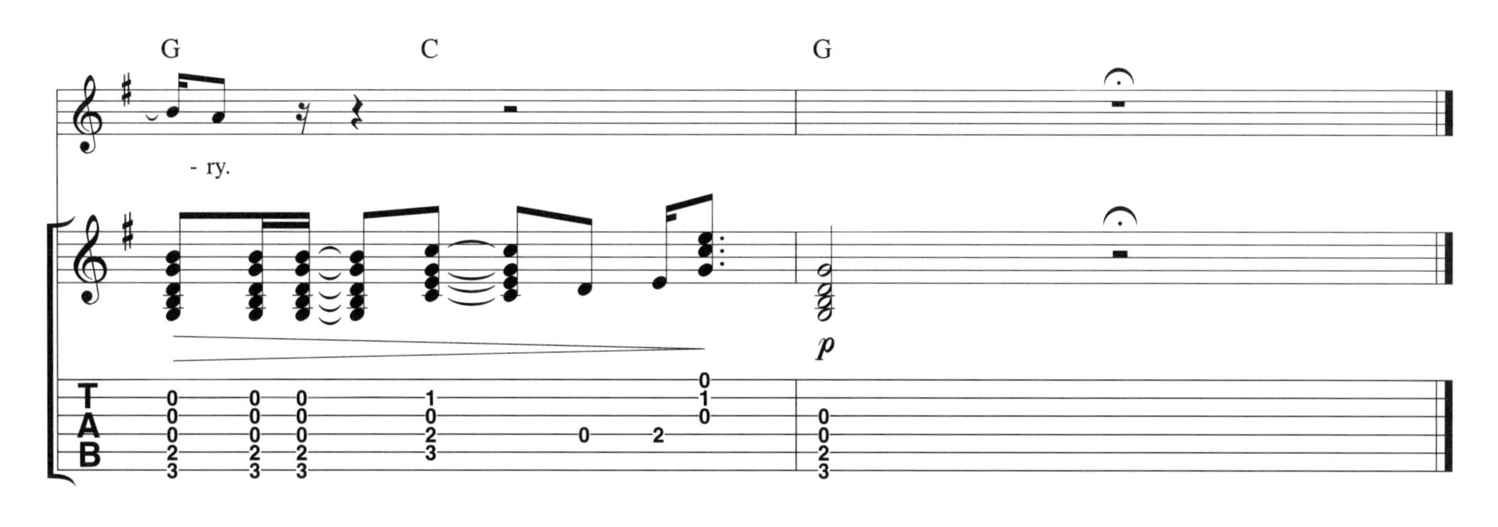
G
C
G
- ry.
p

TOUCH, FEEL & LOSE

Words & Music by Ryan Adams & David Rawlings

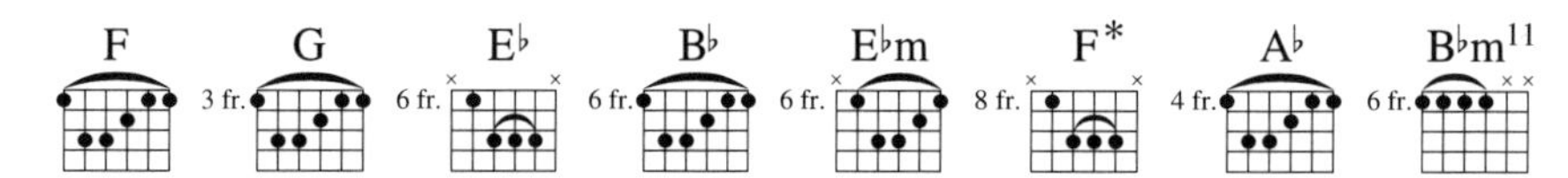

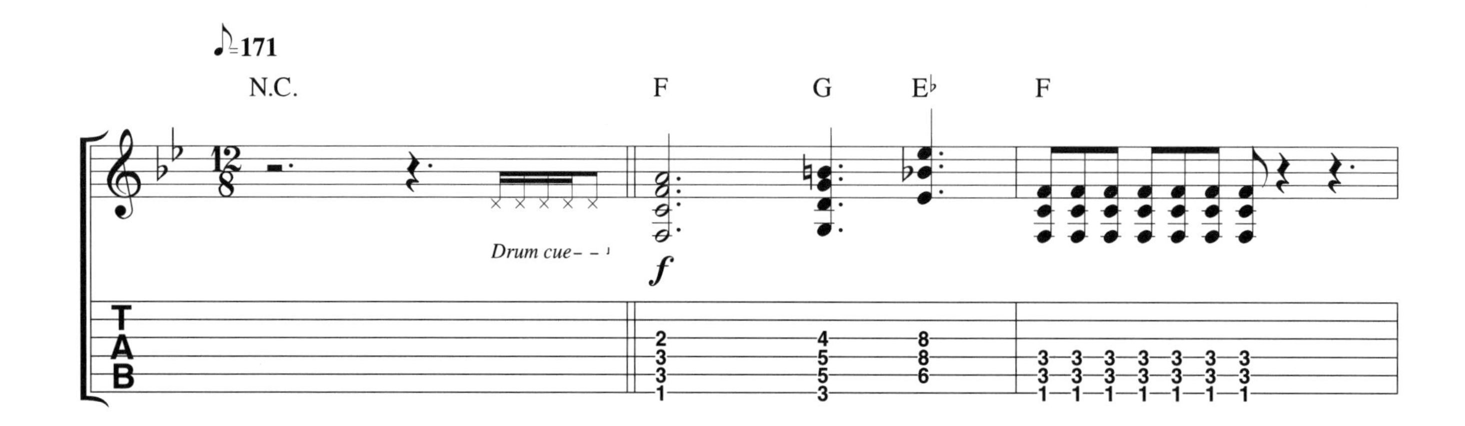

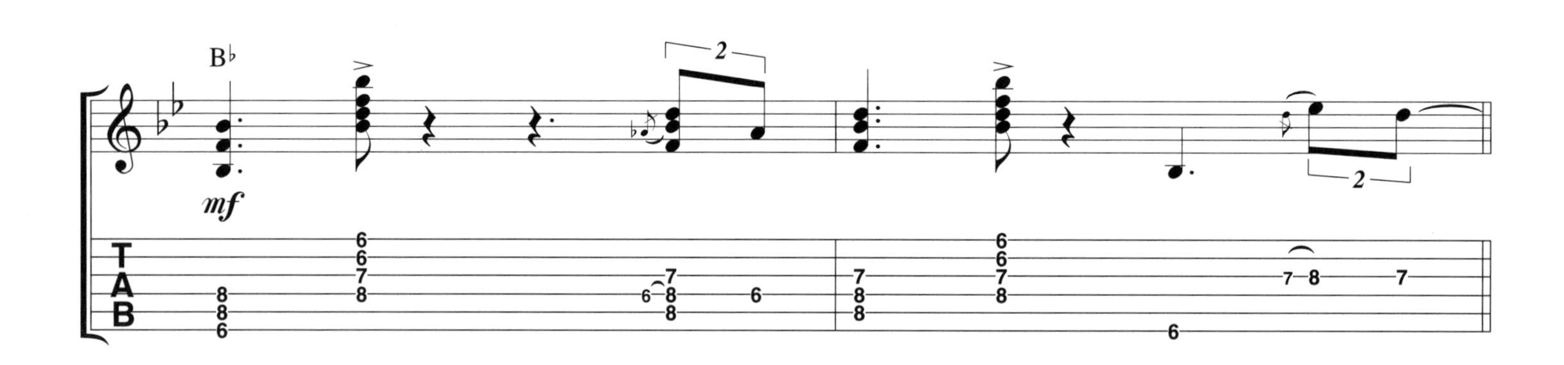

Verse

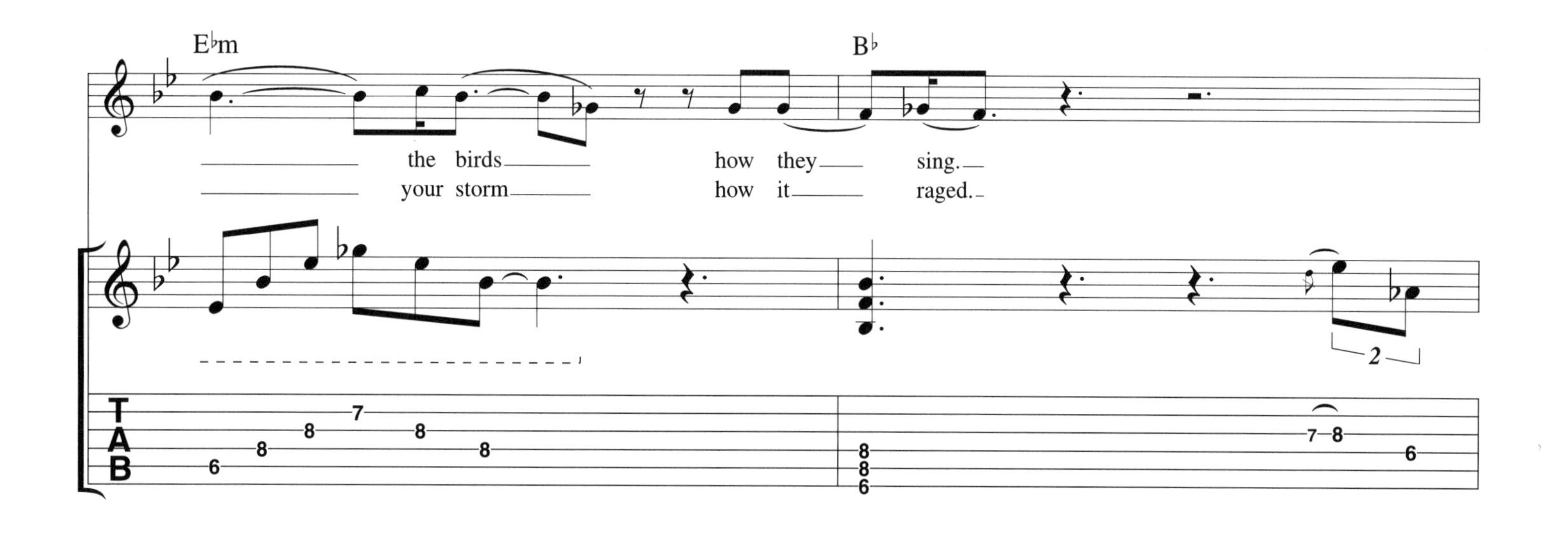
E♭m
B♭
the birds how they sing.
your storm how it raged.
2
T
A
B
7
8 8
8 8
6
8
8
6
7 8
6

E♭
3
3
If you were a bird could you sing me a song of sor - row, 'cos
You know your kis - ses they're like light - ning and thun - der, and your
2
T
A
B
7
8
8
8
8
8
6
8 8
8 8

E♭m
F*
all I know now from you is grief.
smile is sweet and comes down like rain.
T
A
B

Chorus

F G A♭ E♭
But I ne-ver wan-ted to be your rol-ling train,
F G A♭ E♭
I ne-ver wan-ted to be your dan-cing shoes.
F G E♭ F G E♭
I just wan-ted you to love me, I just wan-ted you to love me,
F
touch, feel and
1.
B♭ (A♭)
lose, cry, cry, cry.
f
sfz
mf

E♭
B♭
A♭
Cry, cry, cry.
E♭
2.
F
lose, ho-ney. Ah, ah, ah.
B♭
A♭
E♭
And cry, cry, cry.
B♭
A♭
E♭
And cry, cry, cry.

B♭
A♭
E♭
And cry, cry, cry.
B♭
A♭
E♭
And cry, cry, cry.
F
G
E♭
F
G
E♭
I just wan-ted you to love me,
I just wan-ted you to love me,
F
touch, feel and lose, ho - ney.
sfz > mp

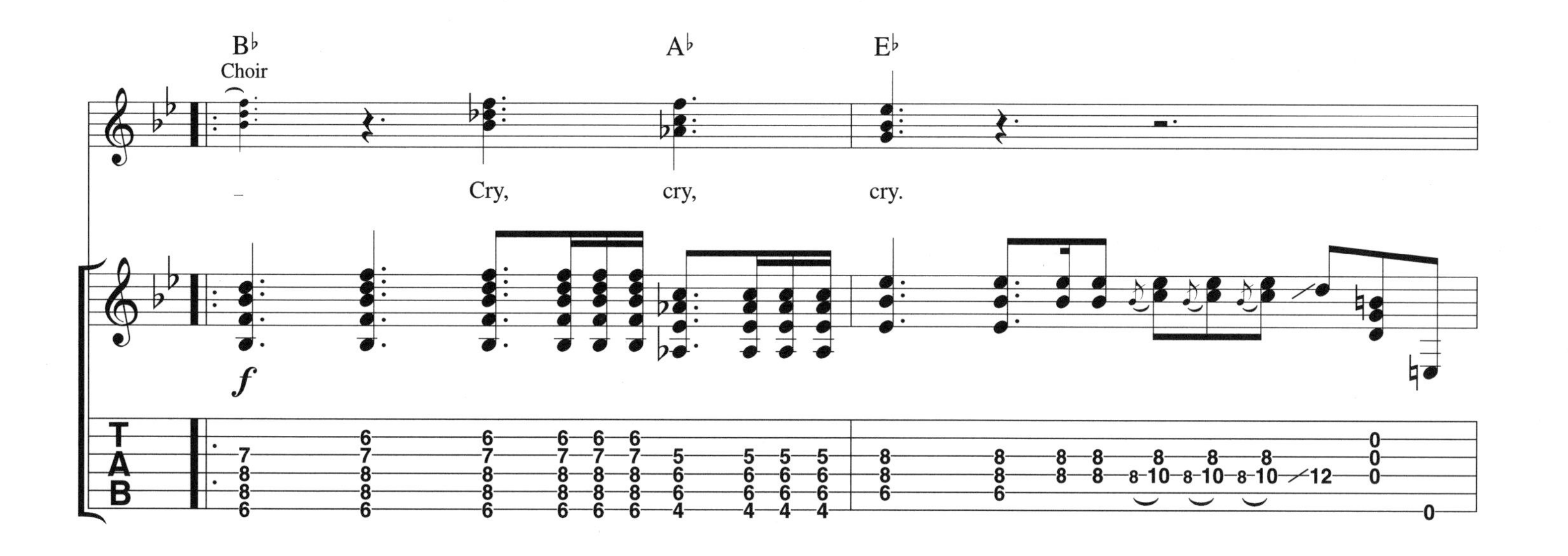
B♭
Choir
A♭
E♭
Cry,
cry,
cry.
f

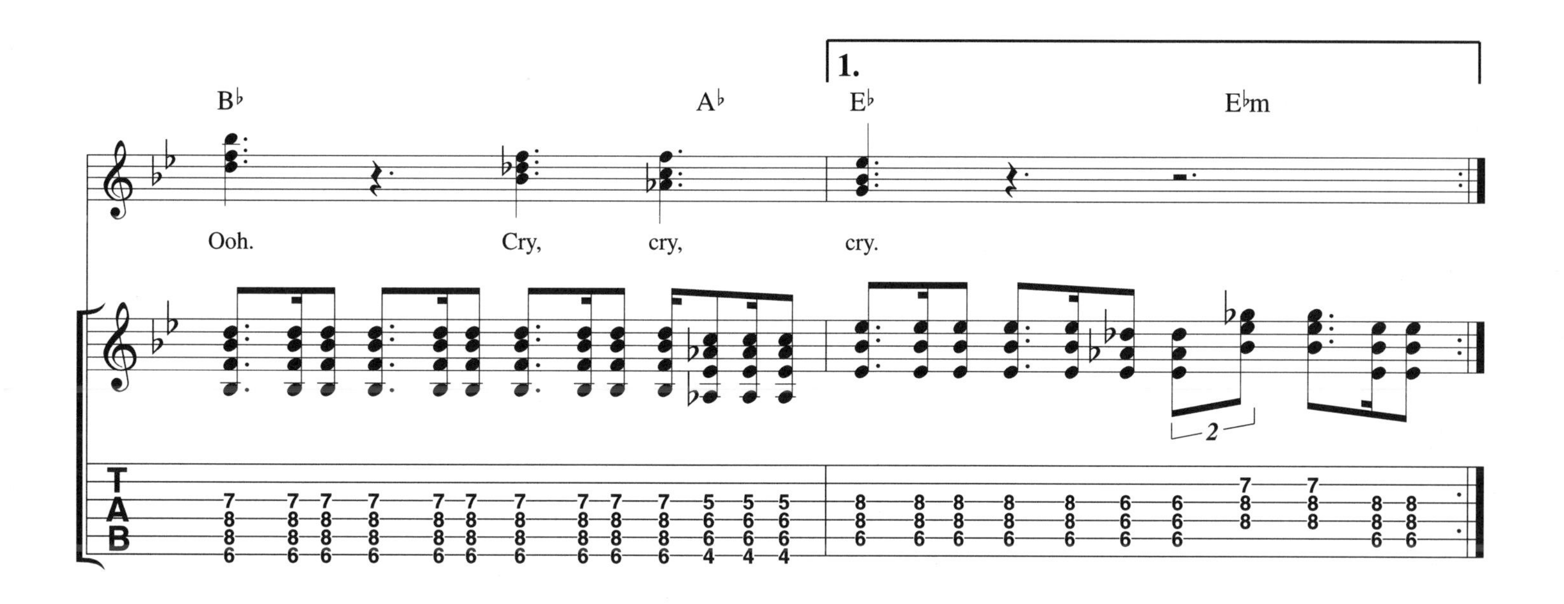
1.
B♭
A♭
E♭
E♭m
Ooh.
Cry,
cry,
cry.

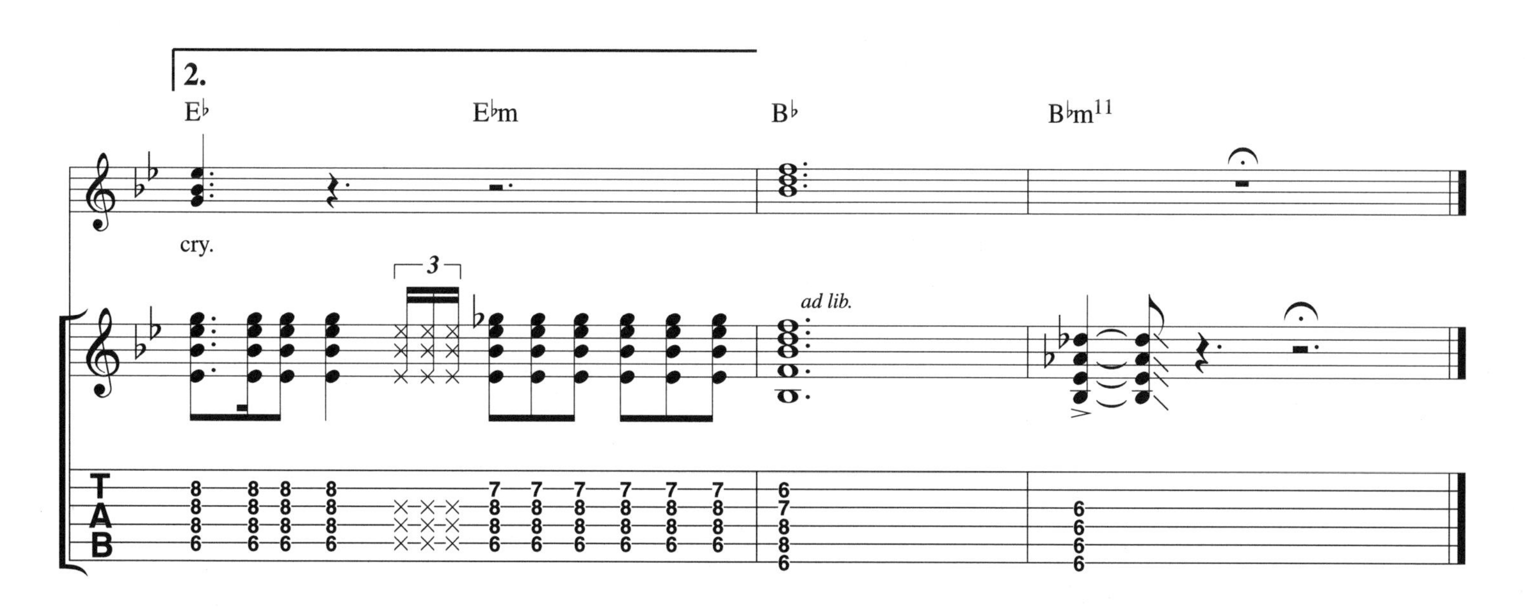
2.
E♭
E♭m
B♭
B♭m11
cry.
ad lib.

TINA TOLEDO'S STREET WALKIN' BLUES

Words & Music by Ryan Adams & Ethan Johns

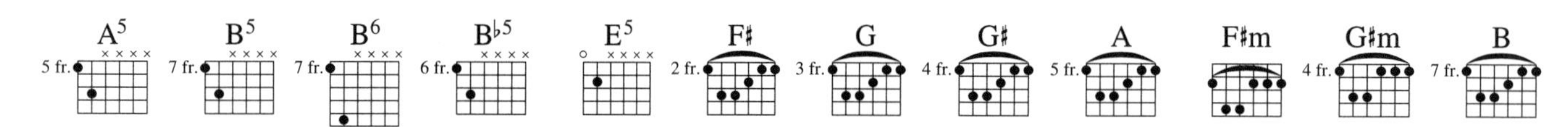

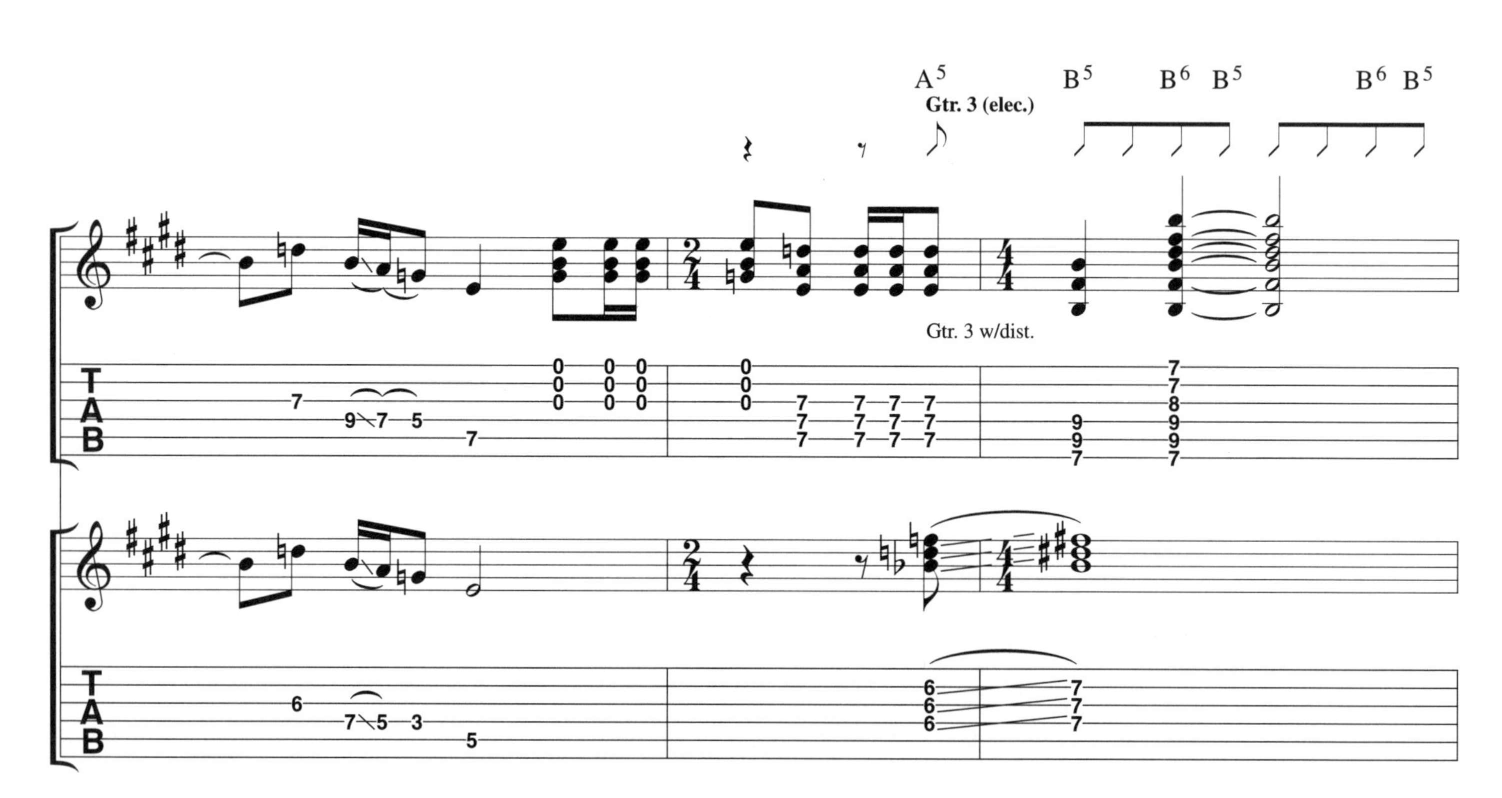

B6 B5 A5 B♭5 B5
cont. sim.
B6 B5 B6 B5 B6 B5 A5 B♭5 B5
B6 B5 B6 B5 B6 B5 A5 B♭5 B5
B
B6 B5 B6 B5 B6 B5 A5 B♭5 B5
Full

Verse
B5 B6 B5 B6 B5 B6 B5 A5 B♭5 B5 B6 B5 B6 B5
1. Sweet talk - in' John - ny push a John quick - er than he spit, street walk - in' Ti - na with a
2. Ti - na To - le - do got a kid that lives with her ma, she take the sub - way af - ter
TAB
TAB

B6 B5 A5 B♭5 B5 B6 B5 A5 E5
crook - ed crown wait - in' for it, there she goes.
school makes up her face, chan - ges clothes, there she goes.
TAB
TAB

G G♯ B E5
B5 B6 B5 B6 B5 B6 B5 A5 B♭5 B5
She born in Bos - ton but the Am - trak took her a - way,
She feels the rain com - ing down on Wash - ing - ton Square,

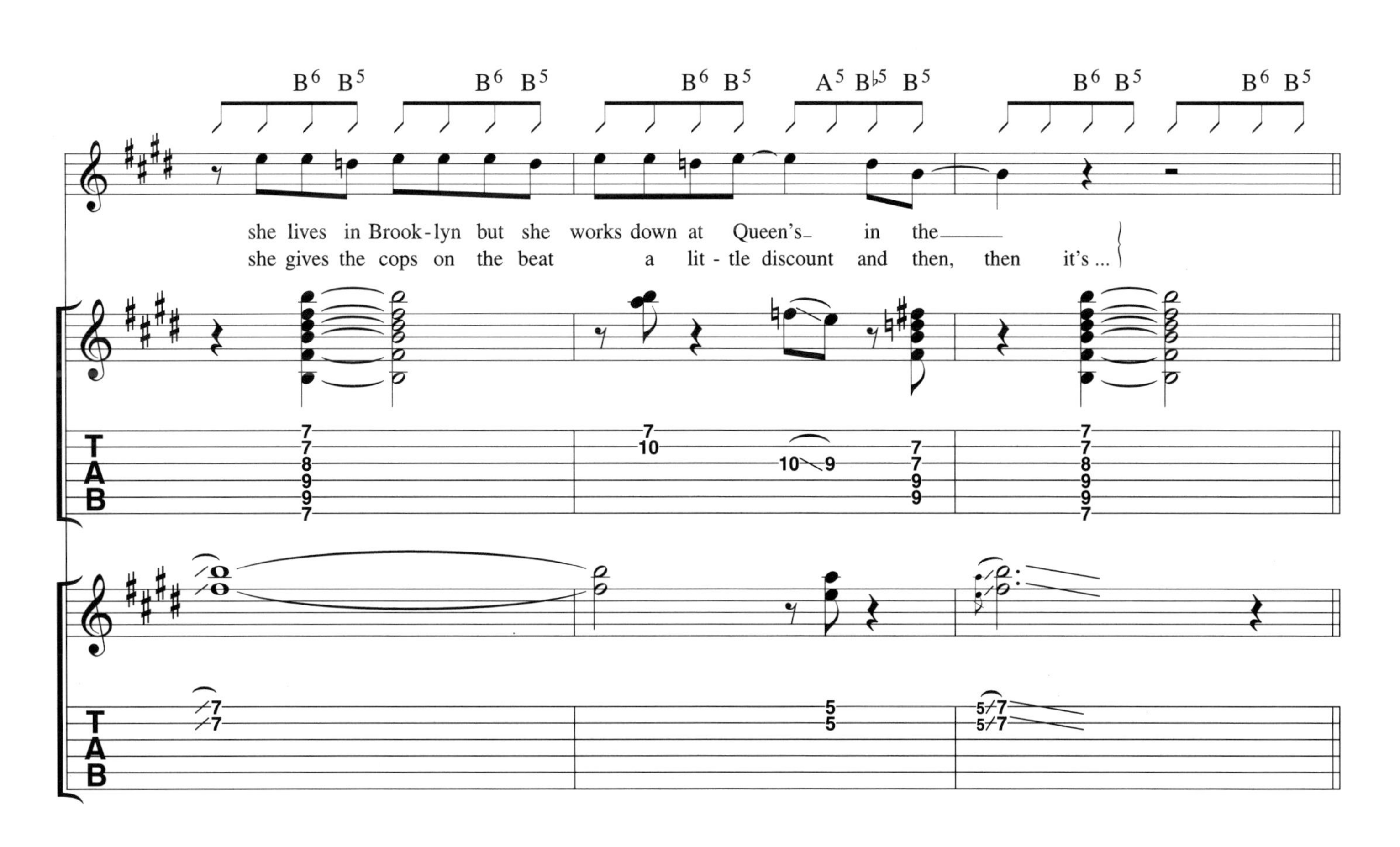
B6 B5 B6 B5 B6 B5 A5 B♭5 B5 B6 B5 B6 B5
she lives in Brook - lyn but she works down at Queen's in the
she gives the cops on the beat a lit - tle discount and then, then it's ...

Chorus

E5
cont. sim.
Black lim-ou-sines,_ mo - ney in the bank._ Black lim-ou-sines,_ mo -
Gtr. 1
TAB

1.
A5 B5 B6 B5 B6 B5
cont. sim.
- ney in_ the bank, send it home.
TAB

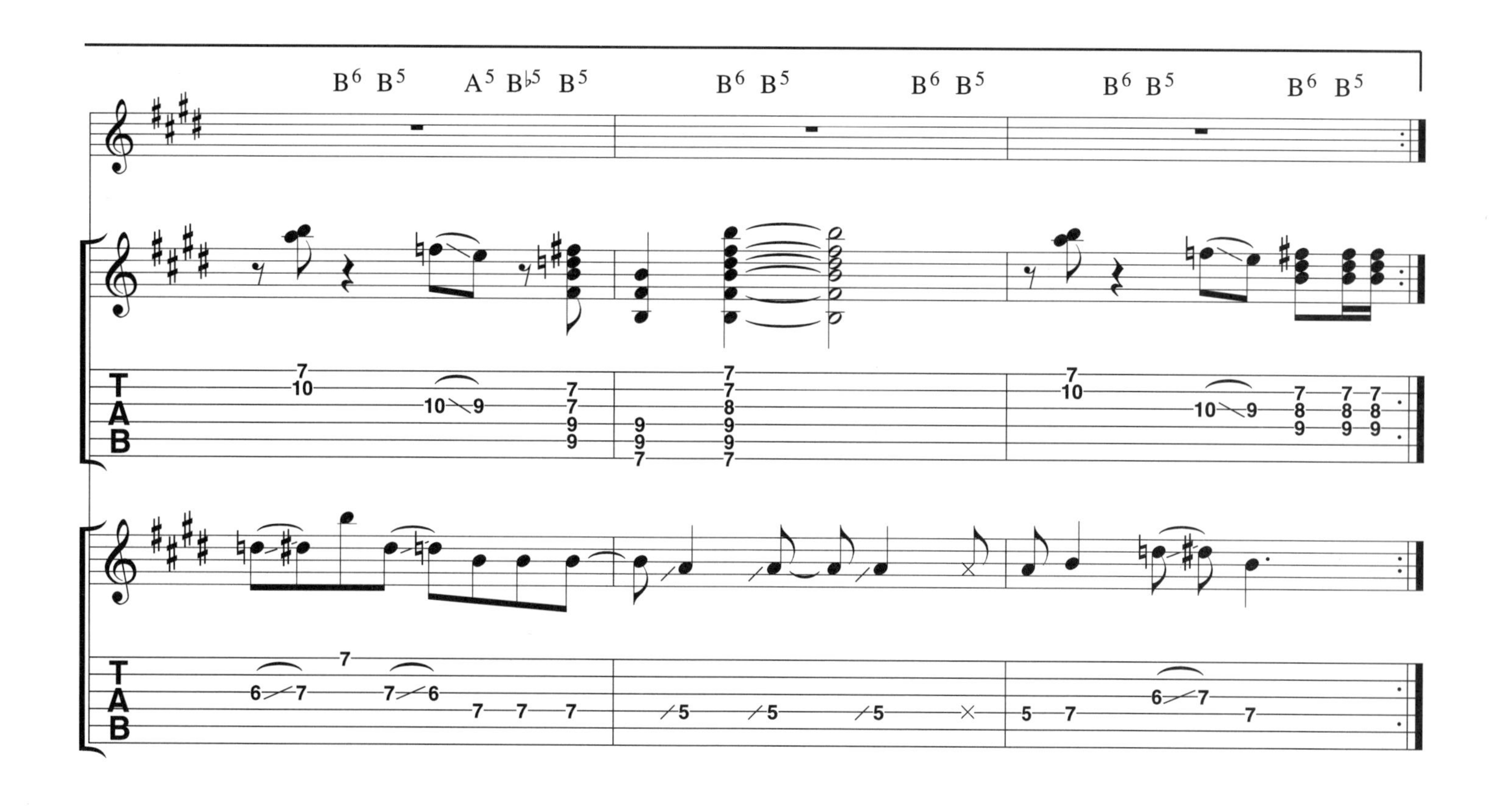
B6 B5 A5 B♭5 B5
B6 B5 B6 B5
B6 B5 B6 B5

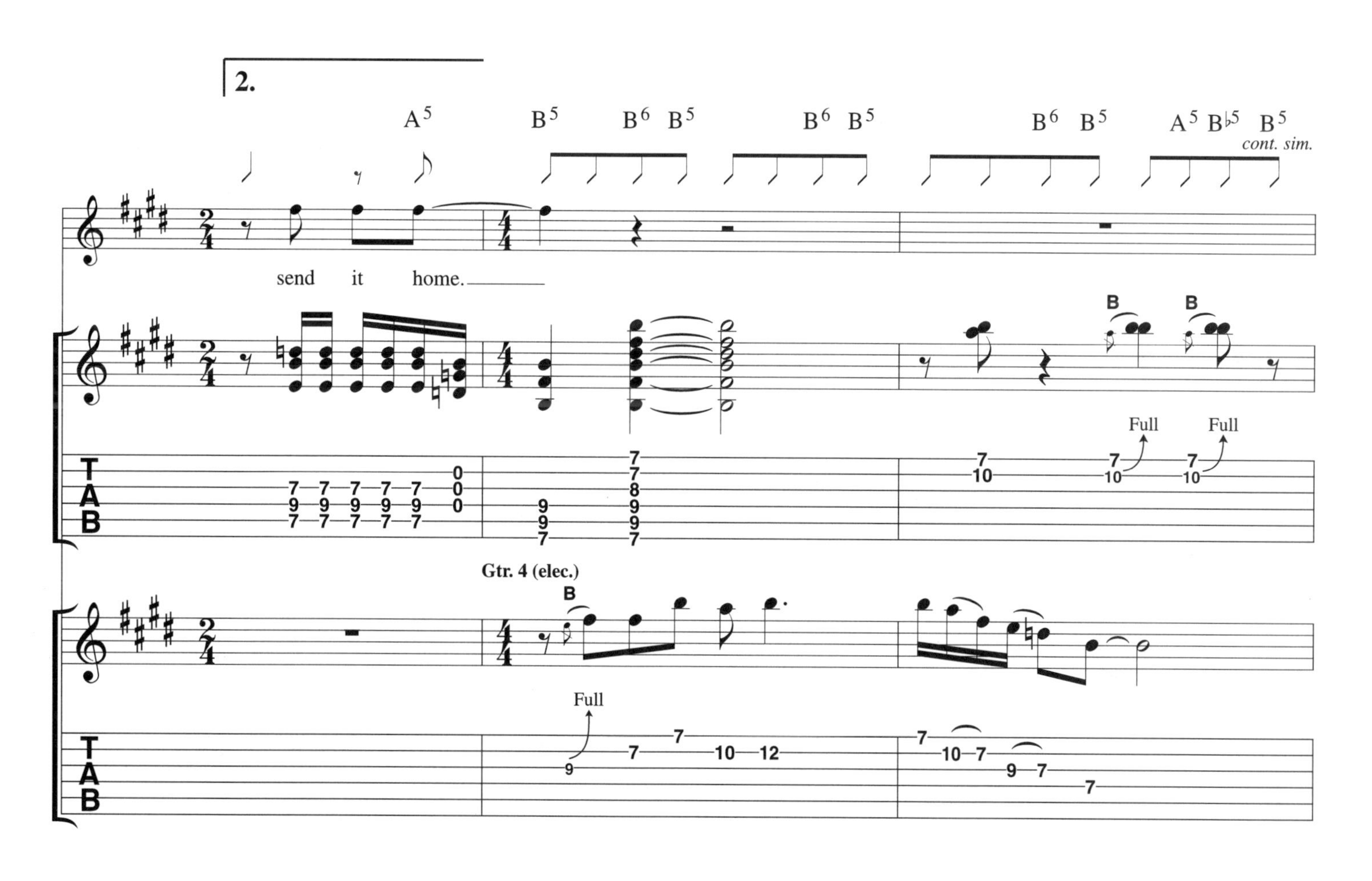
2.
A5 B5 B6 B5 B6 B5 B6 B5 A5 B♭5 B5
cont. sim.
send it home.
Full
Full
Gtr. 4 (elec.)
Full

E5
cont. sim.
Hard on the knees, mo - ney in the bag. Hard on the knees, mo -
Gtr. 2

A5 B5 B6 B5 B6 B5
cont. sim.
- ney in the bag, send it home for me - di - cal school.

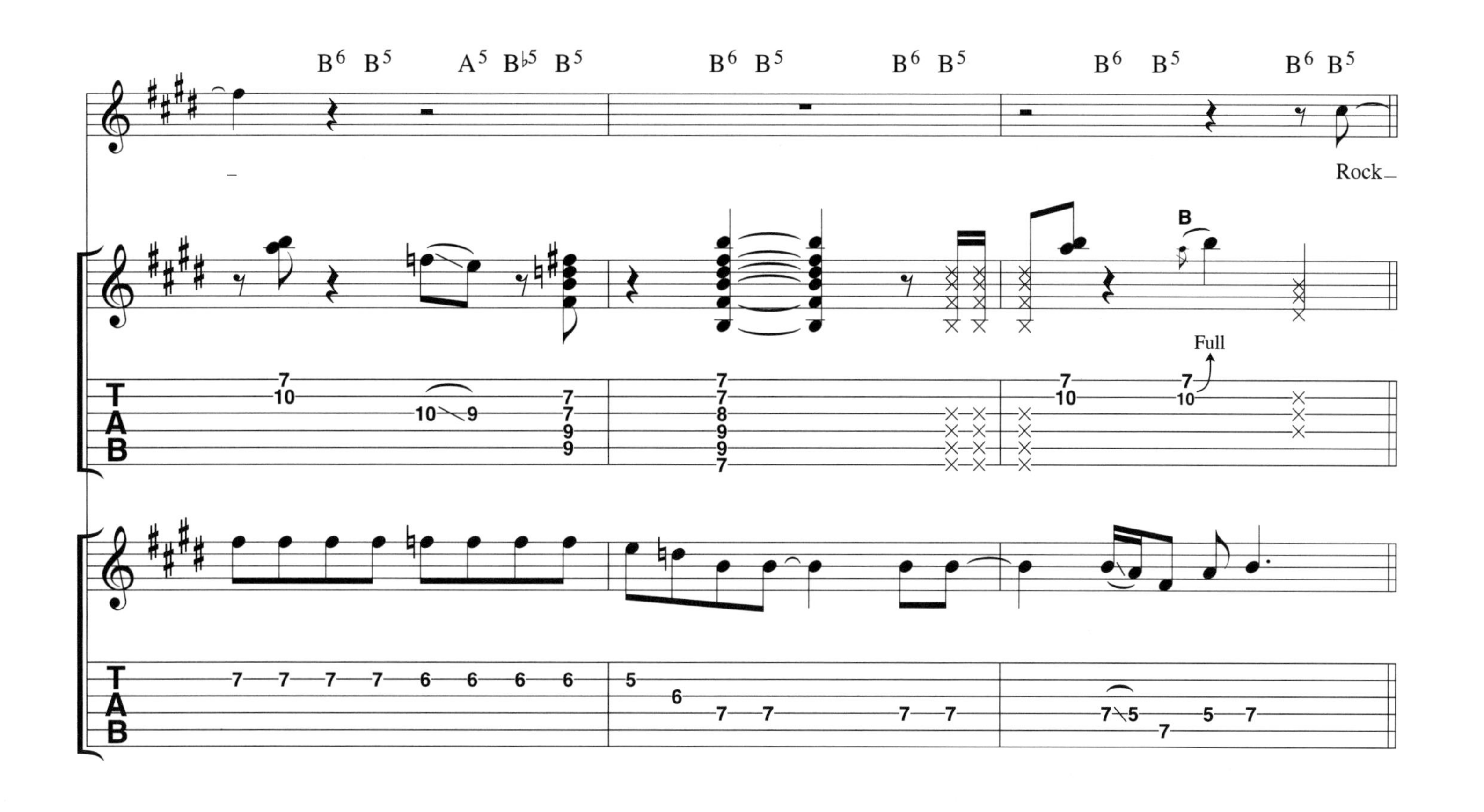
B6 B5 A5 B♭5 B5 B6 B5 B6 B5 B6 B5 B6 B5
Rock
B
Full

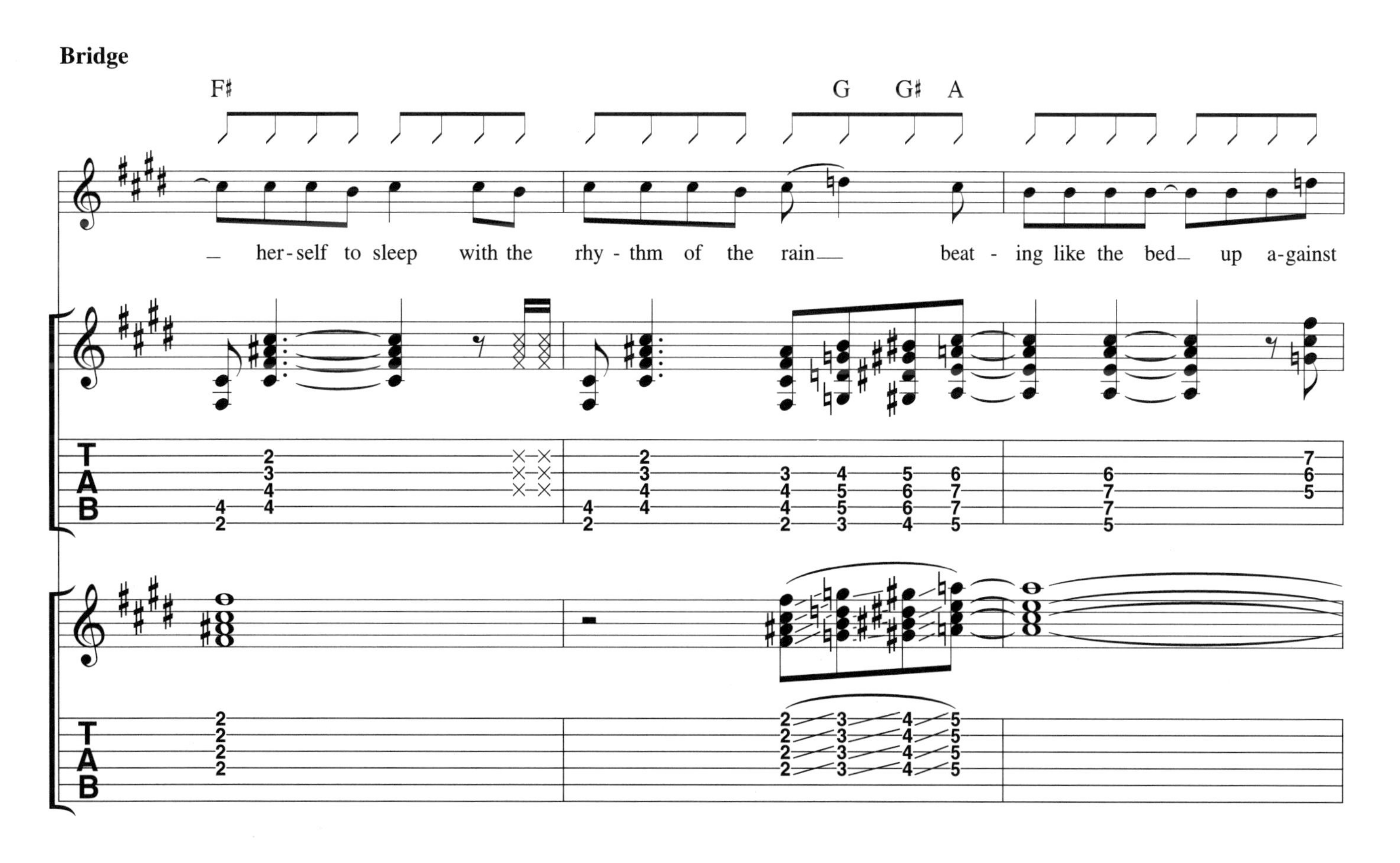
Bridge
F♯ G G♯ A
her-self to sleep with the rhy-thm of the rain beat-ing like the bed up a-gainst

B5
B6 B5
B6 B5
B6 B5
B6 B5
the win-dow frame of the ho - tel room.
w/out slide
T
A
B

B6 B5
B6 B5
B6 B5
B6 B5
F♯
Rock her-self to sleep with the tunes
w/slide
T
A
B

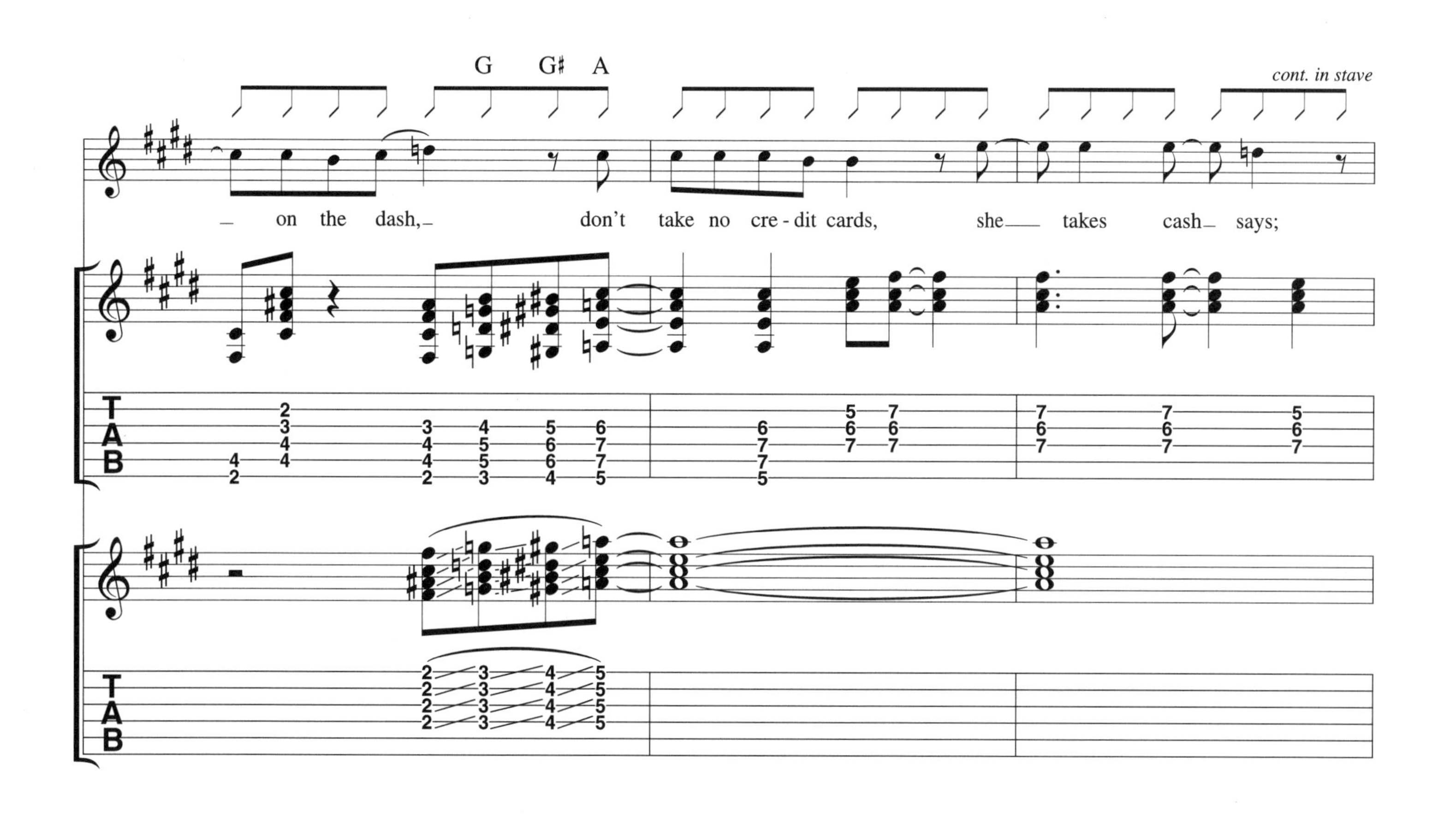
G G♯ A
cont. in stave
on the dash,
don't take no cre-dit cards,
she takes cash says;

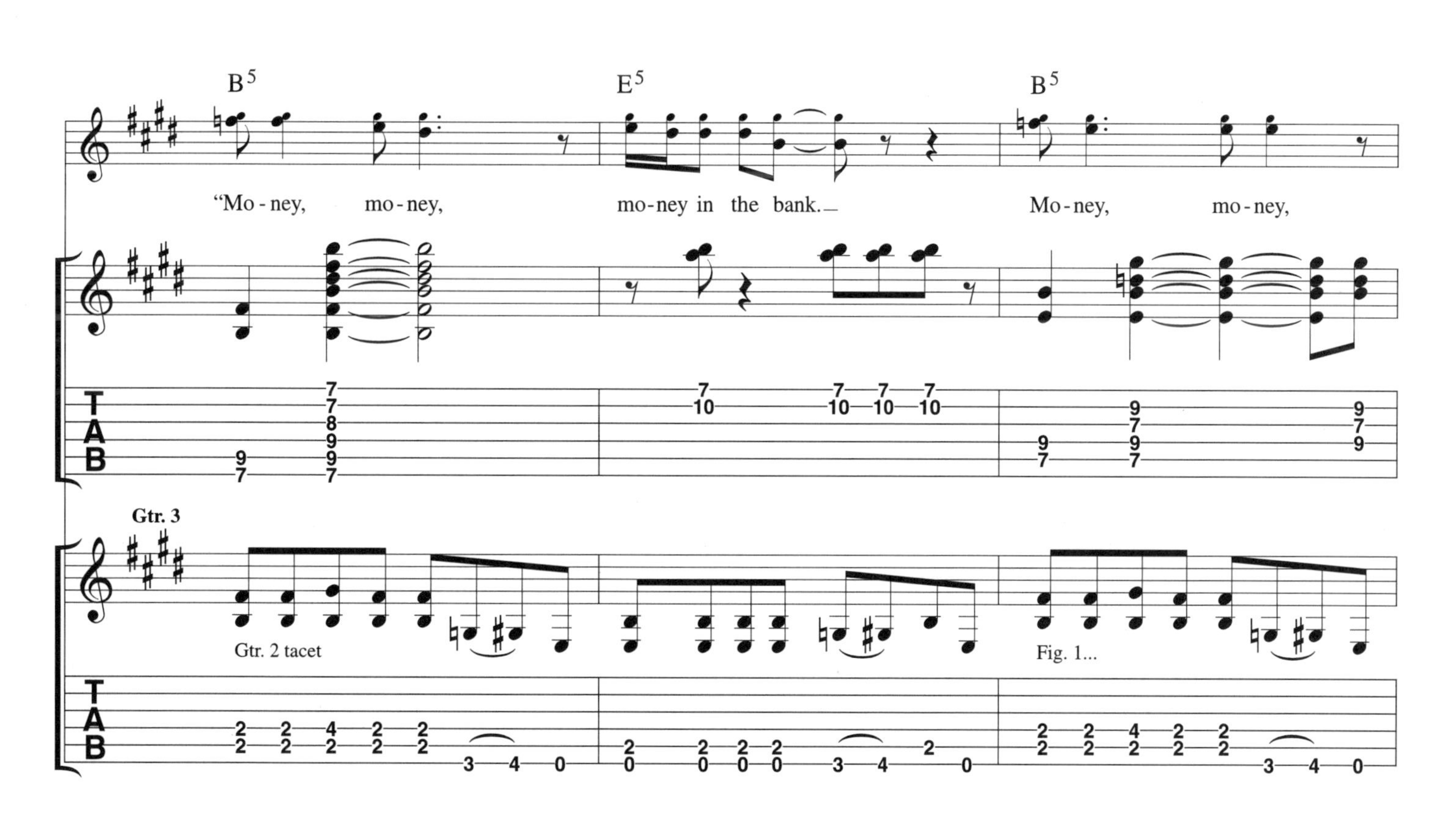
B5
E5
B5
"Mo-ney, mo-ney,
mo-ney in the bank.
Mo-ney, mo-ney,
Gtr. 3
Gtr. 2 tacet
Fig. 1...

E5
B5
E5
mo-ney in the bank. Mo - ney, mo - ney, mo-ney in the bank. Mo -
cont. sim.
...Fig. 1 ends
B5
E5
B5
Gtr. 3
- ney, mo - ney, mo - ney in the bank.
Gtr. 4
Full
Full
Full
Gtr. 3 cont. in slashes
E5
B5
E5
Hey, hey, hey, hey.
Gtr. 3 w/Fig. 1 (x4)
Full
1/4
Full

B5
E5
B5
E5
B
B
Full
Full
Full
Bridge 2
Freely
F♯m
G♯m
A
It ain't no ea - sy life but it pays pret-ty good, keeps her out
Gtr. 3
mp
w/clean tone
Gtrs. 1+4 tacet
a tempo
F♯m
G♯m
of the cold.
It ain't no ea - sy life, but it's sil -
A
B
- ver and gold, sil - ver and gold, sil - ver, sil - ver, sil - ver and gold.
Gtrs. 1+3
cont. in slashes

E5
Gtr. 3
Gtr. 1
mf
Gtr. 3 w/dist.
Gtr. 2
mf
w/distortion + slide
A5
B5
B6
B5
B6
B5
B6
B5
A5
B♭5
B5
E5

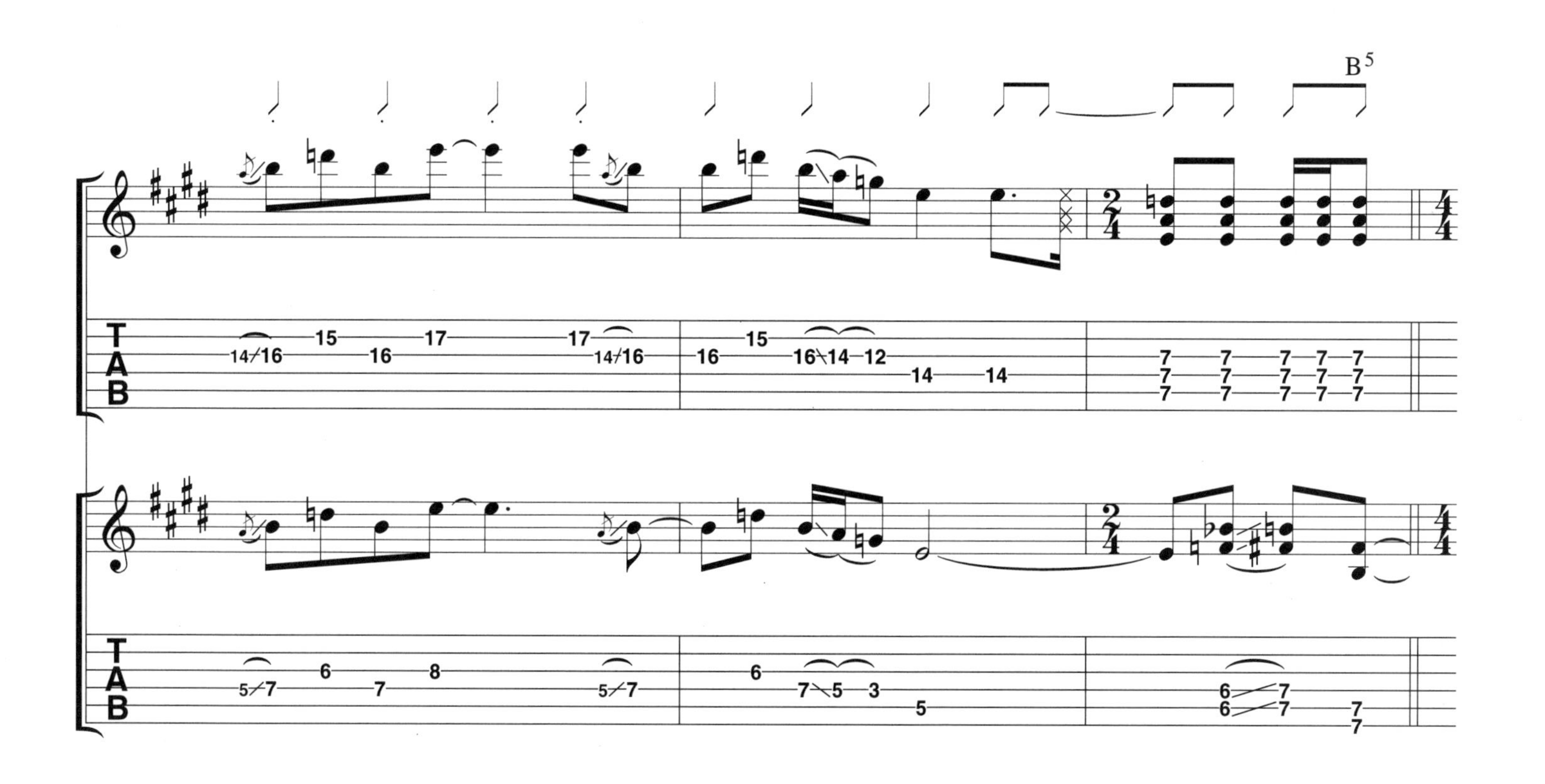
B5

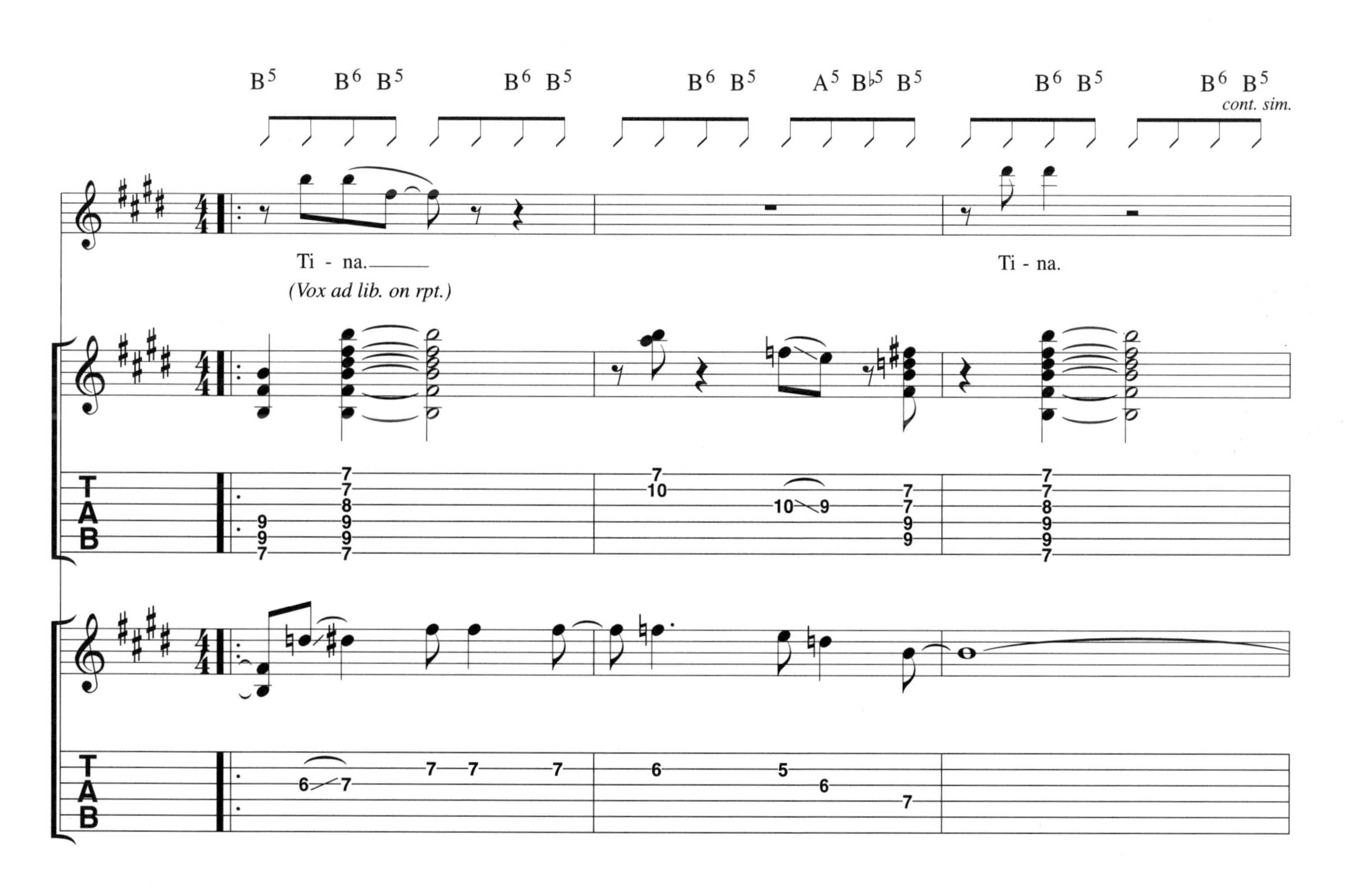
B5
B6 B5
B6 B5
B6 B5
A5 B♭5 B5
B6 B5
B6 B5
cont. sim.
Ti - na.
(Vox ad lib. on rpt.)
Ti - na.

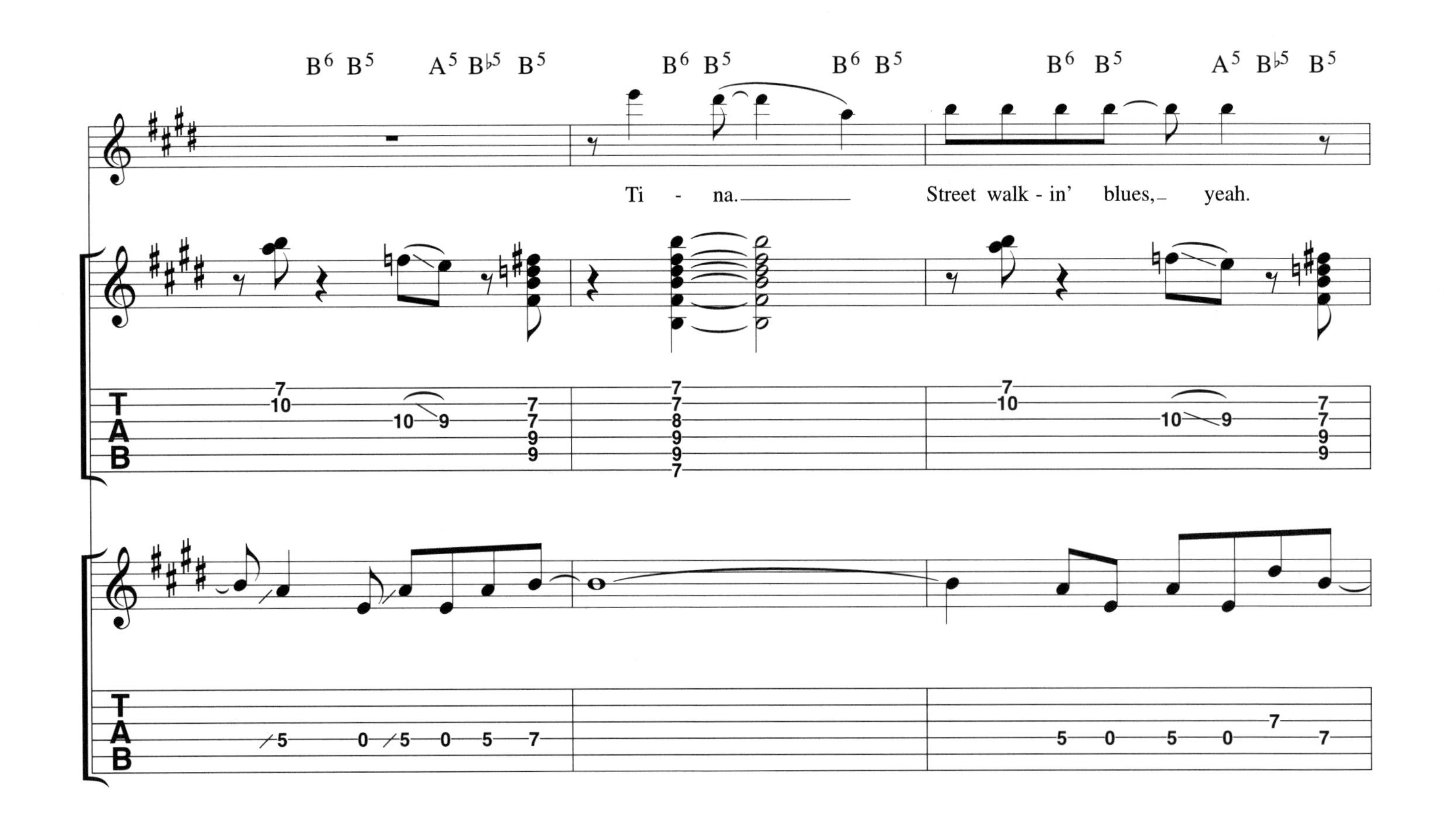
B6 B5 A5 B♭5 B5 B6 B5 B6 B5 B6 B5 A5 B♭5 B5
Ti - na.
Street walk - in' blues, yeah.

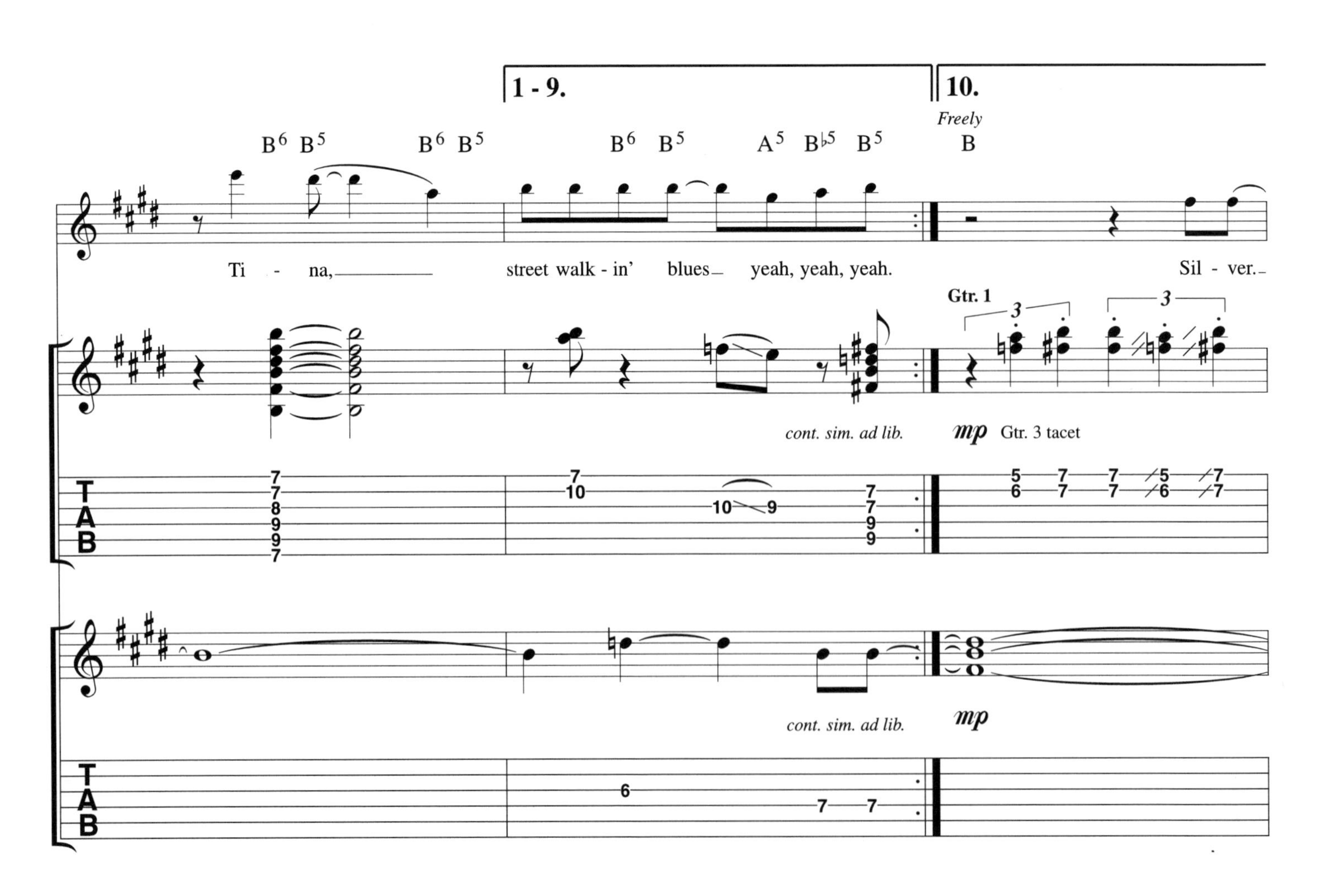
1 - 9.
10.
Freely
B6 B5 B6 B5 B6 B5 A5 B♭5 B5 B
Ti - na,
street walk - in' blues yeah, yeah, yeah.
Sil - ver.
Gtr. 1
cont. sim. ad lib.
mp
Gtr. 3 tacet
cont. sim. ad lib.
mp

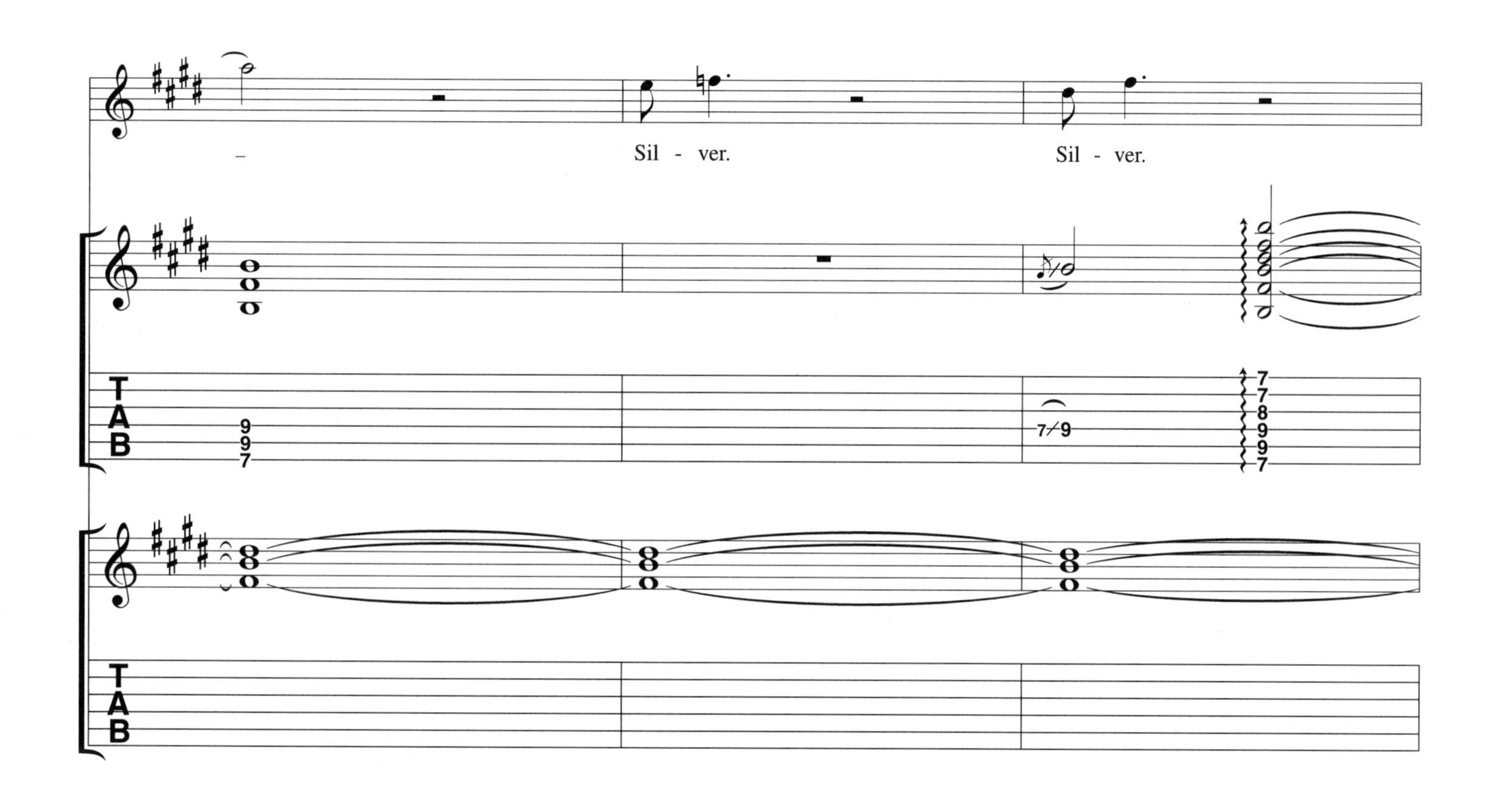
– Sil - ver. Sil - ver.

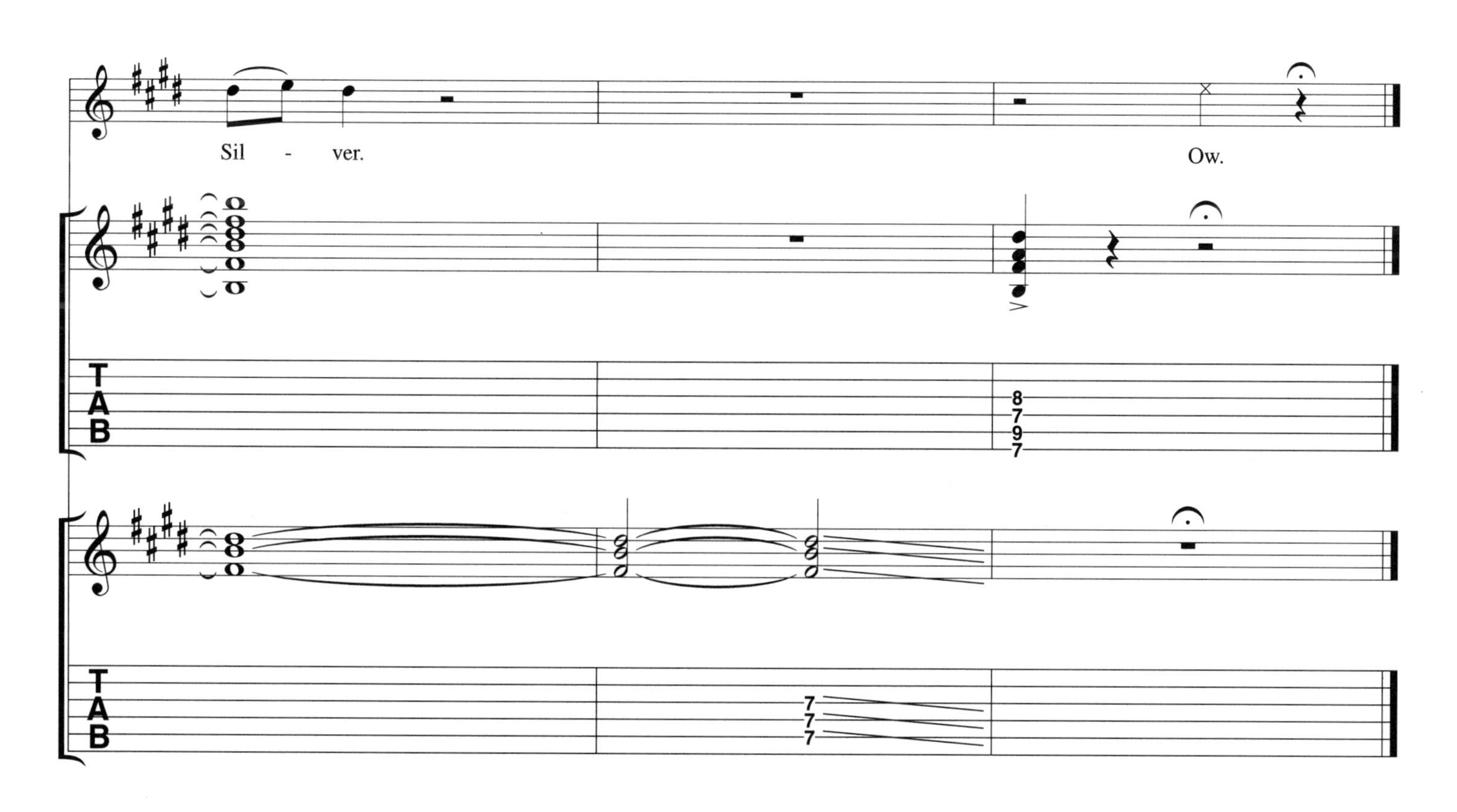
Sil - ver. Ow.

GOODNIGHT, HOLLYWOOD BLVD

Words & Music by Ryan Adams & Richard Causon

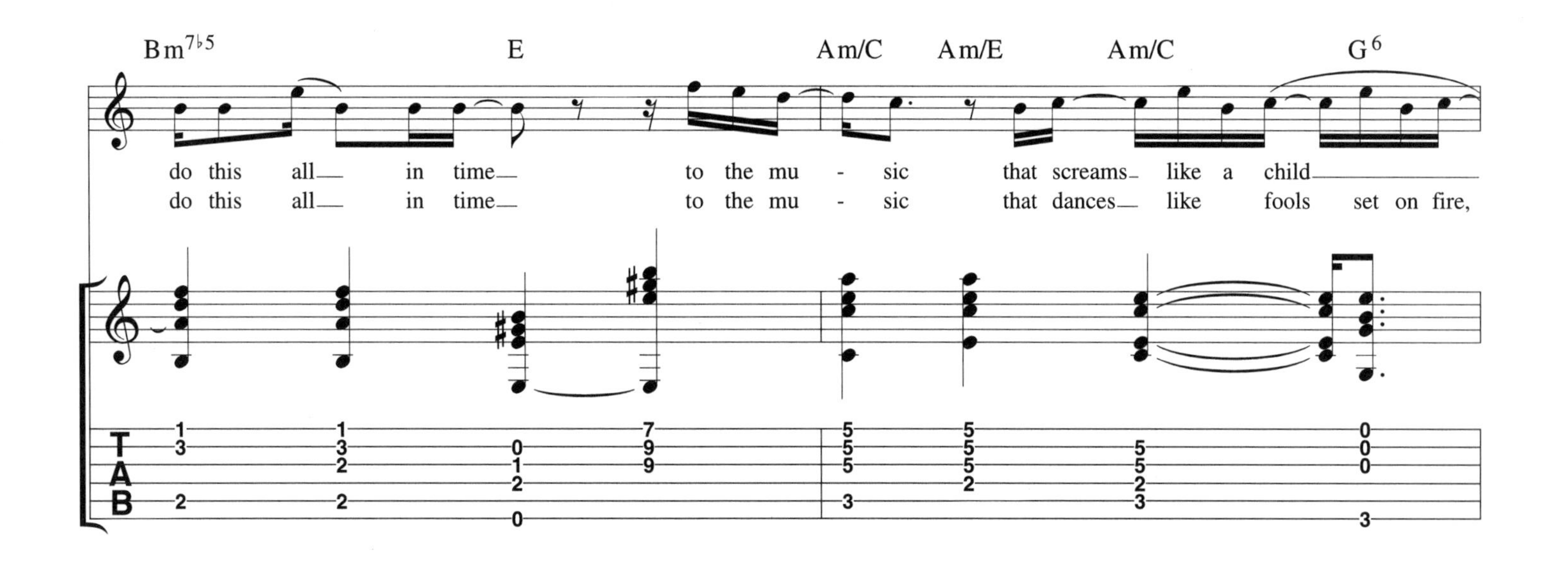

Bm7♭5
E
Am/C
Am/E
Am/C
G6
do this all in time to the mu - sic that screams like a child
do this all in time to the mu - sic that dances like fools set on fire,

F♯m7♭5
Fm6
C
in the back of your mind in a clowns' sa - loon.
flail - ing their arms in a room full of whores.

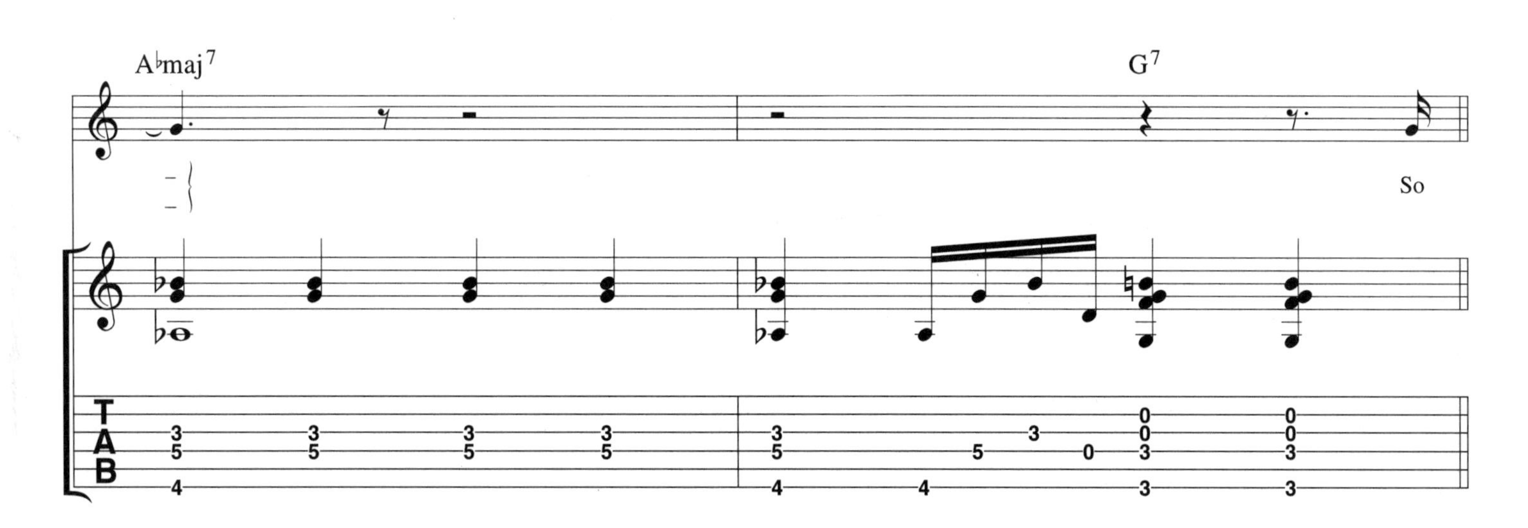

A♭maj7
G7
So

Chorus

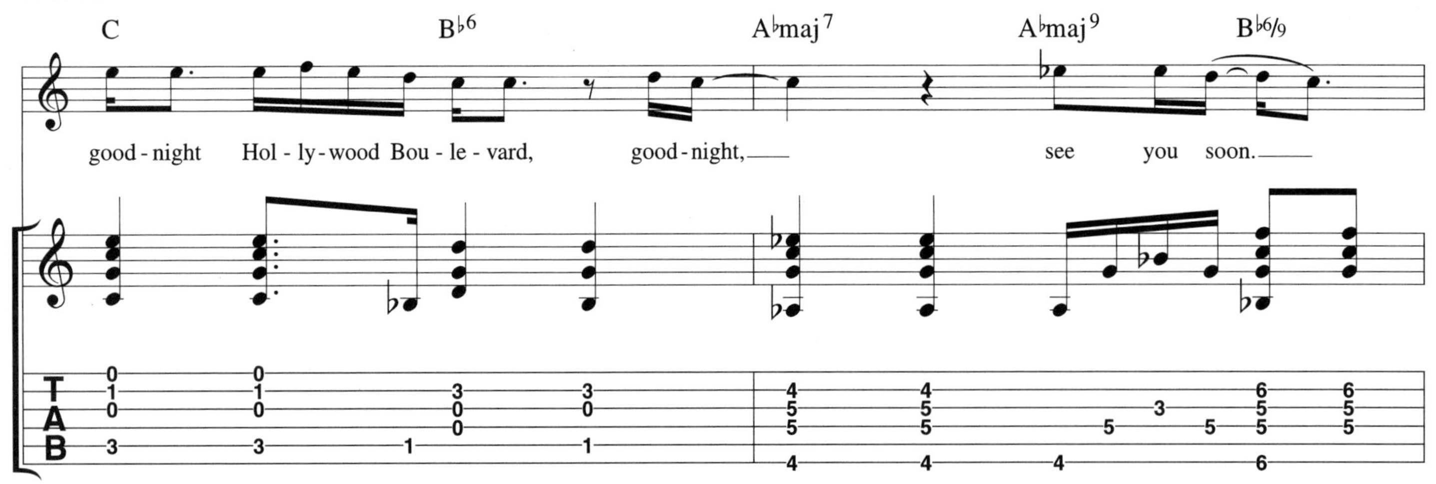
C
B♭6
A♭maj7
A♭maj9
B♭6/9
good - night Hol - ly - wood Bou - le - vard, good - night,
see you soon.

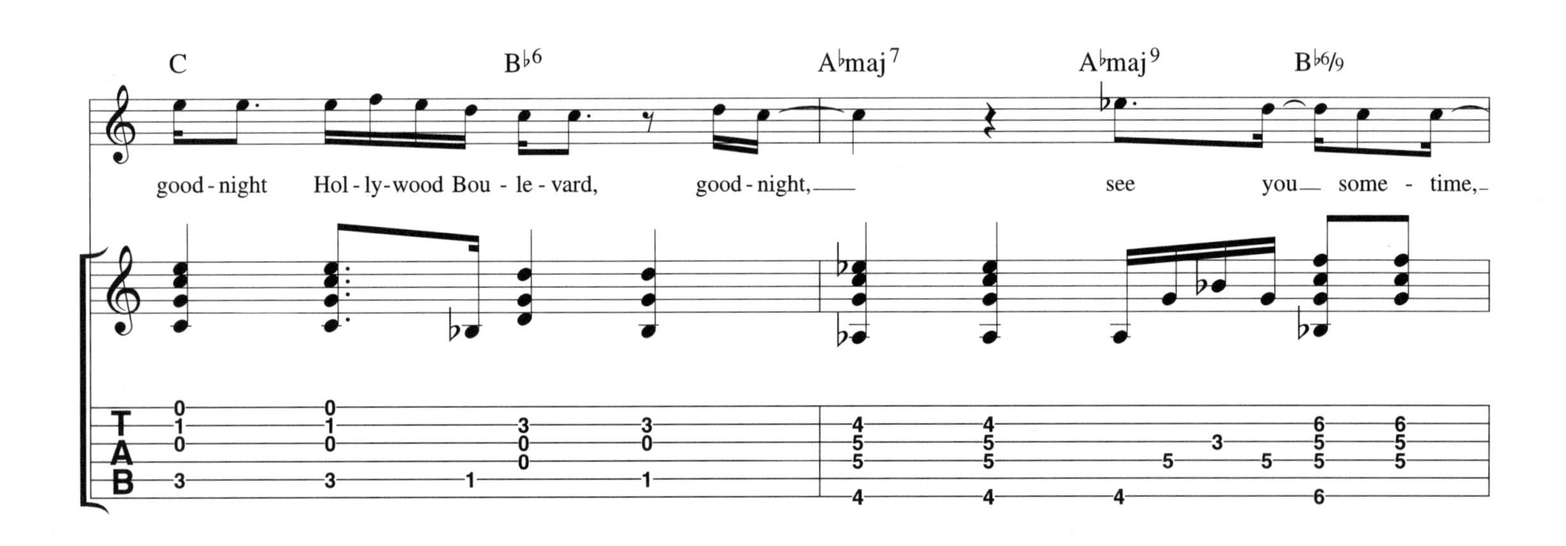
C
B♭6
A♭maj7
A♭maj9
B♭6/9
good - night Hol - ly - wood Bou - le - vard, good - night,
see you some - time,

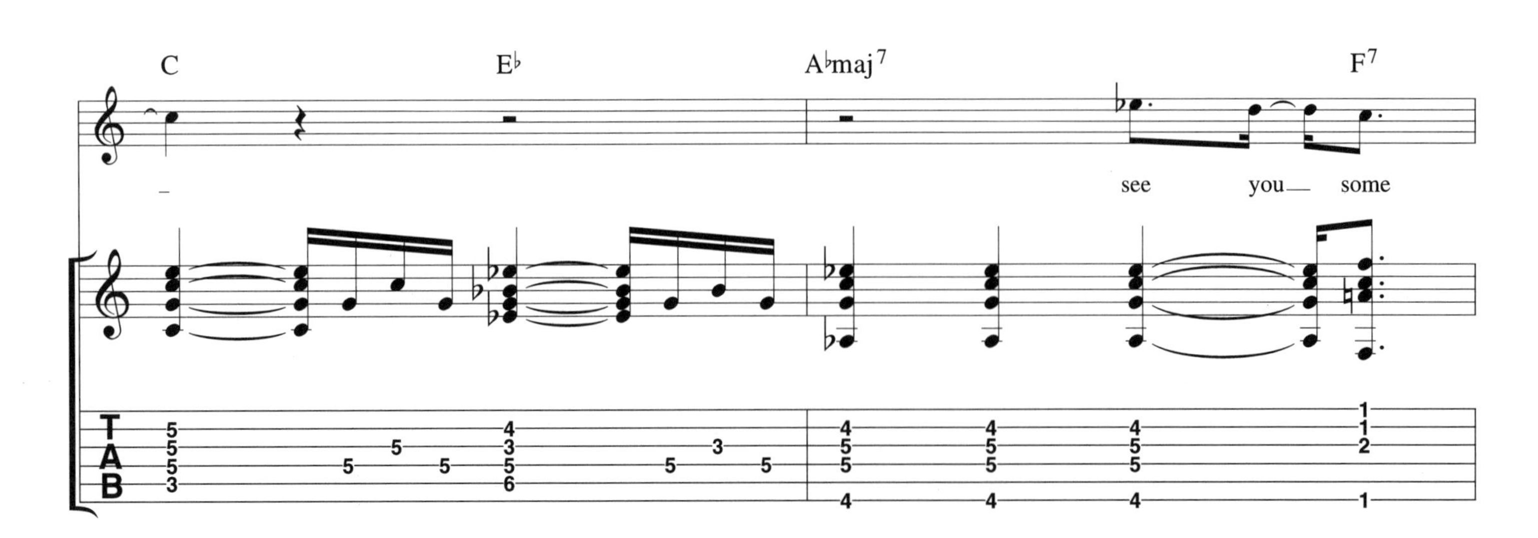
C
E♭
A♭maj7
F7
see you some

E7aug
E♭6
D7
D♭maj7
time.
Yeah
right.
Yeah
T
A
B

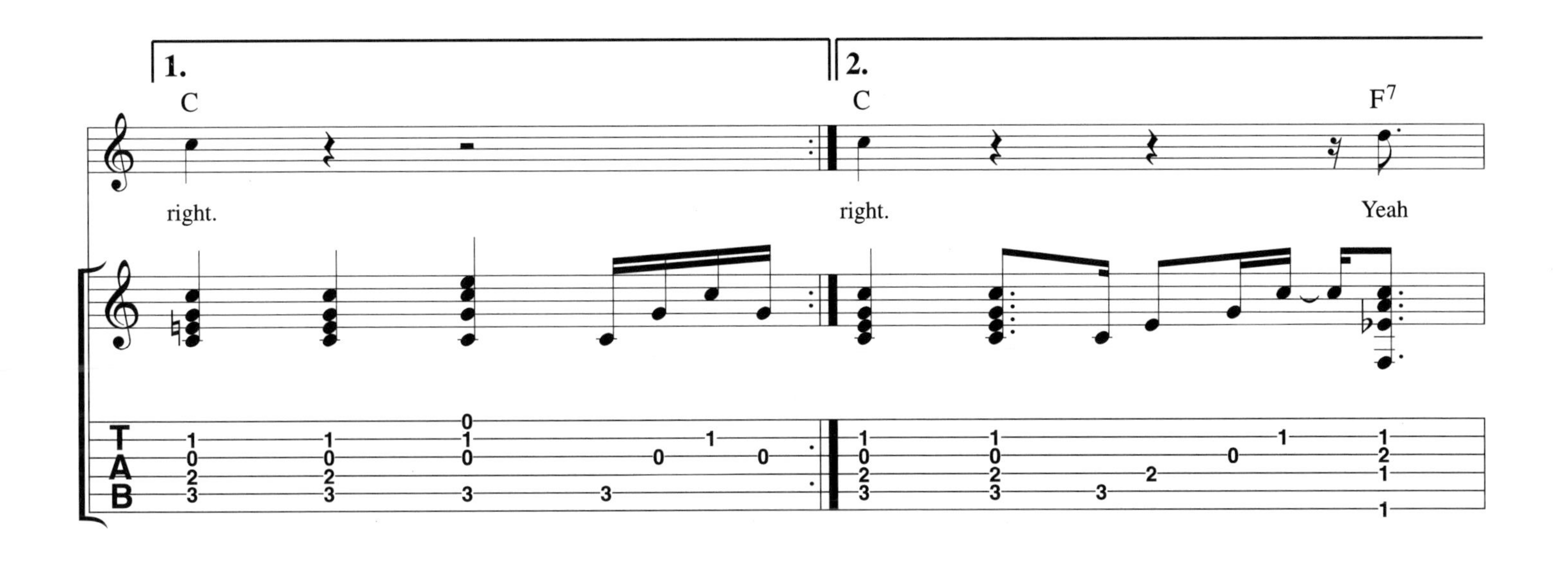
1.
2.
C
C
F7
right.
right.
Yeah
T
A
B

E7aug
E♭6
D7
D♭maj7
C
right.
yeah
right.
Yeah
right.
T
A
B

ROSALIE COME AND GO

Words & Music by Ryan Adams

Verse
E/G♯
D/F♯
A/C♯
E
girl named Ro - sa - lie, we used to hang out in the park, we used to
Gtr. 1
Fig. 2...
score some sys - tem grease from the fel - las af - ter dark. We used to
...Fig. 2 ends
stay on the streets at night, used to hang out in the rain. She had a
Gtr. 2
Gtr. 1 w/Fig. 2
bad time in the bow - ery, and caught a bul - let in her teeth.

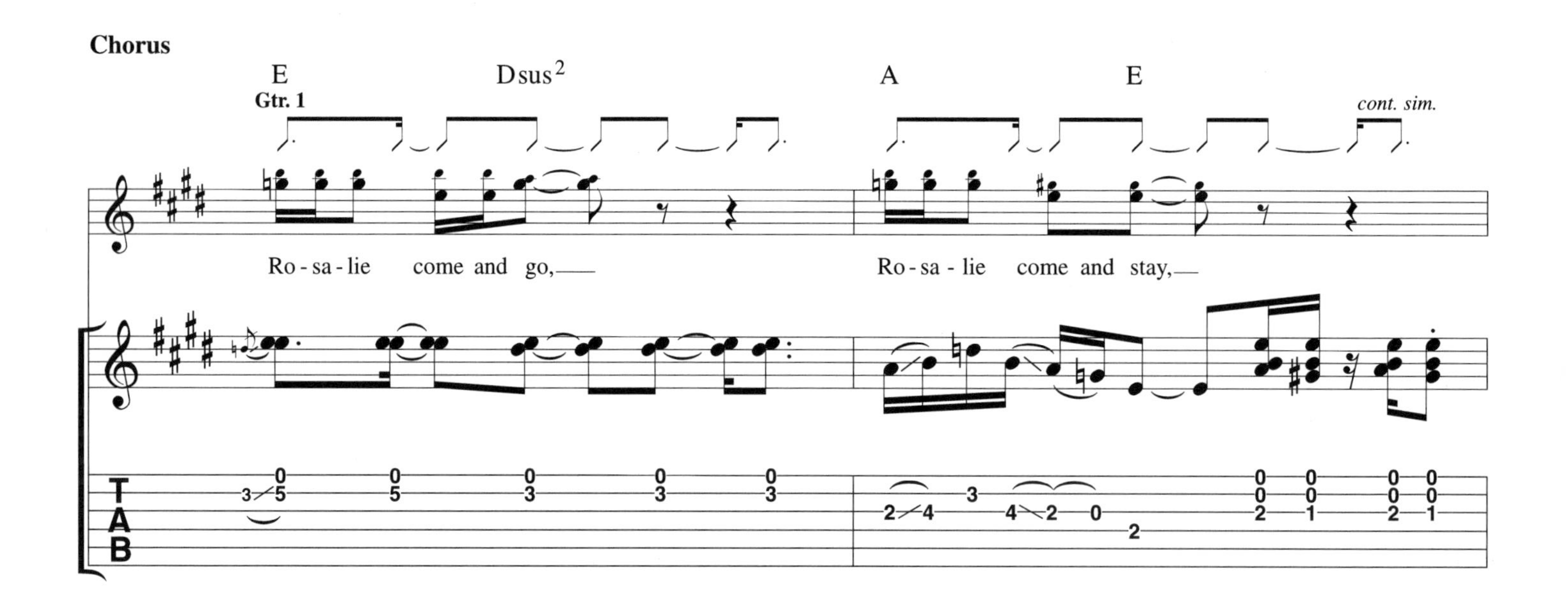
Chorus
E
Dsus2
A
E
Gtr. 1
cont. sim.
Ro-sa-lie come and go,
Ro-sa-lie come and stay,

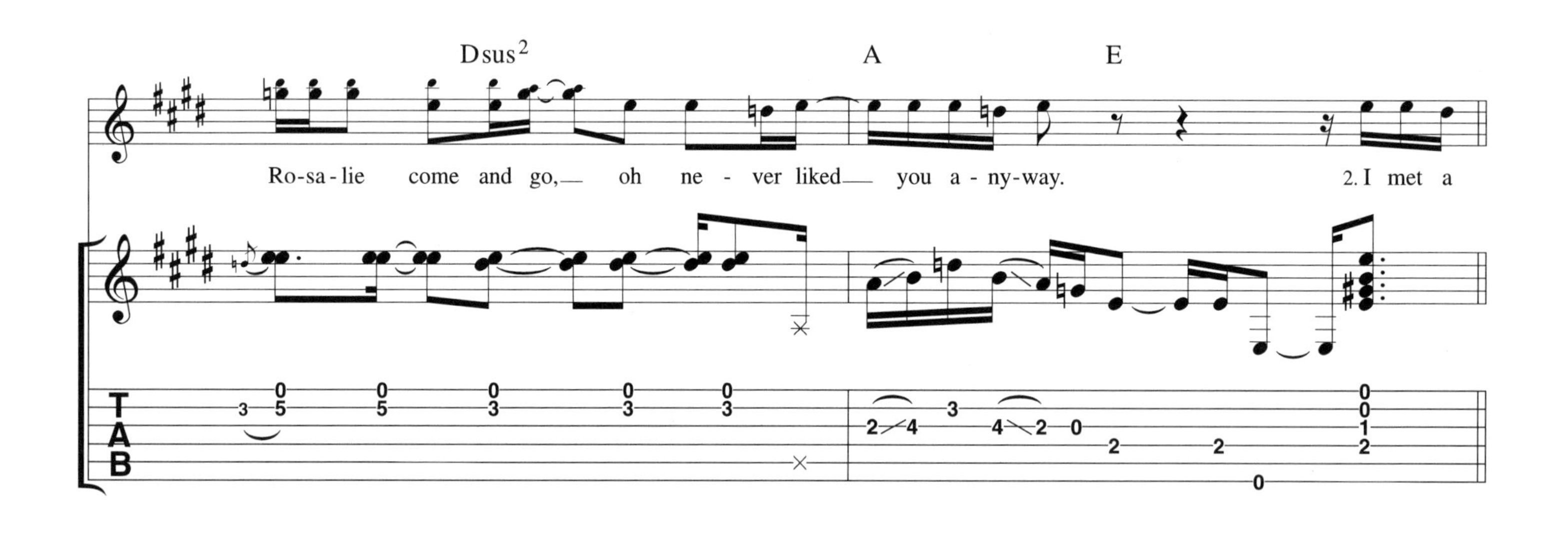
Dsus2
A
E
Ro-sa-lie come and go, oh ne-ver liked you a-ny-way.
2. I met a

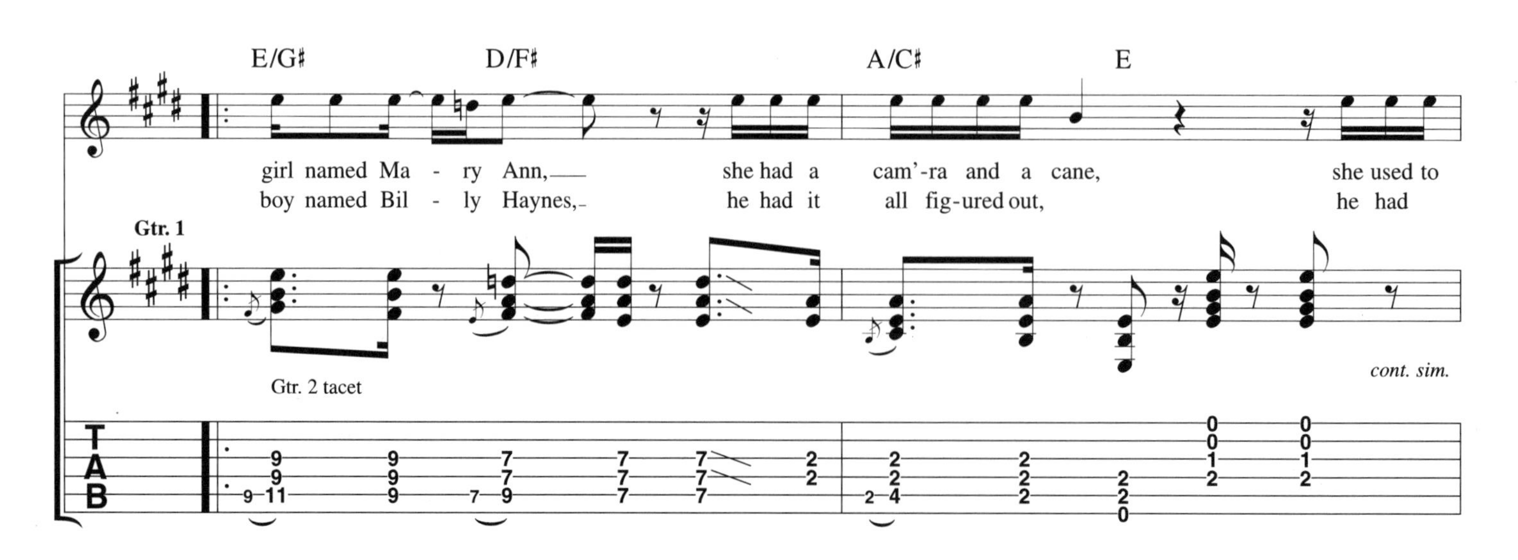
E/G♯
D/F♯
A/C♯
E
girl named Ma-ry Ann, she had a cam'-ra and a cane, she used to
boy named Bil-ly Haynes, he had it all fig-ured out, he had
Gtr. 1
cont. sim.
Gtr. 2 tacet

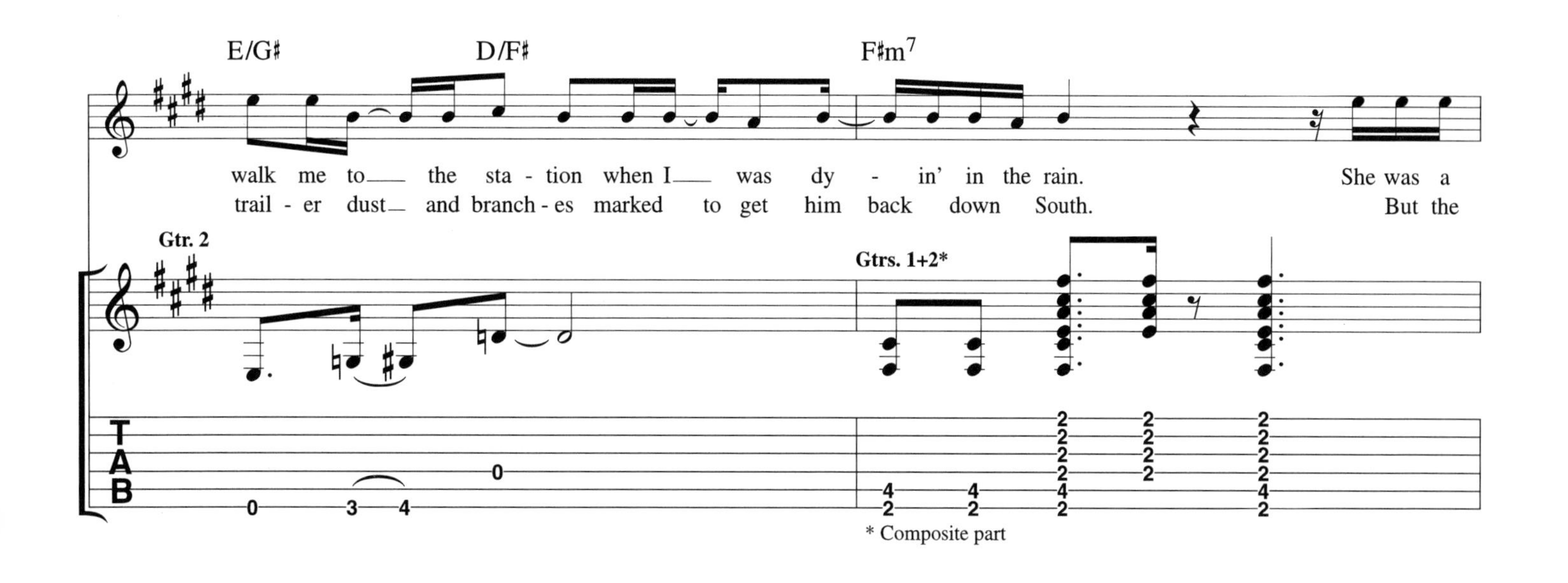
E/G♯
D/F♯
F♯m7
walk me to the sta - tion when I was dy - in' in the rain.
She was a
trail - er dust and branch - es marked to get him back down South.
But the
Gtr. 2
Gtrs. 1+2*
T
A
B
* Composite part

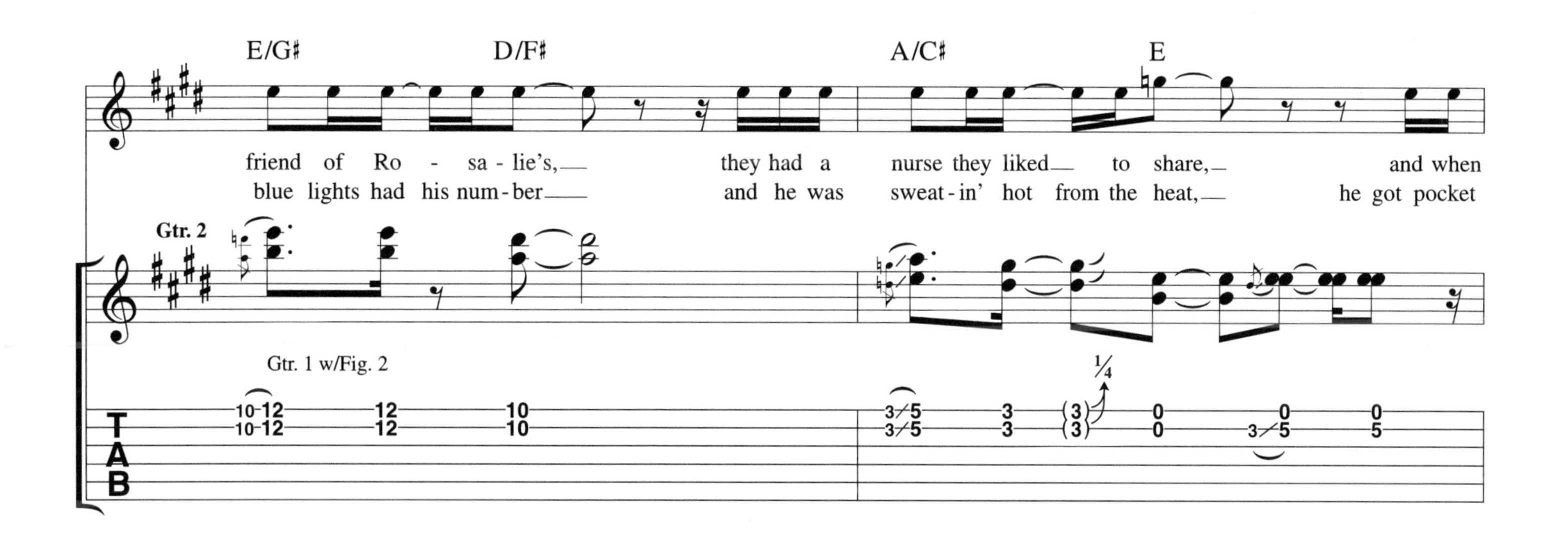
E/G♯
D/F♯
A/C♯
E
friend of Ro - sa - lie's, they had a nurse they liked to share, and when
blue lights had his num - ber and he was sweat - in' hot from the heat, he got pocket
Gtr. 2
Gtr. 1 w/Fig. 2
¼
T
A
B

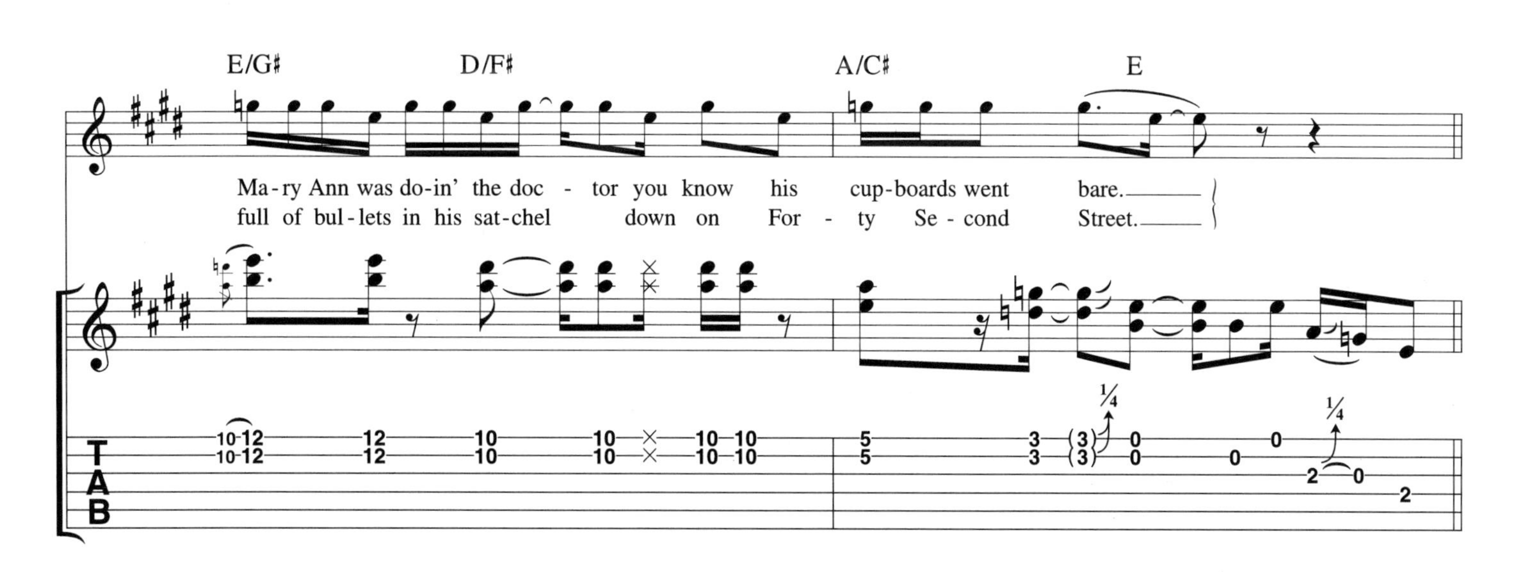
E/G♯
D/F♯
A/C♯
E
Ma - ry Ann was do - in' the doc - tor you know his cup - boards went bare.
full of bul - lets in his sat - chel down on For - ty Se - cond Street.
¼
¼
T
A
B

Chorus
E
Dsus2
A
E
cont. sim.
Gtr. 1
Ro-sa-lie come and go,
Ro-sa-lie come and stay,

Dsus2
A
E
Ro-sa-lie come and go, oh ne-ver liked you a-ny-way.

Dsus2
A
E
Ro-sa-lie come and go, ah-ha, Ro-sa-lie come and stay.

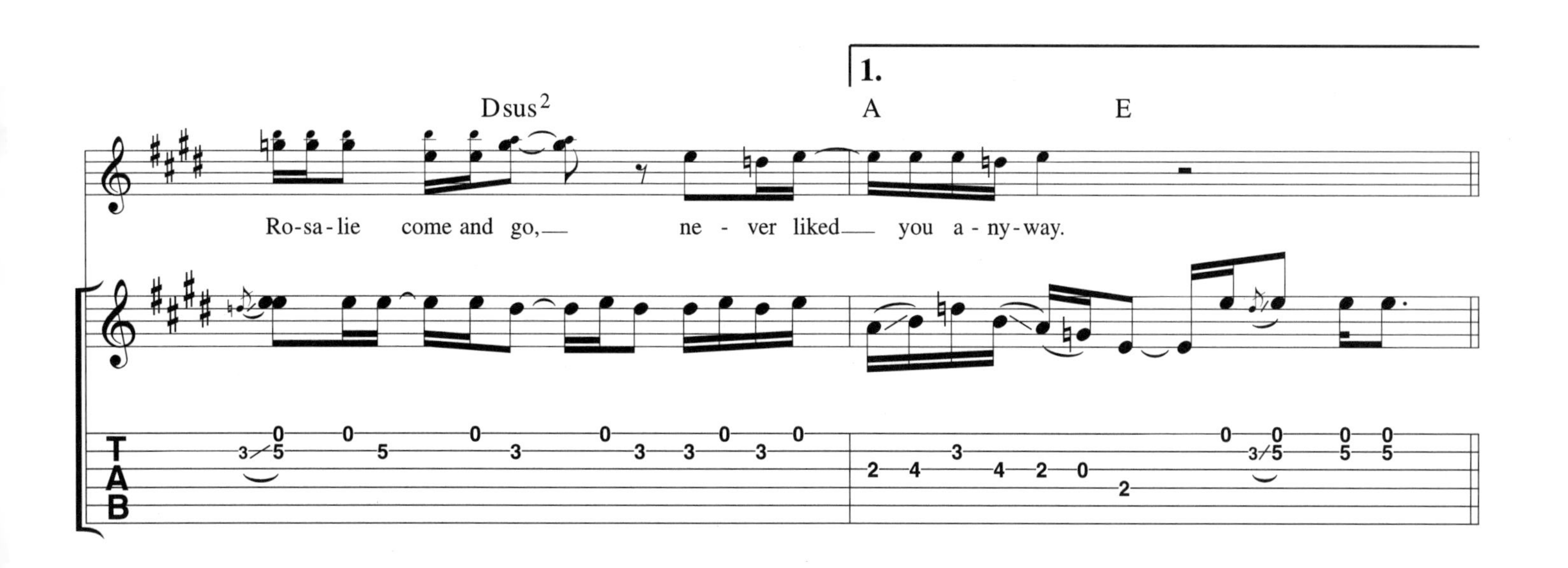
1.
Dsus2
A
E
Ro-sa-lie come and go, ne - ver liked you a-ny-way.
T
A
B

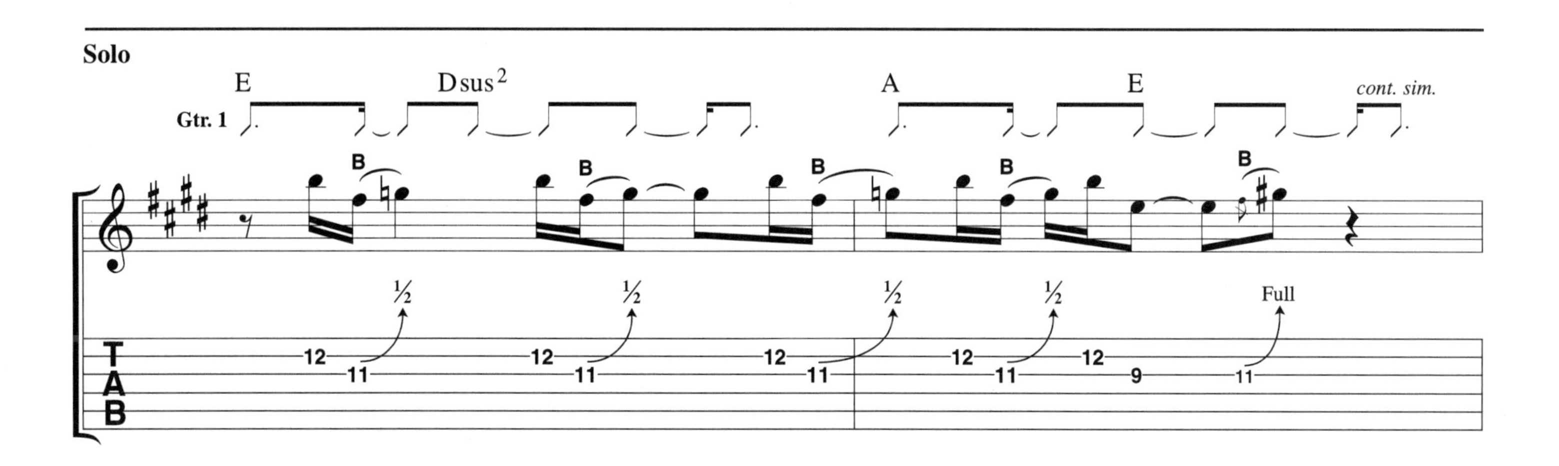
Solo
E
Dsus2
A
E
Gtr. 1
cont. sim.
B
½
Full
T
A
B

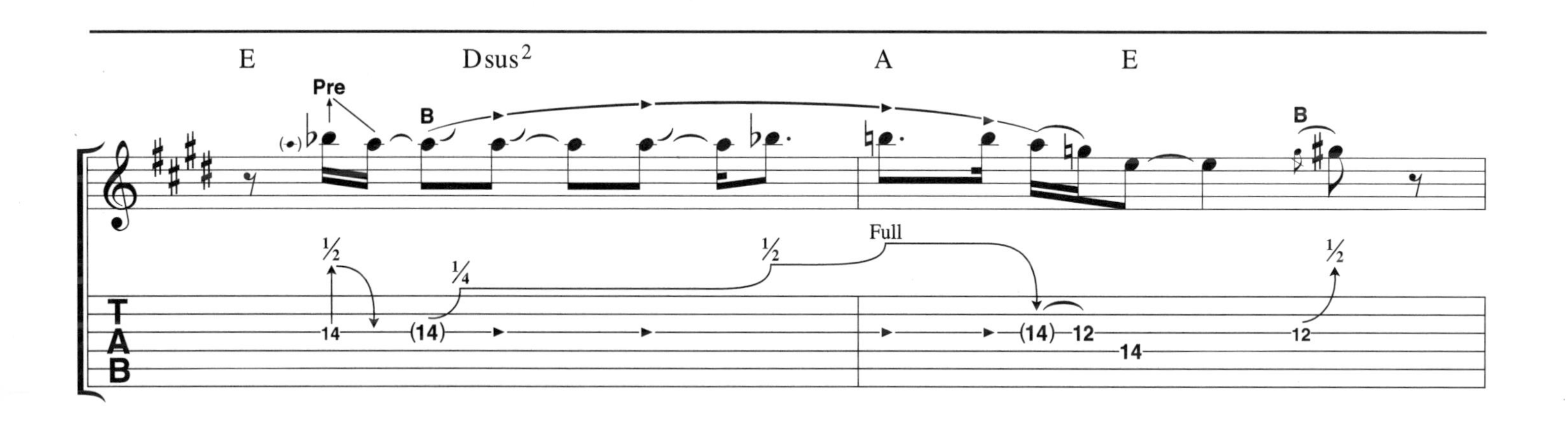
E
Dsus2
A
E
Pre
B
½
¼
Full
T
A
B

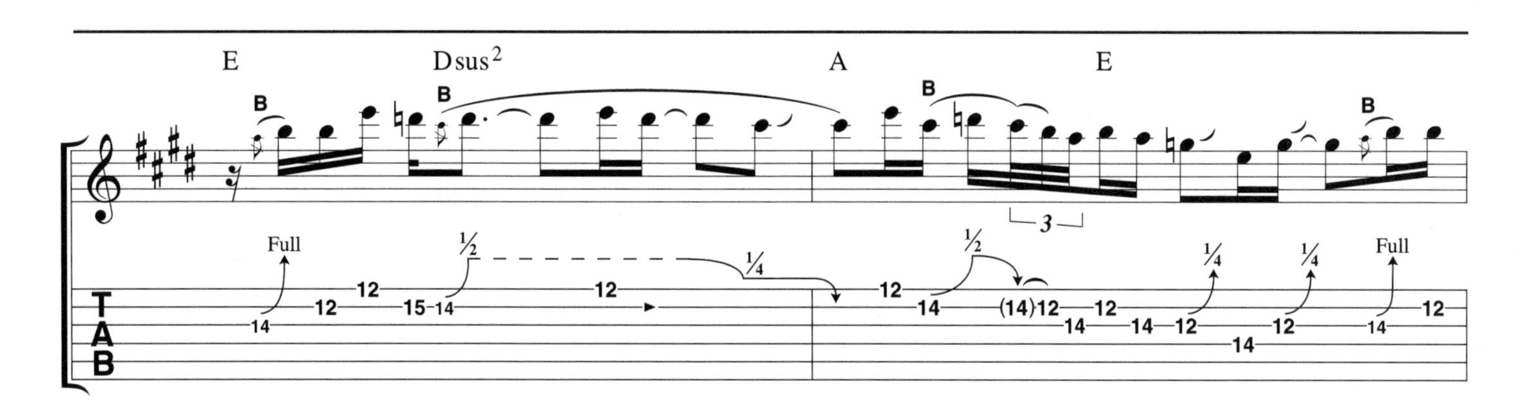
E
Dsus2
A
E
B
Full
½
¼
3
T
A
B

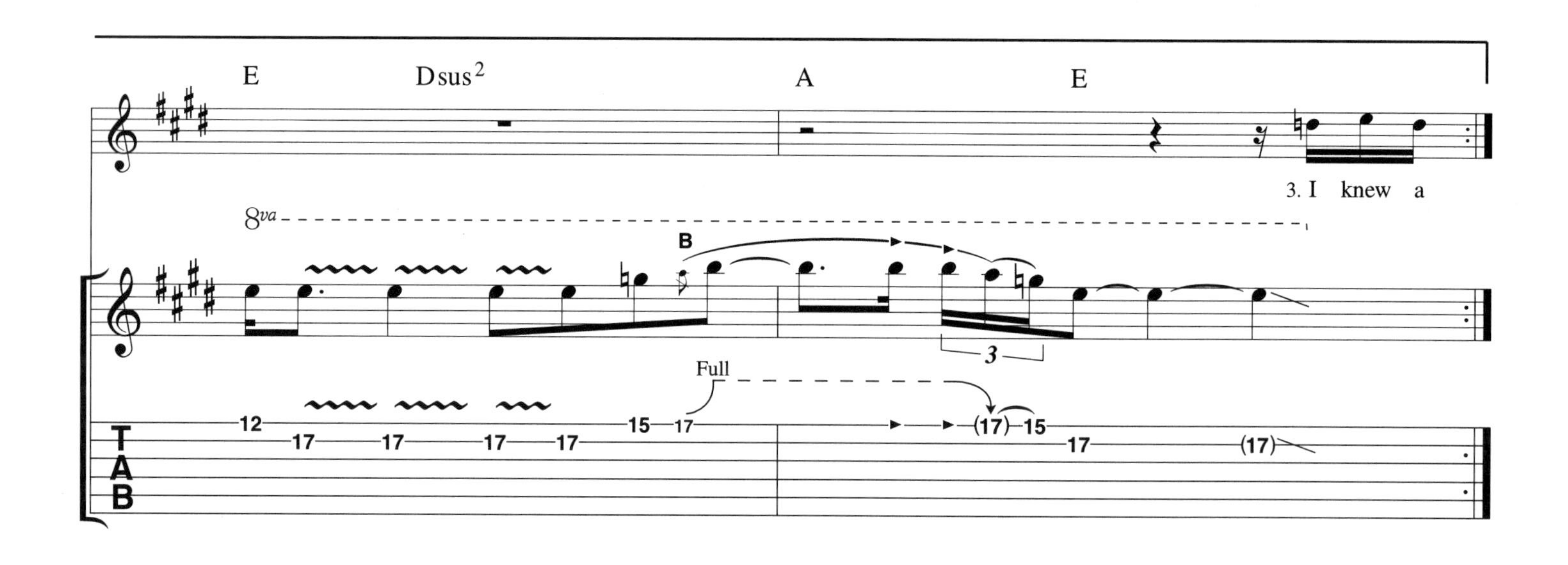
E
Dsus2
A
E
3. I knew a
8va
B
Full
T
A
B

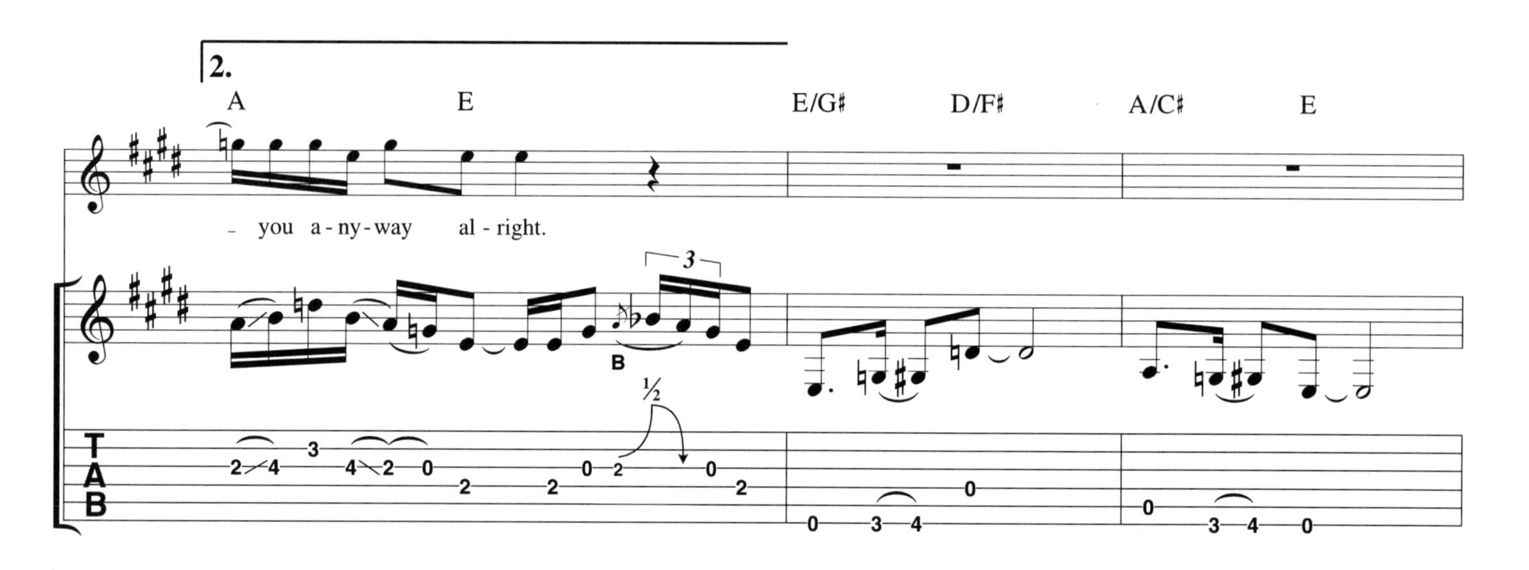
2.
A
E
E/G♯
D/F♯
A/C♯
E
you a-ny-way al-right.
B
½
T
A
B

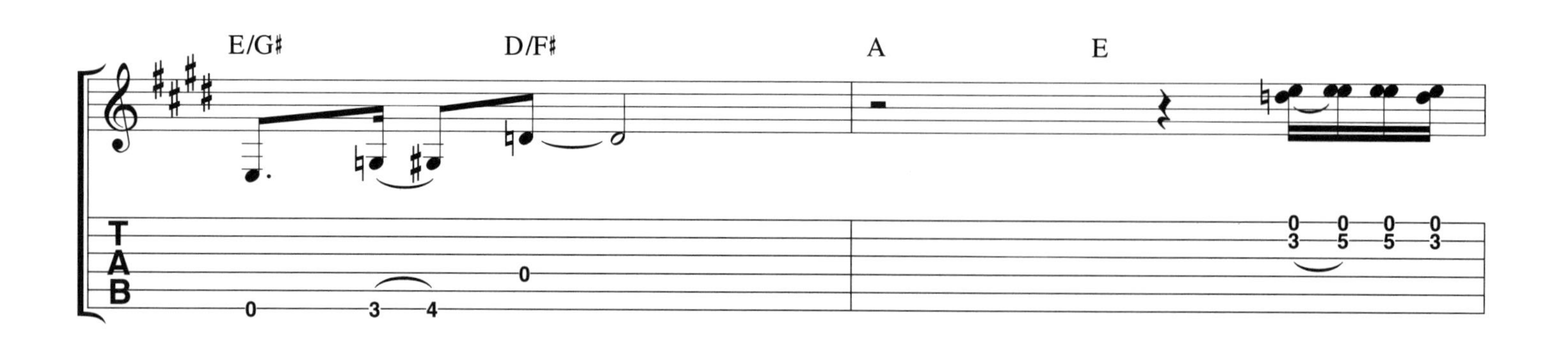
E/G♯
D/F♯
A
E
T
A
B

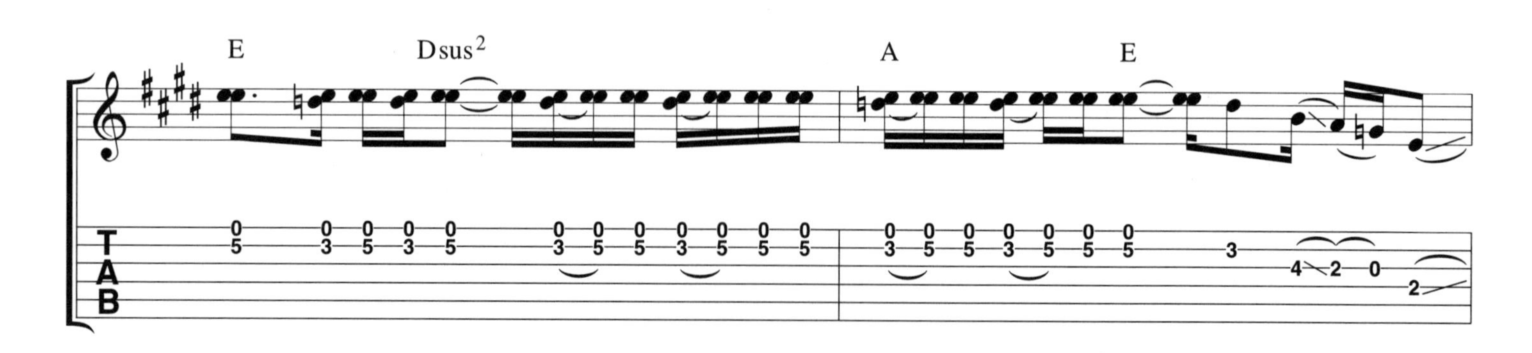
E
Dsus2
A
E
T
A
B

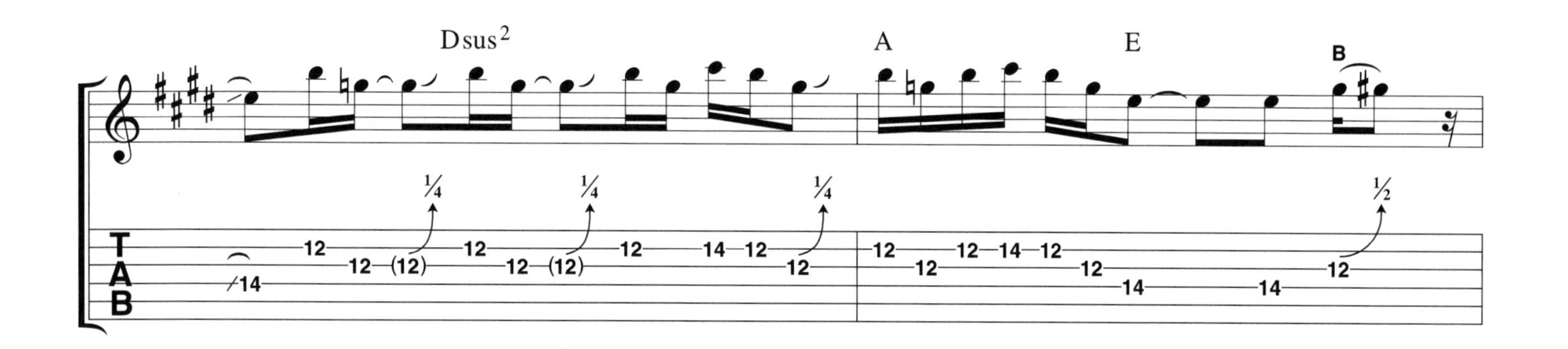
Dsus2
A
E
B
¼
¼
¼
½
12 12 (12) 12 12 (12) 12 14 12 12
14
12 12 12 14 12 12 14 14 12

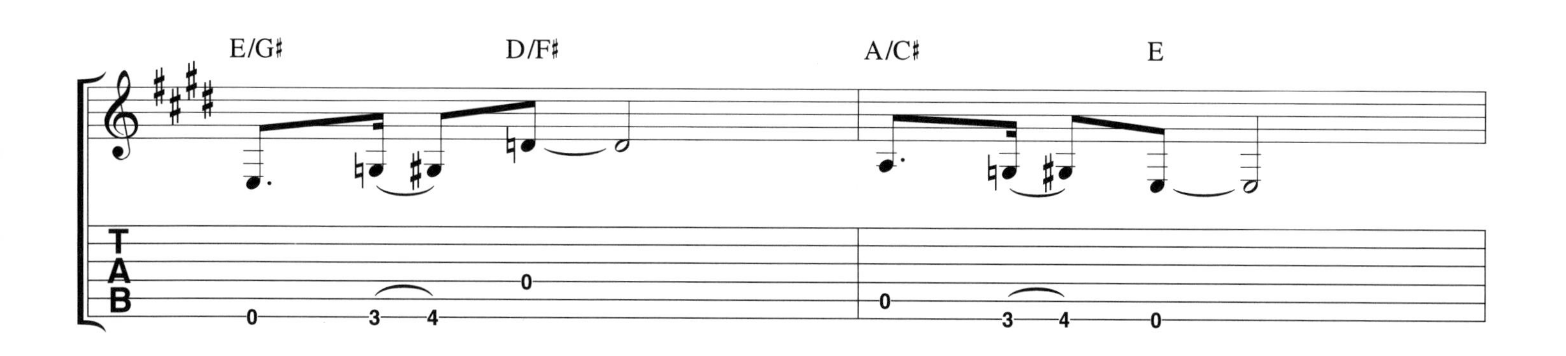
E/G♯
D/F♯
A/C♯
E
0 3 4 0
0 3 4 0

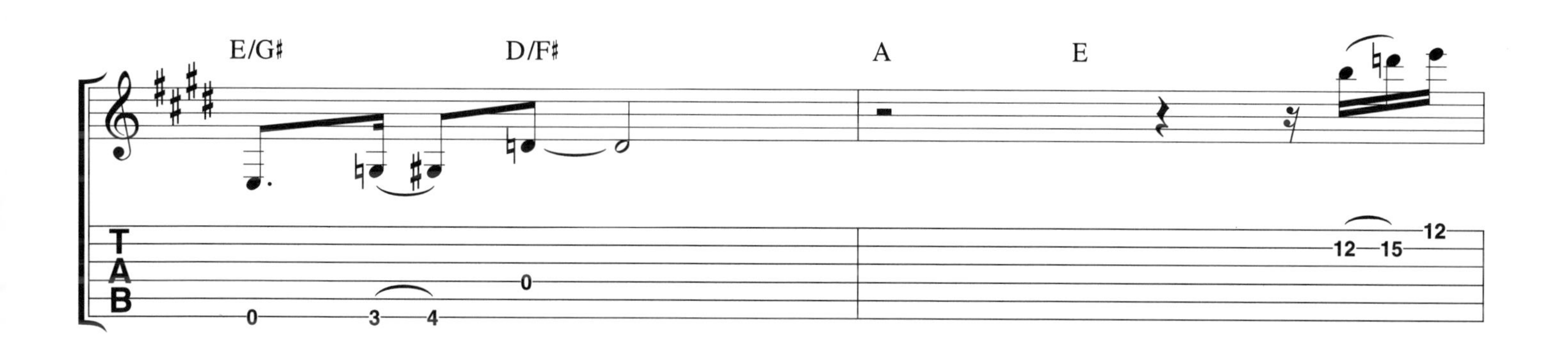
E/G♯
D/F♯
A
E
0 3 4 0
12 15 12

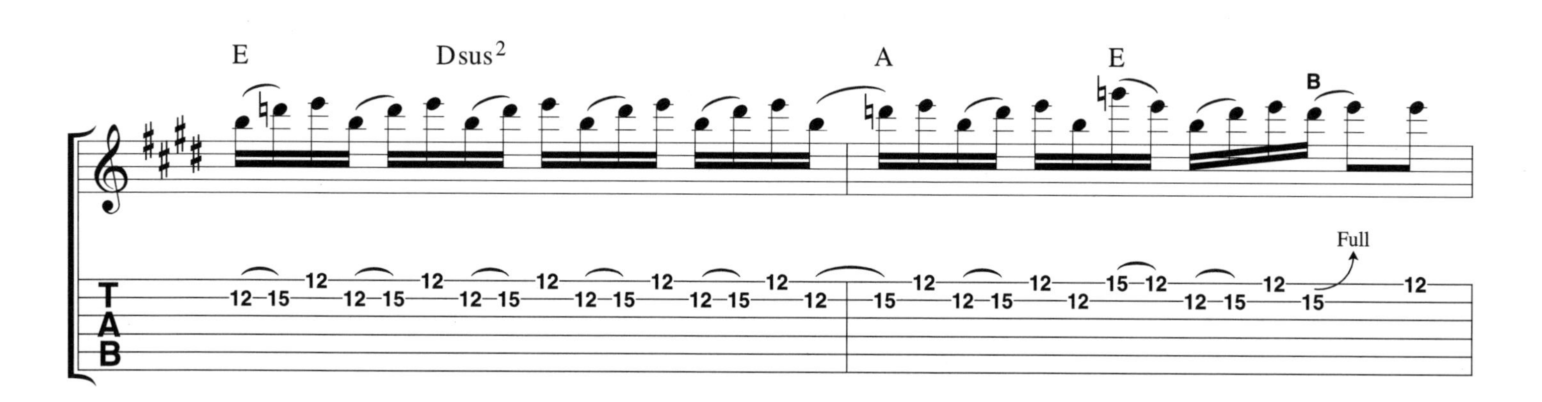
E
Dsus2
A
E
B
Full

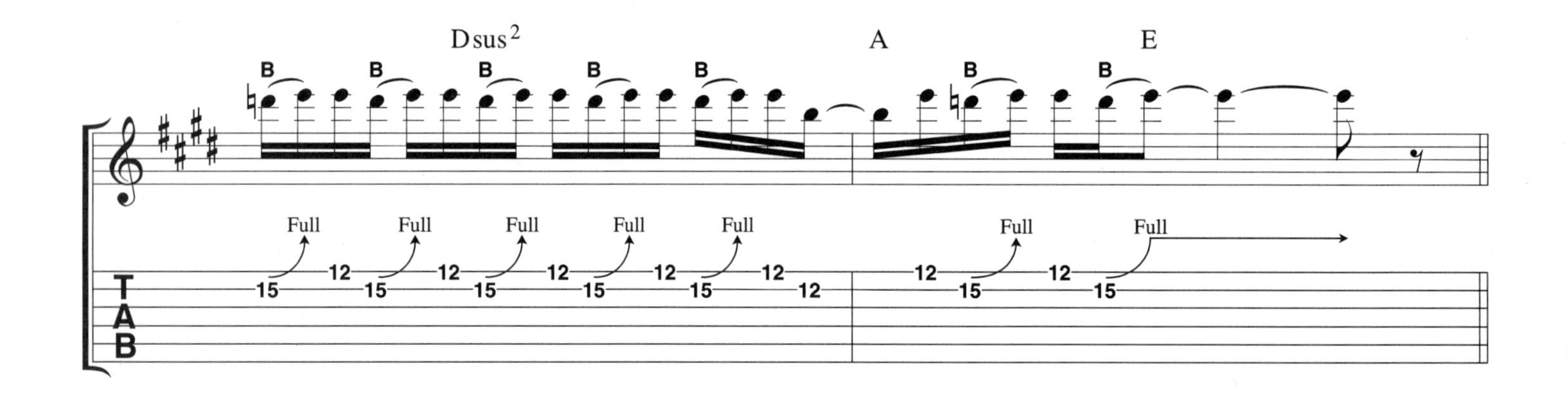
Dsus2
A
E
B
Full
T
A
B

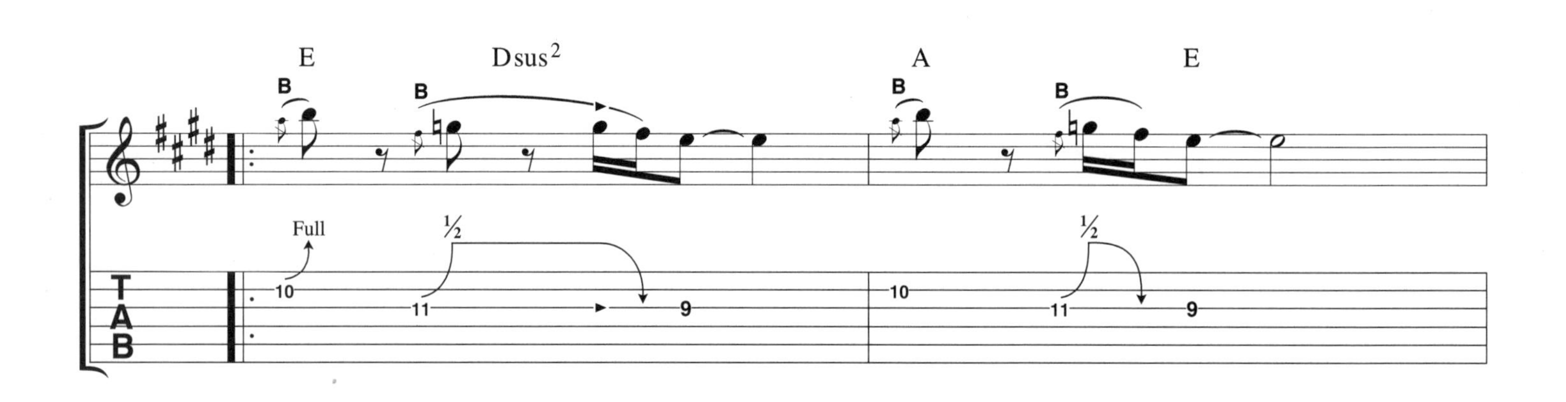
E
Dsus2
A
E
B
Full
½
T
A
B

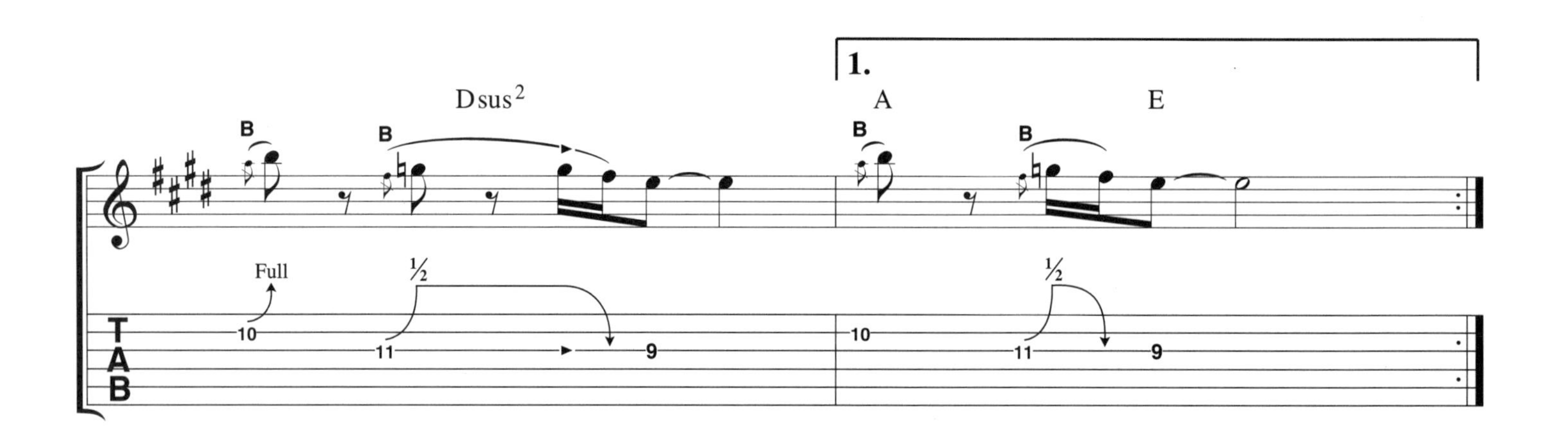
1.
Dsus2
A
E
B
Full
½
T
A
B

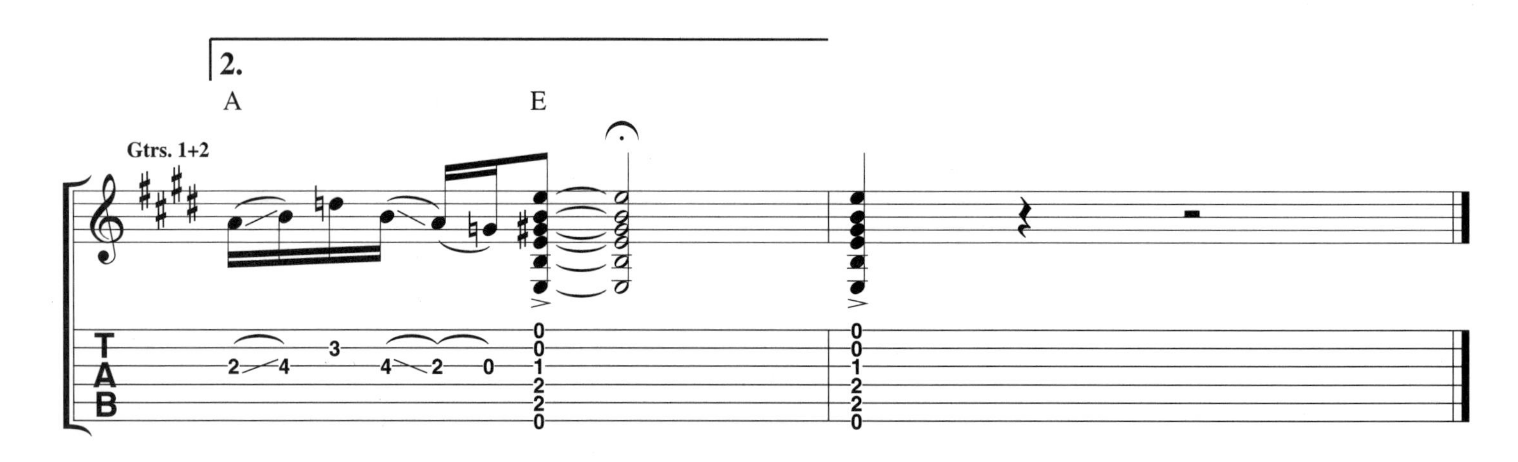
2.
A
E
Gtrs. 1+2
T
A
B